I0889507

Traitors and True Poles

Ohio University Press Polish and Polish-American Studies Series

Series Editor: John J. Bukowczyk

Framing the Polish Home: Postwar Cultural Constructions of Hearth, Nation, and Self, edited by Bożena Shallcross

Traitors and True Poles: Narrating a Polish-American Identity, 1880–1939, by Karen Majewski

Traitors and True Poles

Narrating a Polish-American Identity, 1880–1939

Karen Majewski

OHIO UNIVERSITY PRESS
ATHENS

Ohio University Press, Athens, Ohio 45701

Ohio University Press books are printed on acid-free paper ♾

11 10 09 08 07 06 05 04 03   5 4 3 2 1

Library of Congress Cataloging-in-Publication Data

Majewski, Karen.
Traitors and true Poles : narrating a Polish-American identity, 1880–1939 / by Karen Majewski.
p. cm. — (Ohio University Press Polish and Polish-American studies series)
Includes bibliographical references and index.
ISBN 0-8214-1469-0 (alk. paper) — ISBN 0-8214-1470-4 (pbk. : alk. paper)
1. American literature—Polish American authors—History and criticism. 2. Polish Americans—Intellectual life. 3. Polish Americans in literature. 4. Immigrants in literature. I. Title. II. Series.

PS153.P65 M35 2003
810.9'89185—dc21

2002030711

Cover art: From *Jak można osięgnąć bogactwo i wpływ w Ameryce* (How to acquire money and influence in America) [Toledo: Paryski], 1911.

Publication of books in the Polish and Polish-American Studies Series has been made possible in part by the generous support of the following organizations:

Polish American Historical Association,
Orchard Lake, Michigan

Stanislaus A. Blejwas Endowed Chair in Polish and Polish American Studies, Central Connecticut State University, New Britain, Connecticut

St. Mary's College of Ave Maria University,
Orchard Lake, Michigan

The Polish Institute of Arts and Sciences of America, Inc.,
New York, New York

Additional support for this book has been provided by the Kulczycki Prize awarded by the Polish American Historical Association

To Helena Staś

Contents

Illustrations

Series Editor's Preface

While the literatures of a few immigrant communities already have entered the contemporary American literary canon, literary life within Polonia—the Polish immigrant and ethnic community—remains to date largely terra incognito. Heavily peasant in composition, the Polish immigrants of the late nineteenth and early twentieth centuries often have been portrayed as an inarticulate, undifferentiated mass, silent and rough like the coal many of them dug in the mining towns of industrial America.

In *Traitors and True Poles* Karen Majewski gives us a truly pathbreaking work that decisively dispels the image of the voiceless Polish peasant. A singular expert on the ethnic literary genre, Majewski here reconstructs an entire ethnic literary tradition, one nearly extinguished by the ravages of language loss, the passage of time, and simple neglect. From it, she explores the nationalist and feminist themes that animated immigrant discourse within the Polish ethnic community between the 1880s and the 1930s. Along the way, Majewski also has managed to assemble biographical profiles of hitherto little known Polish émigré writers who formed an influential cultural elite (and, in some measure, political cadre) in turn-of-the-century Polish America: the immigrant intelligentsia.

A thoroughly interdisciplinary work, *Traitors and True Poles* not only speaks to matters literary and cultural but also plumbs the foundations of one ethnic group's "hyphenated American cultural identity." Majewski persuasively argues that literature (and the arts) "were powerful ideological tools in the struggle to define Poland and Polishness, on both sides of the ocean" at a time when the Poles were a submerged and colonized nation (and later, when a post–World War I Poland, recreated as a result of the Treaty of Versailles, was compelled to reinvent itself). Examining a cluster of interlacing literary topics, Majewski shows that this transnational immigrant literature served as "an instrument of national definition and consolidation" during these years and that its audience was not the American or outside world but the immigrant community alone and for itself. *Traitors and True Poles* accordingly stands as a landmark work in the field of immigrant history, outsider literature, and ethnic studies.

Winner of the Polish American Historical Association's prestigious Kulczycki Prize, *Traitors and True Poles* is the second volume in the new Ohio University Press Polish and Polish-American Studies Series. The series revisits the historical and contemporary experience of one of America's largest European ethnic groups and the history of a European homeland that has played a disproportionately important role in twentieth-century world affairs. The series will publish innovative monographs and more general works that investigate under- or unexplored topics or themes or that offer new, critical, revisionist, or comparative perspectives in Polish and Polish-American studies. Interdisciplinary or multidisciplinary in profile, the series seeks manuscripts on Polish immigration and ethnic communities, the country of origin, and its various peoples in history, anthropology, cultural studies, political economy, current politics, and related fields.

Publication of the Ohio University Press Polish and Polish-American Studies Series marks a milestone in the maturation of the Polish studies field and stands as a fitting tribute to the scholars and organizations whose efforts have brought it to fruition. Supported by a series advisory board of accomplished Polonists and Polish-Americanists, the Polish and Polish-American Studies Series has been made possible through generous financial assistance from the Polish American Historical Association, the Polish Institute of Arts and Sciences of America, the Polish Chair at Central Connecticut State University, and St. Mary's College of Ave Maria University and through institutional support from Wayne State University and Ohio University Press. As an ambitious new undertaking, the series meanwhile has benefited from the warm encouragement of a number of persons, including Gillian Berchowitz, the late Stanislaus Blejwas, Thomas Gladsky, Thaddeus Gromada, James S. Pula, David Sanders, and Thaddeus Radzilowski. The moral and material support from all of these institutions and individuals is gratefully acknowledged.

John J. Bukowczyk

Preface

BECAUSE NO RELIABLE bibliography of the Polish immigrant novels and short stories discussed in this study had ever been compiled, primary sources were identified through a painstaking (and ongoing) search, and by the occasional lucky break. While university repositories facilitated the process, it still meant tracking down clues and half-clues about authors and titles buried in Polish-language immigrant histories and memoirs, examining the catalogues and reading the shelves of Polish-American organizational libraries and archives, sorting through knee-deep papers in half-abandoned immigrant bookstores, and scanning hundreds of rolls of microfilmed newspapers. Despite my attempts to be comprehensive, some works have undoubtedly been missed. And because extant copies of several titles could not be located, it is also possible that a small number have been misidentified. It can only be hoped that further research will correct this record.

Early versions of sections of this work have been published as the following:

"Crossings and Double-Crossings: Polish-Language Immigrant Narratives of the Great Migration." In *Multilingual America: Transnationalism, Ethnicity, and the Languages of American Literature,* ed. Werner Sollors. New York: New York University Press, 1998.

"The Politics of Polishness in the United States: American Literature in Polish Before World War II." In *Not English Only: Redefining "American" in American Studies,* ed. Orm Øverland. European Contributions to American Studies 47. Amsterdam: VU University Press, 2001.

A Family Reunion: Love, Sex, and the State of Marriage in Polish-American Literature. Occasional Papers in Polish and Polish American Studies, no. 3. New Britain: Polish Studies Program, Central Connecticut State University, 1997.

"Toward 'A Pedagogical Goal': Home, Nation, and Ethnicity in the Works of Polonia's First Women Writers." In *Something of My Very Own to Say: Women Writers of Polish Descent,* ed. Thomas S. Gladsky and Rita Holmes Gladsky. New York: Columbia University Press, East European Monograph Series, 1997.

"Wayward Wives and Delinquent Daughters: Polish-American Flappers in the Novels of Melania Nesterowicz." *Polish American Studies* 53, 1 (Spring 1996).

To accommodate readers unfamiliar with the Polish language, the first mention of a Polish title is accompanied by a translation. Subsequent references are given in English. Finally, all translations, unless otherwise indicated, are mine.

Acknowledgments

THIS PROJECT COULD not have been completed without the kind help of many people who went out of their way to track down hard-to-find materials: the staff of the Polish Museum of America, including Jan Loryś, Halina Misterka, Małgorzata Kot, Leonard Kurdek, and Violetta Wóżnicka; Ewa Wołyńska of the Connecticut Polish Archives at Central Connecticut State University; Karen Rondestvedt, former director of the Alliance College Collection at the University of Pittsburgh; Jean Dickson and Brenda Battleson at the University of Buffalo; and the staff of the Immigration History Research Center at the University of Minnesota. Thanks also to Monsignor Roman Nir, Sister Angelita, and Krzysztof Tyburski of the Central Archives of Polonia, Orchard Lake, and to my colleagues at the Alumni Memorial Library of St. Mary's College: being allowed to snoop freely among all those old Polish books has immensely enriched this work and my life.

In Poland, Franciszek Lyra facilitated my research at the Polish National Archives. And Danuta Pytlak of the American Studies Department at the University of Warsaw not only searched Polish libraries for primary sources but reminded me through her own work that this project was opening a door that others would also walk through.

I am grateful to those who opened their personal libraries to me and helped me with their professional expertise: Ed Martin, David and Gwidon Chełminski, Tamara Sochacka, Paul Valasek, and Regina Kościelska, as well as to the families of writers and publishers. Mark Yolles generously provided information about his father, Piotr. Basia Kocyan McCoy graciously opened her home and family papers to me as I researched her grandmother Melania Nesterowicz. Paul Paryski and Antony Plutynski enthusiastically shared material on their grandfather, Antoni Paryski.

Among those whose belief in this project most heartened me are my colleagues and friends in the Polish American Historical Association: Mary Cygan, Mary Erdmans, Tom Gladsky, Tom Napierkowski, John Radzilowski, John Bukowczyk, Thad Radzilowski, Bill Galush, the late Stan Blejwas, Anna Kirchman, Thad Gromada, Tony Bukoski, Jim Pula, and Victor Greene. Matt Jacobson, Orm Øverland, Gonul Pultar, Melinda Gray, Dag

Blanck, and Werner Sollors helped pave the way for a field in which my own work could fit. And Gill Berchowitz was an always patient and encouraging editor, even when she didn't have to be.

For financial assistance, I am indebted to those who supported this project in its first incarnation, as my dissertation at the University of Michigan: the Kosciuszko Foundation, the University of Michigan's Center for the Education of Women, the Rackham Graduate School, and the American Culture Program. Sincere appreciation also goes to Anita Norich, Bogdana Carpenter, June Howard, Rosemary Kowalski, and Bill Lockwood.

Much love as well to those who throughout this long project kept me connected to my dancing self, especially to John P., Csiki, Erzsike, and Sala and Andrea.

Finally, thanks to my family. In Poland, my love and gratitude to Ciocia Józia, Józef and Lucyna, and Jadzia. In the United States, to my mother, Gerry; to Mary and John; to my dear Grandpa Chalus; and to all the departed ones—especially my father, John—who somehow set me along this most unexpected path. Thanks too to the Feazells for their always cheerful support. But most of all, I am grateful beyond words to Matt Feazell, for everything.

Abbreviations

KON	National Defense Committee (Komitet Obrony Narodowy)
PNA	Polish National Alliance
PNCC	Polish National Catholic Church
PRCU	Polish Roman Catholic Union of America
PWA	Polish Women's Alliance

Guide to Pronunciation

THE FOLLOWING KEY provides a guide to the pronunciation of Polish words and names.

a is pronounced as in *father*
c as ts in *cats*
ch like a guttural h
cz as hard ch in *church*
g always hard, as in *get*
i as ee
j as y in *yellow*
rz like French j in *jardin*
sz as sh in *ship*
szcz as shch, enunciating both sounds, as in *fresh cheese*
u as oo in *boot*
w as v
ć as soft ch
ś as sh
ż, ź both as zh, the former higher in pitch than the latter
ó as oo in boot
ą as French *on*
ę as French *en*
ł as w
ń changes the combinations -in to -ine, -en to -ene, and -on to -oyne
The accent in Polish words always falls on the penultimate syllable.

Traitors and True Poles

INTRODUCTION |||

Reading the Immigrant

THIS STUDY LOOKS at a forgotten fragment of American literature: immigrant narrative fiction written in Polish and published in the United States before World War II. The purposes of this study are several and necessarily interdisciplinary. It will admit the Polish-language writing of turn-of-the-century immigrants into the scholarly conversation by reopening its long-closed pages, outlining its dimensions, and suggesting its possible significances. It will situate these works within the larger tradition of popular literature and reading in Europe and America alongside which it emerged, and within the context of Polish literary history and American ethnic literary theory, including the newly emerging field of American literature written in languages other than English. But its primary focus will be the role of Polish immigrant, Polish-language fiction in the negotiation of a national and ethnic identity as writers argued the boundaries and obligations of Polishness. If, as Jules Chametzky observed many years later, ethnicity "ain't what you do, or what you are but an image created by what you read,"[1] Polish-language literature, written in the United States and published by Polish American companies, attempted to model a Polish identity for its immigrant readers at the same time that it articulated specifically Polish-American perspectives and experiences.

Despite stereotypes suggesting otherwise, that these immigrants were reading is obvious from the great number of Polish-language newspapers they produced, particularly after 1880, when the immigrant press burgeoned and began branching into other publishing activities. Self-help books, religious tracts, installment fiction, poetry, dramas for the amateur and professional stage:[2] the variety and output were enormous. And so, apparently, was the demand. Nineteenth-century Polish-American newspapers reported the establishment of local reading rooms and lending libraries. As early as 1891 even small towns like Manistee, Michigan, could boast a Polish library. Emil Dunikowski reports that, of the several hundred books owned by a Buffalo Polish reading room, all but a few dozen were checked out at the time of his visit.[3] And Artur Waldo recounts that "when a peddler left a Chicago bookstore carrying a heavy suitcase stuffed with books, after covering one block, not more than twenty or thirty homes, he returned to the publisher's stockroom with his suitcase already empty."[4]

So how is it that, given the flurry of publishing activity and the evident hunger for books in Polonian homes,[5] so little is known about the works written and published on American soil by immigrant Poles and their children? Why could Stanislaus Blejwas, as late as 1988, state that "there does not exist a Polish American literature," or Karol Wachtl, while offering sketches of a score of Polonian writers, claim, "In a strict sense, one cannot yet speak of original Polish-American writing, about a true literature bred among Polish settlements here, blossoming from and maintained by its homegrown, independent talents."[6]

The answers are complex and lie in the juncture between ideology, history, and literary theory. Blejwas and Wachtl were both referring to Polonia's sparsity of professional, English-language writers, who were influenced more by a Polish-American experience and upbringing than a Polish one and who were able to speak for the immigrant and ethnic community to an outside audience. What's more, the 1980s and 1990s saw a flurry of creative fiction that is self-consciously Polish-American. But no English-language study has systematically considered Polish-language literature produced in this country for its intersection with Polonian and American literary scholarship.

Scholars who might have wished to include immigrant texts written in Polish within a more general discussion of Polish-American writing have until now been hampered by several problems. Not only had none of these works been translated into English, but until this study no reliable bibliography of this material has appeared in either English or Polish, and even the most rudimentary scholarly consideration of these Polish-language immigrant texts was lacking.[7] The rare discussion of diasporan literature has tended to concentrate on works by renowned nonimmigrant writers, such as Henryk Sienkiewicz's melodramatic *Za chlebem* (After bread). Or it has neglected the old peasant immigration in favor of writers of the World War II emigré generation.[8] The Polish-American chapter of the Modern Language Association's recently reprinted collection *Ethnic Perspectives in American Literature* notes works about America by Poles, including Sienkiewicz's ubiquitous *After Bread,* and even credits a sixteenth-century political treatise with influencing the Declaration of Independence.[9] But it makes no mention of the treatment of the American experience by Sienkiewicz's contemporaries writing in Polish in this country. Magdalena Zaborowska's more recent study of Polish and Russian immigrant women's narratives is silent on works written in Polish before 1939.[10] These omissions are almost certainly not the result of deliberate choice, but rather evidence of the deep obscurity into which these works have fallen.

This examination of early Polish-American fiction begins with the publication in 1881 of the first known immigrant novel in Polish,[11] and ends in 1939, when the Second World War spurred a fresh wave of immigrants from Poland, necessitating a reevaluation of Polonian identity and goals, and leading to new patterns of immigrant publishing. Even the approximately three hundred novels, novellas, short stories, sketches, and anthologies of short fiction identified here comprise only a portion of the Polish-language works produced by the *stara emigracja,* the old emigration. The inclusion of drama and poetry would make any bibliography several times as long. This study is thus limited to fiction for partly practical reasons. But even within the sizable body of Polish prose fiction written and published in America, a focus on immigrant identity has narrowed the selection.

A number of immigrant works were eliminated from consideration because, although published in the United States, their plots were set outside this country, drawn from exclusively Polish history or world legend. Like their counterparts among other immigrant groups, Polish-American publishers offered their readers works of classic and contemporary literature from Poland, as well as translations of Russian, French, German, English, and American works. *Popular Narratives and Ethnic Identity,* Brent Peterson's study of ethnicity shaped and perpetuated by German-American newspaper fiction, argues convincingly that all literature contributed to the collective identity of its immigrant readers, that it is not "ethnic literature" but "narratives for ethnic readers" that reveal the process of ethnogenesis.[12] And "literary ethnicity" rather than "ethnic literature" is Thomas S. Gladsky's focus in *Princes, Peasants, and Other Polish Selves,* which looks not only at

English-language fiction and poetry written by second- and third-generation Polish-Americans, but also at the literary images of Poles and Polish-Americans created by purely "American" authors, shifting attention to the way in which works "may be read as contributing to the literary creation of ethnic selves and American ethnicity."[13] However, my concern with how this literature specifically and self-consciously engaged its readers as Poles in America and later as Polish-Americans led me to restrict this study to works that attempted to position their readers, however superficially, in the context of American conditions, a phrase contained in the subtitles of so many of these novels. Thus, all works considered here contain at least one Polish character on American soil.[14]

Fiction about Polonia—that is, about the Polish diaspora—but written and published in Poland is also not included here, although several such novels were reprinted by Polish-American publishers and read in immigrant households. Some authors, like journalist Stefan Barszczewski, spent considerable time in the United States before returning to Poland and writing about their experiences. Others, like Józef Watra-Przewłocki, remained in the United States but published their major works in Poland. A comparative analysis of those two bodies of literature has been begun by Bolesław Klimaszewski.[15] But while the works published overseas have already received scholarly attention, at least in Poland, before comparison can be meaningful it will be necessary to know something more about the work that was produced on American soil, work that not only grew out of community concerns but that utilized local publishing resources and networks. On that subject scholarship is still negligible. The works of several immigrant authors who eventually returned to Poland are included, however, when those works were published in the United States before the author's repatriation. Included also are works that were published in both America and Poland, either under joint agreement or in separate editions.[16]

The carefully articulated parameters of this study suggest the complicated nature of ethnic literature and ethnicity in general, as well as the particularities of Polish and Polish-American history. Konstanty Symonolewicz-Symmons raises issues central to the formulation of this study, and indeed to the definition of ethnic literature itself, when he asks, "Who exactly can be considered a Polonian writer":

> Native Poles writing in English, whether Polish subjects play any kind of role in their works or not? Or American literati of Polish extraction, although their works have nothing in common either with Poland or with Polonia? Or authors of Polish nationality who write in English but on Polish subjects? Or writers of Polish nationality or Polish extraction who write in English but on subjects from Polonian life? Or, finally, writers and poets who write in both languages?[17]

Symonolewicz-Symmons problematizes the author's place of birth, choice of subject matter, and ethnic consciousness, all matters of consideration in possible definitions of ethnic literature. But he leaves unchallenged the fundamental assumption, as expressed by Mary Dearborn in 1986, that "the ethnic literary tradition implies, of course, the acquisition of the English language."[18]

Nevertheless, the consideration of non-English-language texts in American literary studies is hardly a new phenomenon, going back to at least 1921, when the *Cambridge History of American Literature* included sections on German, French, Yiddish, and aboriginal language works. Henry Pochmann's classic 1946 essay, "The Mingling of Tongues," acknowledges the "rich and diverse . . . writing by Americans who use tongues other than English."[19] Until recently, however, this inclusive view had been largely forgotten, despite occasional reminders that the function of the scholar of ethnic literature "is to locate, describe, and interpret all the ethnic components in creative works produced by Americans, regardless of the language employed and of the genres employed."[20] Efforts like the Recovering the U.S. Hispanic Literary Heritage Project, and those of Harvard University's Longfellow Institute, devoted to the study of American literatures in languages other than English, demonstrate renewed efforts to define a place in American literary studies for works that do not attempt to fit themselves into an exclusively anglophone cultural network.

It is not surprising, given America's dizzying linguistic diversity and the insularity of many ethnic communities, that non-English texts remain largely unknown. Obviously, a literature written in Polish excluded most non-Poles not only from active participation in the highly charged dialogue through which Polonia voiced itself, but also from the most basic awareness that a dialogue was taking place. This may have been considered fortuitous, since ethnic communities often try to present a unified front to outsiders. Another result, however, is not just the marginalization of this fundamentally transnational literature, but its complete invisibility, since it seems to fit neatly into neither the American nor the Polish literary establishment. Though the plots are set for the most part in the immigrant enclave, Poland and its troubles are just over the horizon. Though the literary patterns are essentially Polish, they are influenced by American models of popular fiction and the needs and experiences of largely urban immigrant readers. The Polish language itself is stretched and adapted to new needs and inflected by English, the language of the dominant culture. Because these conditions are not exclusive to Polonia, but are part of the history of perhaps all non-English-speaking immigrant groups, reconstructing their individual literary histories can also help us piece together a general framework for the study of American literature in languages other than English.

At the same time, we should not lose sight of the particularities of each group's experience. Immigrants brought with them their own specific economic, social, and migratory histories, which they called upon in devising strategies by which to advance their goals in America. Because these histories were reflected in their cultural production as well, any literary analysis that relies primarily on "critical paradigms created by the dominant culture," as Fred Gardaphé points out in his study of Italian-American literature, is bound to end in a "monologistic, methodological trap."[21] To understand the elements that formed the Polish-American community and its literature, it will be necessary to keep in mind not only the circumstances of the life in America that the immigrants faced, but the political and cultural conditions they had left behind in Europe. These European conditions supplied Polonia its terms of struggle and negotiation and shaped its creative impulse. And so we cannot make much sense of Polish immigrant fiction in the face of America's literary trends, historical movements, or mythic self-representations without recognizing the heavy backdrop of Polish history.

David Fine connects ethnic literature with an American cultural tradition.[22] For well-educated writers fluent in English, this may have been so, but for the majority of Polish-language writers in this country, the literary model was doubtless a European one. And for the readers, many of them first-generation literates, literary history for all practical purposes may not have existed. The context into which many readers would have fit these Polish-American works may have been primarily an oral one, alongside songs, folktales, poetry, sermons, declamations, and letters. Even the written word was often oral and communal within peasant and immigrant communities, as newspapers were shared, husbands read books aloud to their families, and letters were community property.[23] Reading was not the solitary, individual act we think of today, but rather a shared activity that brought one into active communication with others. Polonia's early writers, most of them activists for the Polish cause, also employed tactics and meanings developed through a century of cultural oppression in which literature was a major avenue of tacit protest. The "conspiracy of understanding between the author and the reader"[24] that this experience necessitated also provides early Polonian literature with many of its patterns, tropes, and symbols.

Drawing from different historical precedents and expectations of the reading experience, we have to ask the extent to which this literature fits into common paradigms of American ethnic cultural production. Robert Spiller's developmental model—in which ethnic literature advances from personal writing such as letters, autobiographies, and diaries; to the public forum of journalism and other nonfictional forms; to "imitative" literature; and finally to the creation of a new literature out of the community's unique experiences[25]—overlooks ways that the literature of out-groups like working class immigrants can reshape "less mature" forms for sophisticated purposes. It ignores the internal conditions and influences not coming from the mainstream, which were necessarily most relevant to the day-to-day life out of which culture is created. By not considering trends in Poland's own centuries-long literary and cultural history, it misses the very terms in which immigrant authors formed their aesthetics and envisioned their role as writers. What is needed, then, is a more elaborate picture that takes into consideration the diversity of American Polonia and its influences, the internal complexities of its community life, and its essentially transnational political concerns and social and cultural patterns. These provided the literary and linguistic strategies from which Polonian literature derived its forms and upon which it relied for its meaning. Part of our purpose must be, then, to establish the relationship of Polish-language Polish-American literature to established theories of literary ethnicity.

In this literature intended for a Polonian audience, some of the themes and subjects we have come to expect in ethnic, and particularly immigrant, literature seem much less prominent or, more precisely, take forms that express the situation within the Polish-American community. The Polish-language texts, for instance, force us to reconfigure the common immigrant motif of rebirth resulting from confrontation with the host culture, since this host culture is more often American Polonia (or, at its most alien, Irish America) than it is America at large. In Polish-language fiction for Polonian audiences, the role of Anglo-America is often minimal, the debates originating within the Polish community itself, not in its intersection with mainstream American culture. Antagonists are more likely to be Prussian than American, particularly in the period leading up to and during World War I, and Americans less the objects of admiration than of suspicion. Language issues may center around not only the use of English but also the intelligibility of the varied levels and dialects of Polish spoken by a diverse group of immigrants that outsiders perceived as undifferentiatedly Polish.

Given the focus on these apparently European issues, we might even ask whether this literature is ethnic at all, or whether it should be classified as simply a footnote to Polish literature. But while the problems confronted in this literature are often intra-Polonian, the fact remains that Polonia was never Poland, however authors might have attempted to configure it. So although the symbols that Polish writers in Europe used to mobilize and consolidate Polish patriotism were manipulated by Polish-American authors, it was in order to articulate very specific issues of identity and power within an emerging, increasingly distinct American Polonia. In fact, the Polish consciousness and sense of history that immigrant writers attempted to create and manipulate were largely possible because of the American conditions that threw together immigrants from various regions and social strata and gave them relative freedom to speak, at least to each other. These conditions created a distinct American Polonia (or rather, several), which in turn could take its own literary path, while still serving a Polish cause. The inadequacy of European Polish literature, even great Polish literature, to speak for these immigrants is argued in Helena Staś's 1910 novel *Na ludzkim targu* (In the human market): "They don't understand Mickiewicz or Słowacki. . . . But they would understand a literature created for them, based on their lives. That's the only way the national spirit will survive in a foreign land."[26]

Implicit in the argument of Symonolewicz-Symmons and others is the suggestion that the Polish-language works that early Polonia had produced were not worthy of serious consideration as literature. Andrzej Brożek, for instance, writes that "Even Polonian authors . . . realize the low standard of

Polish literary work in America."[27] The sometimes dubious business procedures of some publishers, as well as their cheap production methods, certainly contributed to this perception. But more important, it was the literature itself, usually aimed toward a newly literate audience and serving a polemical purpose, that was dismissed as an artistic failure, despite the general concession that it met and fueled a desire to read within the immigrant community. Not only do these judgments fail to recognize many skillfully composed works, implying that authors resorted to polemics because they were incapable of art, they also delegitimate the experience and consciousness from which these works derived their meaning and expression, and the historical imperatives that guided authorial strategies. A 1918 editorial in Chicago's *Dziennik związkowy* pleads the case for polemics:

> The novel stimulates the mind, it awakens patriotic feeling. It reaches the poorest peasant hut, and if it's a good novel it educates and ennobles its peasant readers. Because of this, novelists have a great responsibility. They must be apostles, high priests of our Polish faith. . . . They must steel the nation to struggles and difficulties, and work tirelessly toward one sacred end—the freedom of our homeland. . . . The novelists of free nations can permit themselves to write "for art's sake" . . . ; we, in threefold slavery, our enemies seeking constantly to inject into our nation the poison that will disintegrate it, cannot permit ourselves such "art."[28]

For the serious consideration of immigrant writing, then, one has had to turn to the Polish-language work of immigrant historians. Wacław Kruszka, Stanisław Osada, Karol Wachtl, and Artur Waldo all devote attention to Polonian literature, not surprisingly, since Osada was the author of two novels; Wachtl was a short-story writer, poet, and playwright; and Waldo a playwright, novelist, and short-story writer. Even the cleric Kruszka included in his voluminous memoirs a sketch set in a future America in which Polish culture dominates.[29] Kruszka's recently translated *A History of the Poles in America* devotes sections to immigrant literature and the press. The future must have looked promising to Kruszka, writing in 1905. In his brief overview of Polish-American writers and their works, he claims the existence of a nascent Polish-American literature, disagreeing with Osada's assertion (before the appearance of his own novels) that Polish-American writing "cannot be considered literature."[30]

Almost forty years later, Wachtl's *Polonia w Ameryce* (Polonia in America) pleaded the need for an English-language Polish-American literature. Wachtl considered the writers of the stara emigracja to be Polish writers merely influenced by their American experiences, and his evaluation of these writers, like Kruszka's, is highly partisan. However, this also makes it useful in understanding Polonia's points of ideological contention. Although disapproving of playwright-novelist Telesfor Chełchowski's sarcastic edge, for instance, Wachtl grants his works a higher purpose: "Often the literary value of these works was not great, but they faithfully render the spirit of Polonia—sincere, self-sacrificing, fiercely patriotic."[31] The patriotism Wachtl was referring to, of course, was directed toward Poland, not America.

Wachtl reserves his sharpest criticism for writers whom he accuses of betraying the Polish-American community by creating divisions within it. He calls anticlericalist Czesław Łukaszkiewicz, for example, "a talent—undeniably brilliant, but unfortunately warped and wasted through his unscrupulous and unjust derision and mockery of everything that was elevated" (230). And he charges Łukaszkiewicz's publisher and colleague, Antoni Paryski, with selling books that were "completely without worth, even harmful, because they sowed the seeds of discontent and set the Polonian community at odds" (227). Paryski's publishing company, early Polonia's most successful, will be discussed in chapter 2. However, it is important to note that Wachtl's highly politicized analysis reflects precisely the value of internal unity that dominated Polonian thought, if not its practice. Although Polonia's own literary scholarship is sketchy and heavily tainted, it does reflect what could be called the received image of Polonian history, full of contradictions and defensive strategies, but shared by its various ideological camps, valuing group cohesiveness but disagreeing about group identity, and linking Polonian to Polish as well as American historical developments.

While Artur Waldo's *Zarys historii literatury polskiej w Ameryce* (Outline history of Polish literature in America) attempts to systematically describe the development and growth of Polish-American literature, it promises more than it delivers. But despite the murkiness of its categories and its somewhat arbitrary divisions, the second project of Waldo's *Outline,* to periodize Polish-American literary production, at least treats its subject as a serious cultural indicator. What is more, Waldo stresses the unfolding relationship between Polonia, Poland, and the United States evident in this literature.

Recognizing Polonia and its cultural expression as legitimately part of both the American and Polish panoramas, and conscious of American stereotypes of Polish immigrants, Waldo encourages the translation of Polish-language Polonian texts into English, as well as the creation of new works in the English language: "We have to give America Polish-American writing, Polish-American literature" in order "to establish a foundation for the power of the Polish spirit in the United States."[32]

The purpose of my own study is not to prove, to Polonia itself or to American readers, that Polish immigrant communities created a "great literature." Nor is it to develop any monolithic definition of Polish-American literature itself. Certainly, equally valid but oppositional definitions may suit specific purposes and highlight particular qualities, not crossing each other out but rather expanding the matrices by which ethnicity is perceived and expressed. Rather, I intend to reopen the pages of these long-forgotten early works in order to consider the uses to which literature was put within Polonia and the possibilities it offered the community for reading itself as Polish in an American context.

This study will consider the diversity of ethnic identities circulated among readers in the Polish immigrant community, in a Polish and Polish-American cultural and historical context. It will attempt to describe a cultural history reconstructed out of the works that Polish America wrote and read, and that reveal the continuing conversation over values, interests, and identity through which the immigrant community shaped itself.

The first chapter will argue the primacy of literature in the creation of a Polish national and Polish-American ethnic consciousness. Chapter 2 takes a detailed look at the history of Polonian literature and publishing. Chapter 3 will investigate the controlling theme of ethnic and family loyalty and betrayal through the prism of popular Polish-American crime and detective narratives, arguing that the threats to inheritance and family continuity that these stories enact can be read as ethnic and national allegories. Chapter 4 considers the same theme of the creation and maintenance of group identity by looking at the ways sagas of immigration and adjustment encourage immigrant readers to interpret their own emigration in the context of Poland's political oppression, and to see themselves as linked to other Poles by a national identity reinforced by shared suffering and exploitation. By showing emigration as a process that leads back to Europe, these works situate their immigrant characters in a continuing relationship to the homeland. Chapter 5 investigates the literary treatment of political direction and institutional corruption, demonstrating the ways opposing factions utilized the same morally charged rhetoric of treason and betrayal to articulate competing ideologies of group identity and strategies for national survival. Chapter 6 shows how immigrant authors explored and resolved questions of collective identity through the drama of sexual attraction and marital alliance, conflating family and nation and investing personal patterns of action with political meaning, in order to model proper ways of reproducing Polishness. The final chapter turns to the question of why this literature did not survive and suggests its relation to the writing and publishing efforts of later immigrants, those from World War II and, particularly, the Solidarity era. It argues that, despite their surface differences, similarities between the stara emigracja and the newest immigrant cohort account for some commonalities of literary form, style, subject, and theme.

In 1938 Artur L. Waldo dedicated his *Outline History of Polish Literature in America* "to the forgotten writers of American Polonia" (4). That he was referring to authors whose works had appeared only within the last several decades, some of whom were still writing and publishing, testifies to the unstable relationship between Polish immigrant writing and the community of immigrant readers these works addressed. If memory of these publications was already fading within Polonia even while, as Waldo asserts, they lay piled by the score in thousands of Polish-American attics, it is small wonder that later ethnic scholars have either remained ignorant of their existence or neglected their study. Waldo himself balked at the enormity of his task, leaving it to future scholars to flesh out the bones of his research. This study is a partial fulfillment of that hope, so long unfulfilled.

Without looking at writing in Polish, one can obtain only a distorted view of the cultural life of American Polonia, which included scores of Polish newspapers, Polish radio programs, active theater companies, and a lively output of various publications, including fiction. With a growing willingness to accept not simply alternative forms of literature such as letters and autobiography, but to acknowledge as American that literature written in languages other than English, a vast field of study is opened that will enable us to gain a much deeper understanding of how immigrant ethnicity was shaped and experienced. It also establishes a counterpoint to the common image of Polish-Americans in native literature, written by those outside the community for an American audience. Even the most sympathetic of these often portray the Polish immigrant as inarticulate, passive, almost primeval, as faceless symbols of a primitive life force and as voiceless victims of social injustice and economic exploitation. Naturally, they may have appeared so to outsiders, with whom they could not easily communicate. But the view from within Polonia was of an active, vibrant, and complex community, and most relevantly the sound from within was not silence but conversation, argument, laughter. The only way to hear these voices is by eavesdropping on the literature these communities produced by and for themselves, with no intention of cultural mediation with America at large, but with very particular agendas relevant to the immigrants themselves, their institutions, and even to the shape of the world map. All this is lost unless we hear them in their own language.

1 ||| Writing Polish

Literature and the Construction of Polishness in America

If America holds a collective portrait of the Polish immigrant landing at Ellis Island, exhausted, bewildered, clutching bundles and children, surrounded by queerly lettered trunks, what, in the popular imagination, do those trunks contain? The featherbed, embroidered linens, a treasured family photograph, flower seeds, a teakettle, practical, homemade clothing, a fistful of village soil . . . Rarely, however, do we imagine a book among the carefully packed belongings, and if we do, it is likely to be a worn prayer book or a *Lives of the Saints.*

Nevertheless, in America these immigrants were producers and consumers of the written word. Polish communities supported an active (and often combative) press, a lively network of amateur and professional theaters, and scores of book publishers. This study concerns itself with just one segment of Polish America's literary output: Polish-language narrative fiction written and published in the United States before World War II. That such a literature existed at all will come as a surprise to many. Yet literature was more than just an obscure element of immigrant cultural life. It was a self-conscious agent of American Polonia's ethnogenesis.

Like their counterparts in Europe, Polish immigrant authors wrote from a sense of national imperative. From 1795 until the end of World War I, during the period of greatest migration, Poland did not exist as a political state, having been divided in a complicated series of partitions between Prussia, Russia, and Austria-Hungary. In partitioned Poland, Norman Davies points out, "the two great themes of the age [were] the preservation of national identity, and the restoration of national independence."[1] Polish literature was enlisted in these causes, and indeed the two primary literary movements of the partition period, romanticism and positivism, are as much political as artistic strategies.

In the United States, immigrant writers persistently and passionately engaged issues of identity and peoplehood, attempting to define a sense of Polishness that would serve an idealized Poland and a developing American Polonia. But there was no consensus on just what that national identity entailed and demanded, and so the struggle for political independence and the consolidation of nationhood resulted in as much infighting as it did cooperation. Accusations of treachery and treason went hand in hand with admonitions to "support your own."[2] Rather than seeing these conflicts as no more than the self-serving and self-defeating positioning of politicians and ideologues, we might look at them as border skirmishes, meant to establish, defend, and secure territory, particularly at its most vulnerable junctures. That the question of just who should be considered a Pole became (and remains) so contentious reveals the potency of familiar historical flash points of collective identity—religion, language, social class, and political belief. And the recurring finger-pointing at accused traitors underscores the conflictedness inherent in these boundaries. One can, after all, be a traitor only to one's own people.

The cause of Polishness, and of Polishness in America, was perceived as threatened from without and from within. But writers reserved the bitterest criticism not for outside antagonists (Prussians, Russians, Irish priests, or American nativists, for example), but for the Poles accused of aiding and abetting them. Polonian literature is full of warnings against witting or unwitting foreign agents disguised as Poles. This imagery of treason and betrayal fell in neatly with the romantic ideology of Polish messianism, which saw Poland as the Christ of nations, betrayed and sacrificed but destined to rise again for the salvation of Western civilization.[3] But it is also heavily invested with Polish positivist ideology, which developed in reaction to and protest against the revolutionary impulses that had led to and fed on messianism. In the wake of the disastrous January Uprising of 1863, positivists tended to shift blame for Poland's demise from its foreign enemies to the factionalism and private interests that made the nation vulnerable, and to formulate practical and workable ways for Polishness, if not Poland, to survive through wide-ranging educational and social development, so-called organic work. Organized efforts began, often clandestinely and under threat of arrest, to educate the peasants and instill in them a sense of national loyalty. Women were especially active in the organic work movement, which turned reading into a political act. According to Davies,

> If the typical Polish "patriot" at any time up to 1864 had been a young man with a sabre or revolver in his hand, the typical patriot at the turn of the century was a young lady of good family with a textbook under her shawl. . . . They were as determined to manufacture "true Poles" as the state authorities were intent on training "real Germans" or "good Russians"; and they had an utter idealist contempt for [those] who, though intelligent, had betrayed the national culture.[4]

Polish positivism and particularly the organic work movement was early Polonia's strongest literary influence. Positivist writers like Henryk Sienkiewicz, Bolesław Prus, Eliza Orzeszkowa, and Maria Konopnicka were among those most often reprinted by Polonian publishers and serialized in Polonian newspapers. In particular, the work of Orzeszkowa and Konopnicka influenced the activists of America's Polish Women's Alliance and prominent immigrant women writers like Helena Staś. However, not all immigrant writers, including Staś, fall neatly into the mold, and positivism went through its own permutations and produced its own offshoots, of which Polonian writers were aware and which their own work reflects. In fact, as Matthew Frye Jacobson asserts, the "strategy of cultural nation-building . . . in effect blended elements of both the positivist and the insurrectionary approaches."[5]

Still, positivism, with its characteristic emphasis on social issues, often bordering on polemics, is readable in the subject, theme, and style of much early Polonian writing. What is more, positivism's strong ties to journalism reflect those of Polish immigrant writers who, in addition to serializing their work in newspapers, contributed articles on social issues and served on editorial staffs. Polonia's most active publishers issued products similar to (and sometimes pirated from) the *literatura ludowa,* people's literature aimed at peasant and urban proletariat readers, with which immigrants were likely to be already familiar.[6] These connections dovetail with Polonian literature's preoccupation with defining and encouraging a Polish identity among readers in America, who were most easily reached through newspapers and cheap

The children's section of a 1910 Polish-American women's magazine, *Ogniwo,* illustrating the connection between women and reading, a legacy of Polish positivism. Courtesy Polish Museum of America, Chicago

imprints. They echo in the carefully stated aims of Polish-American publishers, who were conscious of their difficult position straddling the interests of the immigrant intelligentsia and the peasant majority and who attempted to appeal to both while fending off accusations that they disseminated scandal and calumny rather than knowledge and enlightenment.

Under partition, the very language was weighted with symbolic meaning, as simple names, phrases, and terms like *solidarity* had become nuanced with layers of historical interconnections and ideological reverberations. This capacity has been noted in the later, communist-era literature of the Soviet satellite period. But Polish literature had already honed this "conspiracy of understanding"[7] during the partitions. The terms of the polemics and the literary shape immigrant authors and publishers gave them reflect attempts to straddle two continents, balancing the concrete needs of an immigrant constituency with political and cultural interests in what was perceived by all factions as a fight for the very survival of everything Polish.

Within Polonia's identity politics, the contingencies of regional identity, social class, and religion, all of which affected economic and social opportunities, reflect a kaleidoscopic puzzle of ideologies and agendas, sometimes contradictory, sometimes blended in surprising and unlikely combinations,

Editorial staff of Chicago's *Głos ludowy.* Telesfor Chełchowski, who wrote under the pseudonym Szczypawka, is third from the left. Courtesy Polish Museum of America, Chicago

but growing out of a European as well as an American experience. These divisions, apparent in the literature these immigrants and their children wrote and read, underscore the difficulties of any monolithic, static conception of American Polonia; and the intracommunity power struggles that are a subtext in much of this literature quickly dispel the commonly held perception of a cohesive and conservative immigrant community.

At the same time, because of political freedom and the intermingling of Polish immigrants from various areas of partitioned Poland and from different social levels, the consolidation of a Polish consciousness seemed possible in this country to a greater degree than it had in Europe, and many writers took advantage of this opportunity to try to instill in their readers a sense of peoplehood and national unity. Milwaukee publisher and politician Michał Kruszka wrote that "in the New World we have the best opportunity to exist as Poles, . . . to feel Polish, . . . to establish Polish societies, to pray in Polish." Kruszka and others saw no contradiction between simultaneously held American and Polish identities. "I am an enthusiastic Pole," he wrote, "and at the same time a [loyal] American."[8]

Ethnic identities were being shaped and formed in a continuing personal and collective dialogue within the immigrant settlements, between the immigrants and their native lands, between the host country and the immigrant communities, and among immigrant groups themselves. But the strands of Polishness and Polish-Americanness are often difficult to differentiate and never remained static. Polish-language immigrant literature reveals these changing concerns and aspirations, as well as the varied and permeable meanings of Polishness influenced by shifting conditions on both sides of the ocean. And because of the commercial opportunism of Polish-American publishers, these works also reveal how the immigrants voted with their nickels and dimes for the community values and identities expressed in the literature they bought.

Although Poles have been settling in the United States since the days of Jamestown, their numbers did not become significant until late in the nineteenth century. Before then, isolated pioneer families like the Zaborowskis (later, Zabriskie) and the Sądowskis (Sandusky), had contributed to American settlement, and it is likely that over one hundred Polish-Americans and Poles, including the celebrated generals Tadeusz Kościuszko and Kazimierz Pułaski, fought in the American War of Independence.[9] But the first noticeable wave of immigration from Poland consisted of 234 emigrés from the 1830 insurrection (the November Uprising), followed by smaller groups after the failed insurrections of 1846, 1848, and 1863. It was the November Uprising exiles, in fact, for whom the first Polish-language book in the United States appeared, as well as the first periodical devoted to Polish issues.[10]

However, it was only with the 1854 arrival in Galveston harbor of a group of immigrants from Upper Silesia, in the Prussian area of partitioned Poland, that visibly Polish communities began to take shape in America. The town they founded, Panna Maria, Texas,[11] is generally acknowledged as the first permanent Polish settlement in the New World, followed by settlements in

Michigan (1857) and Wisconsin (1858).[12] These first communities and ones that followed in the 1860s and early 1870s were primarily rural. But by 1867 a Polish parish was forming in Chicago, and in 1871 the first Polish parish in Detroit was established. The last quarter of the nineteenth century would see the transformation of American Polonia from a loose collection of scattered farm towns to a highly organized network of mostly urban neighborhoods.

The first wave of Polish immigrants in what America would call the Great Migration came from Prussian Poland in the 1870s and 1880s, propelled by land consolidation and Kulturkampf hostility to Polish language and culture.[13] In America, these immigrants, many with a Polish national consciousness developed in response to oppression, formed the advance guard of Polonia's emerging leadership. They, along with intellectuals and former insurrectionists who were beginning to arrive from Russian Poland after the January Uprising of 1863, established Polonia's early parishes, businesses, and community organizations.[14] As conditions in Prussia improved, the number of new arrivals dropped considerably, and although they tended to hold positions of power in American Polish communities, Prussian Poles would make up the smallest percentage of Polish immigrants.

In Russian Poland, which constituted the largest remnant of Polish lands, shifting social categories, economic pressures, and political and cultural oppression had by the 1880s fueled an immigration that continued to grow until World War I. Overlapping that wave was immigration from the Austrian-held territory of Galicia, which began in earnest in the mid-1890s and continued unabated until it too was cut off by the outbreak of the war. Polish culture had been freest to develop under Austrian authorities, who after the mid-nineteenth century did not suppress the Polish language or artistic expression, or close Polish universities. But Galician misery had become a byword in the impoverished countryside. Although Poles from all three partitions entered the same urban immigrant enclaves, the newly arrived were at a disadvantage economically and socially, and tensions between them led to conflict:

> The saddest thing was that [the Prussians] called their brothers from the Austrian partition, "You Galician," and those from the Russian partition, "You Russki," taking them for something less than desirable. Those from the Austrian and Russian partitions, taking revenge, called their brothers from under Prussia, "You Prussian!" There wasn't really anything serious

> about it, but you could notice the aversion and bias of one partition for another. The most wronged was the Austrian partition. For them there was no other name but Galician, maybe because they were the poorest.[15]

While the great wave of turn-of-the-century immigration to America tends to be perceived as a distinctly peasant movement prompted by financial necessity, in actuality economic, social, and political factors combined, often indistinguishably, to propel immigration not only from the peasantry but also, although in much smaller numbers, from the petty nobility, the intelligentsia, and the professional middle class. (The landless nobility, in fact, might very well have been poorer than their peasant neighbors.) Still, the enormous Russian and Galician immigrations, making up over 90 percent of the estimated 1.5 million Polish immigrants who arrived between 1891 and 1914, consisted largely of poor peasants.[16]

This presented special problems for patriotic author-activists in American Polonia, Poland's "fourth partition."[17] Not only did Poles arrive in this country as citizens of three autonomous nations, with immigration experiences shaped by distinct historical circumstances that were often sources of rivalry and suspicion, but those from the rural peasantry were unlikely to conceive of themselves as Polish at all. Back in Europe, a highly parochial worldview focused peasant interests within the family, or at most the *okolica* or *parafia,* the immediate neighborhood or parish, rather than within larger collectivities.[18] They might also identify with a geographic and cultural region: regional identities were particularly dominant among, for instance, the Kashubians of northwestern Poland, the Silesians of the southwest, and the *Górale* of south central and southeastern Poland, where dialect and cultural connections with non-Polish-speaking neighbors further differentiated them from other Poles. In 1892 Milwaukee's *Kuryer polski* complained that

> Poles in many Polish colonies are dividing themselves not only into "Prussians," "Austrians," and "Russian Poles," but even into "Varsovians," "Poznanians," "Galicians," "Silesians," "Kashubians," "Mazurians," and so on. Even the papers call them such. We in Milwaukee have not yet reached this "height of civilization." . . . Here one is called nothing but, in the old style, a Pole![19]

However, it was a new phenomenon that these mostly peasant immigrants might be perceived as Poles. Not only did peasants tend to identify themselves with much less abstract collectivities, but until the mid-nineteenth century the identity of Pole had been reserved for the nobility.[20] The distrustful and often adversarial relationship between the Polish gentry and peasantry reflected past exploitations and betrayals and the mutual conviction that their interests were essentially in opposition. And these tensions had been manipulated by the partitioning powers to help defeat Polish independence movements. The insurrections, it was charged, had failed in part because of lack of cooperation—and at times open warfare—between peasants and the gentry, from which the revolutionary movements originated. But while class distinctions, deeply etched in Polish society, continued to be sources of power and influence within Polonia, new opportunities for dialogue and understanding (as well as new reasons for resentment) also became possible as American conditions cast Polish social strata together in closer proximity than ever before.[21] The results would be important not just for the position of the Polish community in America, but would have implications for the status of any future Polish state.

Since most Polish peasant immigrants arrived in this country, like other newcomers from Eastern and Southern Europe, as temporary sojourners, the national ideals and loyalties that immigrant authors encouraged among their readers not only would shape an American-Polonian consciousness, but could be expected to reach their European villages as well. Franciszek Bujak notes the importance of Polish publications from Chicago brought back by returning Galician migrants: "As more and more of such cases appeared in the village, the entire structural organization of the countryside was altered."[22] One of the earliest immigrant works of fiction concerns a peasant who was hanged by Polish insurrectionists for supporting the czar. When a new insurrection against Russia erupts, his sons return from America to redeem the family name by joining the fight for independence. It is in America that the sons have come to perceive their father as a traitor, in America that the family has been transformed from peasants into Poles, prepared to rescue the Polish homeland.[23]

Among all the factors in debates over Polish national identity, however, the thorniest was religion. As a multiethnic state, Poland had been the home of Roman Catholics, Jews, Russian orthodox, Muslims, Lutherans, Calvinists, Baptists, and others. And so while Polishness is now associated almost universally with Roman Catholicism (the result of later historical developments and

Immigrant socialists in Canada, with author Alfons Staniewski ("Ajotes") at front center. The shield at upper left reads, Knowledge Is Power. Source: Casimir J. Mazurkiewicz and Victor Turek, *Alfons J. Staniewski (1879–1941): A Chapter in the History of the Polish-Language Press in Canada* (Toronto: Polish Alliance Press, 1961). Courtesy Polish Alliance Press

political positioning), the significance of religion to ethnic and national identity has at times in Polish and Polish-American history been a matter for heated debate, a disputed claim rather than a clearly designated border. In particular, opinions on the position of the Jew shifted and varied, with neither Jews nor Christians agreeing even among themselves on the Jewish place in national social, cultural, and economic life. Polish positivists largely favored assimilation. But they were opposed by conservative Catholics and Zionists alike, in a debate that became increasingly vitriolic after World War I. In the United States as well there were Jewish Poles active in Polonian institutional and public life and many others who, though they might think of Polish Christians and Polish Jews as distinct peoples, nevertheless relied on a continuing relationship between them.

Immigrant authors themselves represented a range of these positions and backgrounds, as far as can be determined from sometimes inadequate biographical and bibliographical information. For instance, they seem to have come in comparable numbers from all three partitions, with Galicia slightly overrepresented, perhaps because of Austria-Hungary's laissez-faire treatment of Polish culture. Although most authors were probably Roman Catholic, they represent a spectrum of attitudes toward the role of religion in national life, and some of the most prolific had placed themselves outside the Catholic mainstream. Writers emerged from the National Catholic Church, from the Polish Baptist Church, from the Episcopalian faith, and from theosophical circles. Some rejected organized religion altogether. Jews are frequent characters in Polish-American works, and Jewish immigrants wrote prolifically in Yiddish, but only one identifiably Jewish author wrote in Polish for Polish-American publishers. In Poland, Jewish writers tended to write in Yiddish or Hebrew until the interwar period, when a visibly Jewish Polish-language literature began to emerge.[24] No comparable body of literature exists in America, however. With the exception of Piotr Yolles, Jewish immigrant writers seem to have chosen Yiddish or English as their creative language, perhaps because most arrived in the United States too early, and identified too strongly with a multinational Jewish immigrant collectivity, to be significantly influenced by social and cultural trends developing in the new Poland.

As far as it has been possible to determine, most Polish immigrant authors came from Poland's intelligentsia or its emerging professional class. Many were college educated, though a few, like Stanisław Osada and Helena Staś, were largely self-taught.[25] But by the beginning of World War I it was no longer true, as Lwów's *Ruch literacki* had claimed in 1876, that Polonia's authors were simply writers of opportunity rather than vocation.[26] A handful of writers, including Henryk Nagiel, Wojciech Mórawski, Józef Orłowski, Stefania Laudyn, and Czesław Łukaszkiewicz, had begun their literary careers in Europe, while others had at least contributed to European newspapers.

Immigrant writers also represented a range of political positions, from socialists to right-wing "Endeks," followers of Roman Dmowski's National Democratic Movement. Wiktor Karłowski and Kazimierz Neuman had fought in the 1863 uprising. An American right- and left-wing dichotomy sheds little light on the tangle of Polish-American political strategies, however, which

Felicja Romanowska, singer, musician, and author. Courtesy Polish Museum of America, Chicago

sought to balance Polish issues in three rival European empires with immigrant interests in the United States. To understand the rival stances taken by Polonian activists, one must look to European ideological trends, to the varied conceptions of Polishness and strategies for Polish cultural and political survival that competed for followers in partitioned Poland and its diaspora communities.

The debate over who could be called a Pole, far from being a side issue of concern only to immigrant ideologues, was a controlling and shaping element in Polonia's development. It would play a part in settlement patterns, in the establishment of the parishes that would become the dominant feature of Polish-American neighborhoods, and in the creation of Polonia's highly structured organizational life. These matrices of Polishness are reflected in Polonia's earliest institutional rivalries, the most fundamental of which, between the Nationalists, whose first loyalty was to a restored Poland, and the Religionists, who emphasized the Polish Catholic's relationship to America and the Church, was personified in two powerful ethnic fraternals, the Polish National Alliance (PNA) and the Polish Roman Catholic Union of America (PRCU). The PNA (in Polish, Związek Narodowy Polski), founded in 1880,

Editor and author Hieronim Jabłoński. Courtesy Polish National Alliance

and the PRCU (Zjednoczenie Rzymsko-Katolickie w Ameryce), established in 1873, were sharp competitors in their early years, not just for subscribers to their insurance funds, but for the ideological loyalties of larger Polonia, which both organizations claimed to represent. Although tensions lessened over the years, leading rather to differences in degree than in kind, the PNA and PRCU disagreed in essence over the definition of a Pole. For the PRCU, Catholicism was fundamental to Polishness. Like some activists in Europe, however, the early PNA organizers developed an inclusive ideology of Polishness that was meant to unite all inhabitants of the former multiethnic Polish-Lithuanian Commonwealth, regardless of religion, class, political orientation, language, or ethnicity. (To some of those inhabitants, experiencing their own awakening national consciousness, this would come to sound more like Polish hegemony than national unity.)[27] And so the PNA accepted members regardless of religious conviction, resulting in charges of atheist, socialist, and Jewish influence.

The PNA and PRCU were not the only organizational embodiments of Polonia's competing self-conceptions, however. Other political and religious factions formed, with varying and shifting degrees of intercooperation. Eighteen eighty-seven marked the establishment of Polonia's Falcon (Sokół) movement, based on the Czech model of physical fitness and military exercise but with a specifically Polish agenda that emphasized readiness to fight for the Polish cause. In 1898 the Polish Women's Alliance (Związek Polek w Ameryce) was founded, partially in reaction to the PNA's refusal to grant women full membership rights. (This policy changed in 1900, after which the PNA and PWA often cooperated closely.) In its formative years, the PWA was heavily influenced by European feminism and Polish positivism, and most immigrant women writers came from its ranks. Polish-American socialist, communist, and labor organizations also emerged early on and remained significant until the 1950s.[28] And in the late 1890s, but with roots in earlier "church wars" over financial and liturgical control of ethnic parishes, an independent Polish National Catholic Church (PNCC) was taking shape around a populist ideology that combined uncompromising Polishness with an American insistence on autonomy.[29]

These organizations and others grew out of just some of the varying models of Polishness that were developing through dialogue and diatribe taking place on both sides of the ocean, particularly in the years before World War I. Polish immigrant literature, like its European models heavily invested in the national cause, gave voice to these internal debates as it attempted to shape and consolidate a Polish identity among readers from all corners of the former Poland, readers who in all likelihood had never thought of themselves as Polish before arriving in America. Crafting a strategy of national survival did not stop after Poland's resurrection in 1919, however. Rather, it shifted to considerations of Polonia's obligations toward and relationship to the new state, as well as increasingly pressing issues of second-generation ethnicity in America. The imagery of treason continued, even as the belief in an expansive Polishness found new, hopeful expression.

Emil Dunikowski, describing American Polonia in a series of letters originally published in the Galician press, quotes a public speech made by Lithuanian-born PNA activist Julian Andrzejkowicz, in Hazleton, Pennsylvania: "The fact of our homeland's partition, the infamous treaties that divided us up, have been effaced by the Polish people in America. Lithuanians, Rusyns, those from Great Poland, from Mazury, Krakowians, and even Silesians, feel ourselves brothers, and children of one mother—Poland."[30] Andrzejkowicz's optimistic rhetoric reflects not only one of early Polonia's major constellations of national self-representation, but the conviction that in America an idealized Poland was being created, one that admitted internal diversity but emphasized and essentialized an overriding collective loyalty grounded in the imagery of common blood. The work of immigrant writers is evidence of this belief, that the Polish community in America could indeed form the foundation of a Polish national spirit, whatever shape it might take.

2 ||| "Blessed Are the Light Bearers"

Polish-American Publishing before World War II

"ONE CANNOT TALK about Polishness," wrote Artur Waldo in 1938, "without the POLISH BOOK." Waldo was referring not to books imported from Europe, but to ones supplied by American Polonia's own publishers.[1] Common perceptions of low rates of literacy and lack of interest in or leisure for reading notwithstanding, the immigrant publishing industry, from its tentative beginnings in the 1870s, had mushroomed by the early twentieth century to include scores of companies producing tens of thousands of titles, including many written by immigrants themselves.

Who were these publishers of Polish-language books in America, and what sorts of materials did they offer their immigrant readers? What political, ideological, and economic factors guided their choice of titles, and how did these decisions shape American Polonia's ethnic consciousness and national loyalties? Finally why, by the mid-1920s, were companies forced to consolidate already diminishing energies and resources, leaving by 1938, Waldo's "Year of the Polish Book," only a handful of struggling publishers? Polish-American publishing followed the growth and decline of immigration itself, but numbers of new arrivals alone fail to account for the changes in book production. Implicated in patterns of reading, writing, and publishing are Polonia's varied but interacting ideological positions and purposes, as well as fluctuating political, social, and historical circumstances in Europe and America.

Polish-American publishing, situated within the general movement toward the popularization and commodification of cultural production, developed along patterns common to the American and European popular book industry. Like the American cheap fiction Michael Denning describes, and the work of Polish positivists of the same era, immigrant publishing, including that by Poles, had strong ties to journalism, sharing the same technologies, distribution methods, writers, and readers. According to Werner Sollors, these ties are so universal that it is "appropriate to focus an account of America's polyethnic literature not merely on the development of books but on the centrality of journalism in the literature of practically all ethnic groups."[2]

This connection to the press helped shape the physical forms, literary styles, and thematic content of the literature offered to and created by the immigrant communities, taking on particular coloring within each ethnic context. In the Polish case, it encouraged an emphasis on polemics and partisanship that reflected the divisions within Poland and Polonia even as the literature argued for proper avenues of unification.[3] If literature and journalism were intertwined, so were journalism and politics, and so the literature reflects these affiliations and rivalries, as well as the inevitable intraorganizational struggles for power and focus.

Printery of *Robotnik polski,* published by the Polish Socialist Party, Chicago, circa 1900. The paper, which also printed immigrant fiction, later moved to New York. Courtesy Polish Museum of America, Chicago

Immigrant literary efforts were not only published in book or pamphlet format by publishers who were often affiliated with newspapers, but also printed in the columns of these same, sometimes highly partisan, papers. Just as every major Polonian organization was represented by its own newspaper, the journalistic arm of a fraternal or other community organization might also take up book publishing: for instance, *Dziennik zjednoczony,* the PRCU's official paper, published several of Artur Waldo's works, including the novel *Czar miasta Kościuszko* (The charm of the town of Kosciuszko) and the collection of short stories about Gen. Józef Haller's Blue Army, which Waldo edited, *Czyn zbrojny Polonii Stanów Zjednoczonych w nowelkach, gawędach, i opowiadaniach wojskowych* (The armed effort of U.S. Polonia in novellas, tales, and short stories).[4] The paper put out by the Resurrectionist Order of Catholic priests, *Dziennik chicagoski,* besides printing Polish-American fiction in its columns, published works by Karol Wachtl and popular playwright Szczęsny Zahajkiewicz. In addition, its affiliate, the Polish Publishing Company (Spółka Wydawnictwa Polskiego), issued works under its own imprint.

Among other institutions and their affiliate newspapers that branched into publishing was the Polish National Catholic Church. Its newspapers, *Rola Boża* and *Straż,* and the Towarzystwo Przyjaciół Polskiej Narodowej Szkoły (Society of Friends of the Polish National School) issued works supporting the National Church and its fraternal, Spójna. One of these was PNCC founder Franciszek Hodur's apocalyptic novella *Faryzeusze i Saduceusze* (The Pharisees and the Sadduccees). Another newspaper that branched into book publishing was the socialist *Dziennik ludowy,* along with its satirical supplement, *Bicz Boży,* and its affiliate bookstore, Księgarnia Ludowa.[5] The Smulski Company published not only *Gazeta katolicka* and parochial school textbooks, but works by Karol Wachtl, Stanisław Osada, Iza Pobóg, and Stefania Laudyn, long-standing editor of the PWA's *Głos Polek.* Milwaukee's *Nowiny polskie,* another staunchly Roman Catholic paper, published novels by conservative activist Józef Orłowski.

Other newspapers that published or printed literature by Polonian authors before World War II include New Britain, Connecticut's *Przewodnik katolicki;* Baltimore's *Jedność-Polonia* and the affiliated Markiewicz i Pula company; Bay City, Michigan's *Prawda;* Pittsburgh's *Gwiazda;* Winona, Minnesota's *Wiarus;* New York's *Telegram codzienny;* Buffalo's *Dziennik*

Staff of Polak Amerykański Press, Buffalo, 1901; Stanisław Slisz is on chair in front. Courtesy State University of New York at Buffalo, University Libraries Polish Collection

dla wszystkich, Telegram, and *Polak w Ameryce;* and Chicago's *Dziennik narodowy.* A handful of newspapers like New York's *Nowy świat* and *Ognisko* and Cleveland's *Jutrzenka,* as well as magazines like the women's and children's monthly *Ogniwo* (Chicago) and the literary and current affairs journal *Jaskółka* (Stevens Point, Wisconsin) also published Polish-American works in their columns that were never released under separate imprint.

Although newspaper publishers played the greatest role in Polish-American book production, it must be added that a dozen or so publishers operated independently of the press: in Chicago and Niles, Illinois; in Detroit; in South Bend, Indiana; in Pittsburgh; and in Pulaski and Milwaukee, Wisconsin. Some of these, like Bolesław Straszyński of Chicago and J. Sobierajski of Detroit, produced only a few volumes. Others, like the Sajewski Company of Chicago, were well established and long-lived.[6] Books were published by institutions like Detroit's Polish Seminary and its later Orchard

Lake, Michigan, complex, and by ephemeral organizations like the Polski Klub Artystyczny (Polish Arts Club) and the Zjednoczenie Prasy Polskiej w Ameryce (Associated Polish Press of America). Although the difficulty of compiling a complete bibliography of post-1900 Polonian publications makes any conclusions tentative, between eighty and one hundred book publishers appear to have operated in American Polonia before World War II, some of them very short-lived and small-scale, some extraordinarily prolific.[7] About a third of these included in their catalogs literary works by members of the immigrant community, including poetry and drama.

Even during the most prolific years of Polonian publishing, this original writing by immigrants was only a tiny portion of its total output. But occasionally organizations or publishers sponsored literary contests to encourage local writers. One of the earliest was the 1893–94 Copernicus competition, which called for "short stories, novels, satires, plays, and scientific treatises . . . written in Polish, using Polish-American life as the background." The need for a distinct Polish-American literature had developed because

> our general character has changed. . . . So have our habits of thought changed, our manners and customs, even our language, which has acquired new virtues and new faults. Thus, the literature of our homeland is no longer adequate, and a real need arises for the creation of our own literature, based on the lives of our countrymen here in America. Such a literature will constitute a school that will teach a greater love for drama and books, at the same time giving our brethren across the sea a better opportunity of acquainting themselves with us, thus strengthening the bonds between ourselves and our homeland.

Immigrant authors would make similar pleas, but the publication of immigrant works continued to be constrained by ideological disagreements and political opportunism. The Copernicus contest resulted in controversy, for instance, when the first prize winner turned out to be Zygmunt Słupski, a member of the awards committee and the originator of the contest. The second prize winner wished to remain anonymous, but requested that any monetary award be made to the same Mr. Słupski.[8]

A 1903 competition sponsored by the Polish National Alliance was plagued with similar problems: it drew just three submissions, which were promptly awarded first, second, and third places. The top prize of fifty dollars went to

Office of the Polish National Alliance's *Zgoda,* circa 1910. Courtesy Polish Museum of America, Chicago

Stanisława Romanowska for *Nad Michiganem* (On Lake Michigan), a highly partisan novella about immigrant politics in Chicago.[9] Romanowska was a music teacher with two boarders, both of them journalists. One was in fact Tomasz Siemiradzki, editor of the PNA weekly *Zgoda* and also a contest judge. Only one other work by Romanowska has turned up: a short story printed in the PNA almanac for 1910. The possibility has to be considered that others may have had a hand in Romanowska's work.[10]

The most successful book publishers, however, were connected to "independent" newspapers, not aligned with any political, religious, or fraternal camp. The Worzałła company of Stevens Point, Wisconsin, was a very active publisher of books in addition to several papers, of which *Gwiazda polarna,* established in 1908, still survives. But the most prolific were Władysław Dyniewicz of Chicago and Antoni Paryski of Toledo, Ohio, publishers of *Gazeta polska narodowa/Gazeta polska w Chicago,* and *Ameryka-Echo,* respectively.[11] Despite, or because of, the partisan debates and infighting within the Polish community, the independence of Dyniewicz, Paryski, and the Worzałła brothers was the key to their success—a political act and a marketing strategy addressing the needs of the immigrant community but grounded in European philosophies. It allowed them to position themselves staunchly as Polish patriots, continuing the educational work begun among peasants in the old country among the transplanted peasants of the American colony. Dyniewicz described his pioneering role in Polonian journalism and publishing in terms of national evangelism: "For my whole life I stood faithfully by the national flag and sincerely defended the Polish emigrants. . . . I often think of it, that the pen which I put down was picked up by other hands, to work for the honor and benefit of the Polish nation."[12]

At the same time, Andrzej Kłossowski calls Dyniewicz "the first modern capitalist Polish publisher in the United States."[13] His *Gazeta polska narodowa* had its beginnings in 1873, and Dyniewicz began publishing books three years later. After he retired in 1913, the reorganized Polish American Publishing Company managed to continue into the 1950s. By the early years of the twentieth century, however, business was already booming for Antoni Paryski, Dyniewicz's onetime typesetter and already a steady contributor to Polish-American and mainstream American newspapers, under various pseudonyms.[14] It was Paryski who most deliberately manipulated the power of the press and of modern advertising and promotional methods to sell himself and his publications, taking his cue from American journalism and American and European models of popular book production. Using a carefully articulated populist rhetoric, Paryski took pains to situate himself as an independent voice for the common people, outside the sphere of clerical and partisan interests that fragmented the community, particularly during Paryski's boom years, before World War I. Reviled from the pulpit for his anticlericalism, he wore proudly the claim that priests had refused the sacraments to *Ameryka-Echo* readers.[15] In particular, Paryski exploited Polish class divisions to align himself with his largest potential audience of consumers, the mass of peasant immigrants who began arriving from Russian and Austrian Poland in the 1890s and early 1900s.

Like many of Polonia's founding journalists and writers, Paryski, though he came from an illiterate peasant family, had belonged to the emerging urban professional class before emigrating in 1883, allegedly when the Warsaw judge for whom he had been a clerk was arrested for revolution-

Antoni Paryski, not long after his arrival in the United States. Source: [Rosiński], *Antoni A. Paryski: Życie, prace, i czyny.* Courtesy Paryski family

ary activity.[16] Struggling for a living in America and educating himself (he entered the University of Michigan in the early 1880s but was forced to give up his studies for lack of funds), he became a Knights of Labor organizer among the immigrants, rising to an executive position. But at an 1887 executive meeting, in a characteristically confrontational move, Paryski reportedly resigned his post, accusing Terrence Powderly of "venality and dishonesty" in a Chicago stockyards strike.[17]

Whatever his origins, Paryski carefully and deliberately positioned himself on the side of the immigrant masses, warning his readers against exploitation and betrayal by those who claimed to serve their interests, and calling attention to the power relationships that wound through Polonia's attempts to create and control a unified community. Czesław Łukaszkiewicz, whose novels Paryski published, eulogized his colleague as "The Teacher of the [Polish] Emigration" and "The Champion of the People."[18] Others called him an agent of discontent and dissension. Paryski's career is a complicated, carefully measured mix of opportunism and idealism that made his the success story of Polish-American publishing. Writing in the 1930s, a factory worker claimed, "Everything I know today I owe to the publisher A. A. Paryski, because I read his books by the stack."[19]

Mindful that most of his customers had only a minimal education and little or no acquaintance with Polish high culture, Paryski worked meticulously to maneuver even the most questionable of his publications into the category of educational material, addressing his argument at two audiences: peasant immigrants, who would contrast Paryski's sanctioning—however patronizing—of their choice of simple reading material with the sanctimonious disdain of the intelligentsia, and Polonia's intellectual leadership, who would have to grant Paryski's nobility of purpose and utility of strategy. Paryski journalist Stefan Nesterowicz characterizes his employer in the language of positivism:

> Long years of experience have taught him that one must first teach the people to read, then put the simplest books, even childish ones, into their hands, and then gradually encourage them to read things more and more serious, more and more worthwhile. . . . The man who today bought himself the tales of *The Thousand and One Nights* will tomorrow require a crime novel, the day after tomorrow a novel of manners, then a historical novel; later he will buy himself a history text. This book will encourage him to study geography, then physics, and in this way his hunger for knowledge will awaken.[20]

Paryski walked a careful line between educator and businessman, and the works he published sometimes blurred the boundaries between literature, polemics, and advertising. The newly arrived immigrant in *Sen na jawie* (The daydream) is promised "Salvation, Prosperity, Equality, the Homeland, [and] Absolute Freedom,"[21] but he must first align himself with one of Polonia's ideological factions. He is disillusioned by each in turn: by a debauched clergy, by cynically faithless socialists, and by German and Irish union leaders in the pay of the bosses.[22] The self-styled Patriots are so contentious, the immigrant decides, that their newspaper, *Concordia,* should be called *Discordia*—a clear reference to the Polish National Alliance weekly *Zgoda,* or Harmony.[23] Only *Ameryka-Echo* speaks with an honest voice: "Paryski teaches people to follow their own mind, walk under their own power, and not be led like children" (42).

Paryski's assessment of his own importance may have been more than

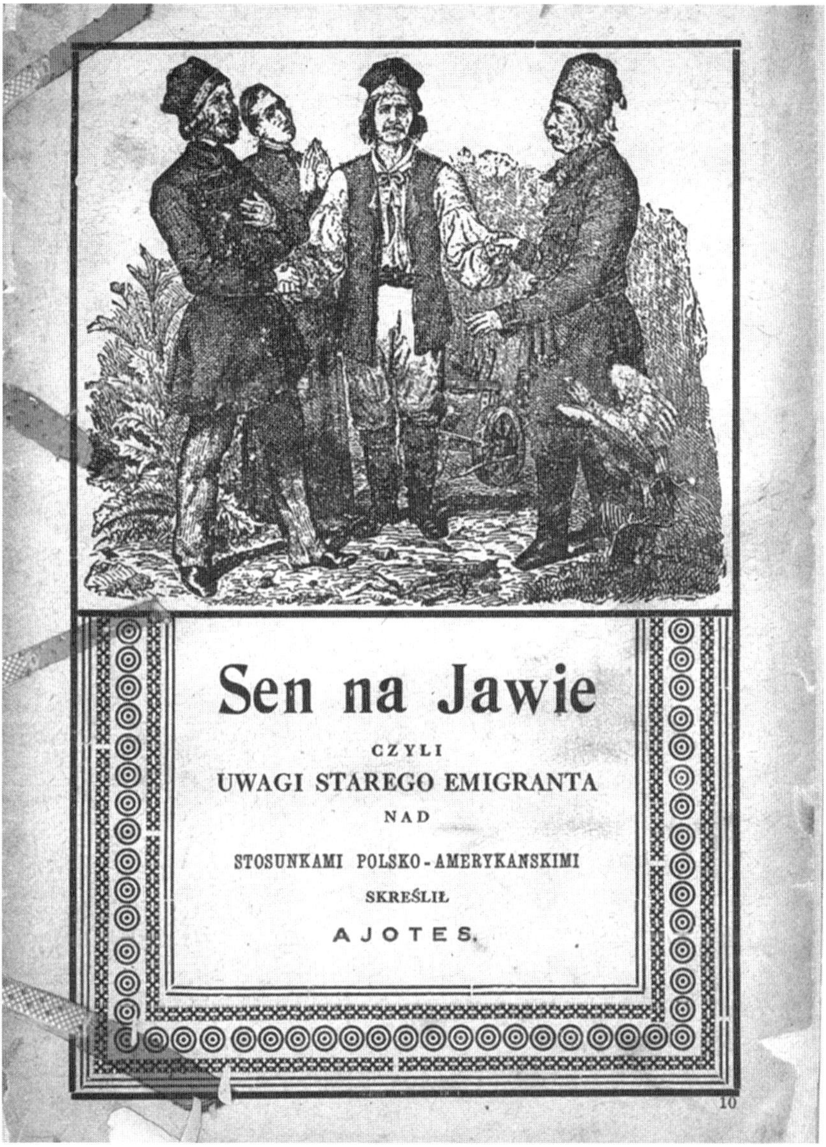

Cover of Alfons J. Staniewski's *The Daydream* (1911). An immigrant is pulled by competing representatives of Polishness: the socialist, the religionist, and the revolutionary.

self-promotion. Numerous immigrant memoirs solicited by the restored Polish government in the 1930s cite his influence. A factory worker writes: "I got the paper *Ameryka-Echo* and went home and read while my wife listened. I have to admit that at that time the paper was rather progressive. I once read an article from the pen of the now departed Mr. Paryski that people arrive at knowledge and prosperity through reading, that it doesn't matter what they read as long as they read and read and read some more. I listened to that advice."[24]

Another laborer recalls the new ideas reading inspired as the source of an awakened national consciousness (and, no doubt, conflict):

> When I got to America I went to church every Sunday and holy day for a year, during which time I wasn't interested in papers and books. After meeting the fellows who were living with me at my sister's, who owned several dozen books and got the papers every day, I started to read *Ameryka-Echo* and *Gwiazda Polarna*. . . . I liked reading [*Ameryka-Echo*] so much, and reading in general, that I couldn't wait to get home from work to see what was new in the paper. I borrowed books from the fellows and in the factory I read on the sly. There was [Sienkiewicz's] *Potop, Ogniem i mieczem, Krzyżacy, Pan Wołodyjowski,* and other little brochures. Those books and newspapers opened my eyes, so that from then on I felt what I was and what Poland was, what a series of battles she went through for her national unity, about the heroes and traitors. I wanted to know everything at once, so I didn't have time to go to church because I preferred to finish reading my book or start a new one.[25]

Paryski, Dyniewicz, and other journalist-publishers were able to operate so successfully in part because the business of journalism facilitated book production. First, it was expedited and made less expensive by the use of technologies and distribution networks already in place for the production of newspapers. Not only did Paryski, for example, offer subscribers book premiums (along with silverware, razors, and curative "electro-chemical" jewelry), but he and other publishers often issued in book form novels and short stories that they also serialized in their papers.[26]

A high-volume newspaper business (Chojnacki reports a circulation of more than one hundred thousand for the daily *Ameryka-Echo* by World War I) also made possible the purchase of state-of-the-art equipment and the employment of a specialized workforce.[27] While other newspaper editors might

Toledo printing plant of *Ameryka-Echo* and the Paryski company. Source: [Rosiński], *Antoni A. Paryski: Życie, prace, i czyny.* Courtesy Paryski family

be writing (or, as critics charged, clipping) copy, setting type, running presses, and sweeping floors, in 1911 Paryski employed seventy men and women in his printery alone.[28] In conjunction with newspaper publishing, book production could be very cheap, and very profitable.

That these works were so often produced by newspaper publishers also accounts in part for their ephemerality, and perhaps for a perception of their artistic inferiority. Most books appeared on cheap newsprint in chapbook editions, many fewer than one hundred pages long. Relatively few books, rarely works of immigrant fiction, were published in hardcover. But it was these low production values that made literature available to an enormous number of Polish immigrants on very limited incomes, facilitating the emergence of a populace of reader-consumers. Of three hundred forty items in Paryski's 1911 catalog, nearly half were priced at from five to ten cents. Dyniewicz's 1913 prices averaged only slightly higher. Given that *Ameryka-Echo* offered readers one dollar's worth of books for each newspaper subscription, these books must have been distributed in large numbers. Paryski alone, it is estimated, was responsible for twenty-five hundred separate titles, amounting to up to eight million pieces.[29] Distrust of the clergy did not prevent him from publishing religious volumes, either, including Roman Catholic prayer books. The market-conscious Paryski, like Dyniewicz, priced these popular items higher than his other publications. His *Lives of the Saints,* for instance, sold for five dollars, and his fanciest Bible for an astounding twenty-five dollars.[30]

Whatever the success of certain publishers, journalism could be a precarious profession. Julian Czupka, in "W jaki sposób zostałem literatem" (How I became a writer), describes the precarious existence of a Polish literary magazine in 1890s New York. For his investment in the enterprise, Czupka is paid four dollars a week "with the right to sleep on a table in the editorial office."[31] The workers live off handouts from their advertisers, and every week their manager has to win the money for newsprint at the card table: "When he won, the paper came out; when he lost, the world was deprived of that week's pearl of literature."[32]

Almost no evidence exists of how much authors were paid for their work, as company records are rare, but the financial possibilities for immigrant writers were certainly limited.[33] Although Paryski claimed, in 1891, to have paid Alfons Chrostowski $150 for his novel *Uwiedziona* (copies of which sold for thirty-five cents), other writers complained that they weren't paid at all. Stanisław Osada admitted, "It is indeed rare to hear of a case in which the author received some money for his work. As a rule, he would be presented with a few copies. Very often the author himself would cover the cost of publishing his book."[34]

In 1907 Helena Staś blamed the Polish-American press and publishers for undermining the development of Polonian literature, and of national consciousness, by refusing to compensate contributors: "I'm sure that more than one youth in America has tried his literary powers in the Polish papers, but when his work was exploited, and other papers repeatedly criticized it, he transferred his efforts to a foreign field, because there they value it and pay for it. If in these circumstances the youth is denationalized, whose fault is it?" It is no wonder, given publishers' economic exigencies, ideological requirements, or simple power plays, that many Polish-language authors who were determined to see their work in print were forced to publish it themselves.[35]

Staś claimed to have no choice but to "turn away from my countrymen. . . . Rather than my own, I have to learn a foreign language; rather than by my own, I must be moved by a foreign spirit."[36] She was to repeat charges like these, and worse, in her self-published 1910 novel *In the Human Market,* bitter with criticism of institutional leadership in general, and of the immigrant press and publishing industry in particular. In this and other works, Staś pleads for a distinctly Polish-American literature that addresses readers' experiences and concerns while serving national and community ideals.

But struggling immigrant authors were at a disadvantage, because publishers had a steady supply of literary material for which they did not have to pay at all. Book pirating was widespread among Polish-American publishing houses. In fact, even after the 1891 enactment of copyright laws, Russian Poland was still not under copyright agreement with the United States.[37] Again, Dyniewicz and Paryski were the most blatant offenders. Paryski, for instance, issued Polish-language editions of *The Adventures of Robinson Crusoe* (without crediting an author), along with works by Arthur Conan Doyle, Alexander Dumas, Robert Louis Stevenson, Harriet Beecher Stowe, Mark Twain, Jules Verne, Upton Sinclair, and Leo Tolstoy, as well as by contemporary and classic Polish authors. The matter seems to have given immigrant publishers very little concern, as evidenced by Paryski's reprint of a Warsaw newspaper's description of his company, in which the correspondent reveals that

> [Polish-]American publishers reprint without paying the European authors for their works, unless the author takes out a copyright in Washington for a given work. . . . T[adeusz] Korzon didn't get any material benefit at all from the fact that ten thousand copies of his general history were distributed in America. [Kazimierz] Gorzycki was suffering dire poverty while tens of thousands of copies of his "Social History of Poland" were being reprinted. [Yet] neither of these authors would be one jot richer if those reprints did not exist; as for the distribution of their books in America, they have a certain moral satisfaction that their works are entering the consciousness of the nation.[38]

Publishers were probably convinced that they would not be prosecuted by Polish authors and copyright holders across the ocean, and that non-Polish authors would not even be aware that their works were being released in Polish-language editions. Still, occasional attempts were made to protect authors. In his Winona, Minnesota, newspaper, Hieronim Derdowski alerted writers in Poland that their works were being reprinted in America and advised them that they had legal recourse. He even offered an English-language sample letter enabling them to request a copy of American copyright laws from the Library of Congress.[39] *Gwiazda polarna* was threatened with a lawsuit when Polish Nobel Prize winner Władysław Reymont, on a trip to the United States, discovered his novel *Chłopi* being serialized in its pages. When the publishers were forced to pay him a settlement, spiteful critics reportedly rejoiced that "at least one writer made something off them."[40] But piracy was so lucrative, and the efforts to stop it so haphazard, that it continued unabated until World War I.

If unpaid immigrant writers and pirated European ones were to take comfort in the knowledge that they were contributing to Polonia's enlightenment, the same blend of business strategy and national mission is discernible in publishers' promotional techniques. Besides offering their publications in bookstores (in Dyniewicz's case, one he himself owned) and through newspaper mail order advertisements, large publishers used networks of newspaper subscription canvassers to publicize and sell books as well. These "education agents," combining organic work with traveling salesmanship, traversed Polish settlements, visiting immigrants in their homes and suggesting reading material in addition to the newspapers they were promoting. Wiktor Rosiński, one of *Ameryka-Echo*'s editors after Paryski's death in 1935, described the work of the company's twenty-five hundred agents: "More than one of them, working hard for the cause and sometimes hungry, read selections aloud from [Sienkiewicz's] *Trylogia,* or [Prus's] *Faraon* to workers gathered in a boardinghouse room in the remote hamlets of Pennsylvania or Massachusetts."[41] A 1911 report describes how "an agent meets workers coming out of the factory or sitting in the tavern on Sunday, spreads out his brochures and books, pushes a five-cent booklet, and gets a promise that the customer will read through it; . . . if an interest in reading is awakened, he has another purchaser and a subscriber to *Ameryka-Echo.*" The approximately one hundred fifty agents in Paryski's employ, the report continues, earned 50 percent of the price of their sales, averaging salaries of around $15 a week, or $780 a year, though some agents earned even more by hiring their own hawkers.[42] According to Paryski, however, agents earned from one to five thousand dollars a year.[43] At any rate, the incentive to sell Paryski's books was surely made more urgent by the fact that the agents purchased up front the merchandise they carried.

These traveling agents are also narrators in some of the advertising fiction through which Paryski promoted his newspaper and books, and which sell the very act of reading, often by linking it to family and community cohesiveness. In these tales, reading is a social force for bringing together divided families. Rather than an individual act isolating each reader within a private experience, reading is communal, reinforcing a shared cultural framework and mutual responsibilities and expectations. Whether the readers are weary miners in a boardinghouse or husband and wife in their bedroom, they are participating in a shared act of mutual consciousness that was an important mechanism of community formation and regeneration. One humorous story, Wójcik's "Przygody agenta" (The adventures of an agent), relates how a clever book agent is able to get a reluctant wife to sleep with her simpleminded husband by selling him a subscription to *Ameryka-Echo.* Finally convinced of her husband's worthiness, the wife reads to him in bed from Paryski's edition of *The Thousand and One Nights.* Next, with a Paryski cookbook, she plans a feast for her neighbors and family, for the priest who married them, and for the book agent who brought them together.[44]

Polish literary critic Julian Krzyżanowski calls the positivists "worshippers of light,"[45] and Helena Staś's promotional tale, "Wspomnienia z agentury Ameryki-Echa: Błogosławieni" (Reminiscences of an *Ameryka-Echo* agent: The blessed) makes particular use of this positivist imagery. It also offers a poignantly ambiguous portrait of the Polish-American counterpart to Davies's "young lady of good family with a textbook under her shawl." Like Wójcik's tale, it argues for reading as the catalyst for domestic accord, but it is also marked by the isolation that independent women face in many Polonian narratives. In a miserable tenement household a wife would rather her husband drink his money away than spend it on a newspaper. "I don't want him to read. . . . I don't like reading," she tells the woman book agent. But driven by desperation at her husband's nightly retreat to the saloon, the wife finally agrees to subscribe to *Ameryka-Echo* and to buy a copy of *Lives of the Saints.* "Will the day come when darkness and evil will yield, and husband and wife in the golden rays of consciousness will join hands and be one desire, one love, one soul?" the agent wonders. Returning several weeks later to find the husband reading aloud to his wife, she steals away from the door rather than disturb them. Then, finding a rare extra nickel in her purse, she wonders what to do with it: "If I had been a man, I certainly would have had a drink." Instead, she goes to a five-cent show, where the presentation is a living tableau of Jesus, bearing "Love and Light." Her joy will not allow her to sleep, and as day breaks she rejoices, "Blessed are the Light Bearers! Blessed!"[46]

For Wójcik, the secrets of the marriage bed are community concerns. But for Staś, even a glimpse of the reading couple is indiscreet. Her narrator is isolated, although she moves through public spaces and participates in communal events. She is not invited to the marriage feast. Part of the difference lies no doubt in Staś's own bitter experience as a struggling writer. But the sphere of activity for a woman book agent, of which there were very few, along with her ability to make a living, must have been especially limited and precarious.[47] It is unlikely that she would have been able, for instance, to read Sienkiewicz to miners in their rented rooms, or sell books over a Sunday beer in the local tavern. Even visiting strangers' homes must have been cause for some suspicion. And the life experiences that would have propelled an immigrant woman into this profession—widowhood, separation, divorce, even higher education or intellectual ambition not directed toward church or fraternal activity—are likely to have also set her apart within the community, though not necessarily to have removed her from it. It is no surprise, then, that Staś's narrator moves about alone, even through her own territory. She and other immigrant women authors and journalists struggled against institutional barriers that their male colleagues not only did not face, but sometimes deliberately placed in their paths.

Since most Polish-American authors maneuvered within a relatively limited network of other journalist-authors who often circulated from paper to paper, intra-Polonian prejudices and rivalries could play an important part in their careers and reflect the ideological stances toward proper Polishness that they attempted to model in their fiction. Stefania Laudyn's short story "Biały murzyn" (The white Negro) concerns a newspaper editor fired from his position and forced into accepting a rival paper's offer, even though he has been a vocal opponent of the paper's politics. In the anti-Semitic *Trzech pachciarzy* (Three Jewish tenants), by "Stary Związkowiec," to be discussed in more detail in chapter 5, an insurrectionist-turned-journalist is betrayed by a political opponent. But shaky economics and simple opportunism may also have contributed to the peripatetic careers of many journalist-authors: in the seven years he spent in this country, novelist Henryk Nagiel worked on eight newspapers of widely varying persuasions. Stanisław Osada, whose prolific output includes two important novels, went from *Sztandar* and *Zgoda* (Chicago) to *Reforma* (Buffalo), to *Kuryer polski, Dziennik milwaucki,* and *Tygodnik milwaucki* (Milwaukee), to *Dziennik polski* and *Free Poland* (Chicago), and finally to *Sokół polski* (Pittsburgh)—papers ranging from the socialist to the staunchly conservative—all the while contributing to other Polonian and European newspapers and publishing several lengthy

Melania Nesterowicz. Courtesy Basia Kocyan McCoy

historical studies. But despite the instability and infighting, for most authors it was these newspapers and their publishing arms that made up the social and professional networks that enabled them to appear in print in America.

It was probably in response to political factionalism and social strictures that many writers published their works under pseudonyms, or even anonymously. While the significance of some of these authorial disguises is not always certain, they occasionally locate their holders in deliberate relation to the touchstones of Polishness in America. Kazimierz Neuman wrote under code names from his revolutionary days. Paryski, whose original name was Panek, sometimes wrote under the name Łowiczanin, which highlighted his origin in the area around the Polish town of Łowicz. Melania Nesterowicz began her journalistic career writing under a male pseudonym and even as a well-established editor often serialized her novels anonymously. Detroit's *Dziennik polski* suggested an explanation: "Maybe it was a female inferiority complex. Maybe she lacked the manly courage to look the cruel demands of life bravely in the eye."[48] Considering the range of social issues that Nesterowicz confronted in her writing, it is far more likely that she believed her work would be taken more seriously if it were thought to be written by a man. Committed to speaking out on issues she considered important to her readers, Nesterowicz also submitted anonymous articles to rival papers when she disagreed with the editorial stance of her own.[49]

The heyday for Paryski and for Polish-American publishing, particularly of fiction, occurred before World War I. A series of factors led to its swift decline in the 1920s and 1930s. Most important, Poland's rebirth at the end of the war brought the immigrant community to a crisis of commitment over its relationship to the reborn homeland that had repercussions for all Polonia, including the publishing industry. But with a restored Polish state, Polonia's intellectuals, many of whom had claimed political oppression as their motivation for immigrating, now had an open road to return. Some of Polonia's most prominent writers did return to Poland in the 1920s, but the expected mass repatriation from America failed to materialize—the "fourth partition" was establishing its own independence. After peaking in 1921 at a little over forty-two thousand, the number of returnees dwindled to fewer than five hundred persons a year after 1934.[50] And like the soldiers from Haller's Army who had resettled in the old country after the war, only to return in disillusionment, some of the repatriated writers reemigrated to America as well. Although emotional ties and an active and vocal sense of Polish advocacy survived, for Polonia the restoration of Polish nationhood led to a general stocktaking of loyalties that, combined with the changing demographics of a maturing immigrant community, resulted in a shift toward American concerns and a more gradual tendency toward English as a literary language.

Polonia's ideological transformations and aging immigrant population, as well as economic hardship in the United States, produced a new literary profile as well. Not only were fewer titles published, but the nature of those publications, particularly the fiction, was changing. Gone were the days of wholesale book pirating and massive printings of thousands of titles. Though Polish classics were still being reprinted, the medieval legends and tales from *The Thousand and One Nights* had perhaps outlived their usefulness for turn-of-the-century immigrants and for their children educated in American and Polish-American (parochial) schools. Gone too were the cheaply printed satires, exposés, and instructional tales by a large number of Polonian authors. Fewer new works of fiction were appearing, and the field of authors was narrowing. Generally speaking, those authors still active were producing longer and more sustained works, and producing them regularly.

Immigrant communities supported their own bookstores. This one, run by a Mr. Zalewski, was one of several in Chicago circa 1910. Courtesy Polish Museum of America, Chicago

As publishing outlets diminished, however, many of these new works were never released in book form but appeared only in extended serialization. Melania Nesterowicz serialized all her postwar novels in the Buffalo newspaper she edited. Likewise, Bronisław Wrotnowski printed his novels in the monthly literary magazine that he edited.[51]

During the 1920s and 1930s, the Paryski company appears to have published the works of only one Polonian novelist, Czesław Łukaszkiewicz, whose anticlerical and anti-institutional satires were evidently very popular.[52] When Antoni Paryski died in 1935, his children and sons-in-law took over the company, but although *Ameryka-Echo* continued as a weekly into the 1970s, with the printing-house operating as an independent jobber until it closed in 1973, the company's greatest success was already in the past.

A new company did enter the field in the late 1930s, but its connection with the turn-of-the-century immigrant community was marginal. Formerly of Warsaw, New York's Roy Publishers (Rój na Wygnaniu; Roy in Exile) printed mainly works by the Polish intellectuals scattered throughout Europe immediately before and after the Second World War, and so never filled the same niche as the earlier companies.[53] It belonged, rather, to the new growth of emigré publishing houses, most of them based in Western Europe, that emerged out of the Second World War. In the 1950s the Roy Company was merged with the old Polish American Book Publishing Company, and finally both failed.

In 1935, after an extended visit to the United States, Polish writer Wacław Gąsiorowski admitted that Polonian books had their own "long history, a history now and then vexing for Polish authors, but fertile and full of confused efforts." He speculated on the cause of their demise, blaming it on personal temperaments inadequate to the challenge; on a lack of enterprising booksellers, committed activists, and skillful publishers; on poor support from the Polish press; and on the comparative "poverty of the typographical garment." Still, he concluded, "It's hard to blame a group of five million across the ocean, when in the thirty-million-strong motherland the Polish book goes begging."[54]

The designation of 1938 as the Year of the Polish Book in America was an admitted reaction to the deteriorating state of book production and consumption within Polonia. In addition to efforts to make books from Poland available in America and to promote reading through the establishment of

Cover of Artur L. Waldo's *The Charm of the Town of Kosciuszko* (1936), a novel celebrating the centennial of the founding of Kosciuszko, Mississippi. Courtesy Alumni Memorial Library, St. Mary's College of Ave Maria University

book clubs and the awarding of books as premiums and prizes, Waldo proposed measures that would have given Polish-American works a wider profile and made them available to a broader audience. Besides calling for the return of the house-to-house book agent and for more extensive advertising and critical reviewing, he proposed a Polish-American library committee that would publish in book form works that were then appearing only in newspapers, and, perhaps most importantly, a translation project to introduce Polish-American works to an American market. The project, he appealed, was both patriotic and commercial. But only one Polish-American book, in Polish, was published under the project's auspices, the Waldo-edited collection of memoirs and short stories of Haller's Army, *The Armed Effort of U.S. Polonia.* Despite Waldo's efforts and the continued operation of major publishers, as Gąsiorowski had concluded, "The fine times of Dyniewicz, Michał Kruszka, and Paryski have passed, never to return" (97).

3 ılı Crime, Punishment, Atonement

A Family Plot

Surely among the publications Paryski's many critics had in mind when they accused him of pandering to his customer's lowest tastes, and of degrading rather than uplifting the peasant immigrant's spirit and intellect, were the crime novels to which we now turn. Crime and detective fiction, although not usually considered a major category of ethnic literature, is fairly well represented within Polish-American literary production. Not only were European works reprinted and serialized, but immigrant authors and publishers produced Polish-American contributions to the genre. In addition to their general appeal, these stories contained particular resonances for immigrants that help account for the genre's popularity and longevity. Even when lacking the trappings of an immigrant social reality, the Polish-American detective narrative replays the basic tensions over group loyalty and betrayal from within that mark so much other Polonian writing. Rather than standing as an aberration in Polonia's literary history, it restages these conflicts on the most fundamental level of common peoplehood—the family. Within the changing literary forms and styles these works demonstrate, it is possible to trace Polonia's shifting political and social emphases, as well as changes in the Polish-American publishing business itself.

As early as the 1890s and up to World War I, Polonian newspapers were serializing and Polonian companies were publishing American and European crime and detective stories, including those of Polish author Walery Przyborowski and, in translation, Arthur Conan Doyle. But American Polonia also had its own fictional detective stories. The earliest of these is journalist Henryk Nagiel's *Kara Boża idzie przez oceany* (God's punishment crosses the ocean), first published in 1896. Before turning to the complexities of this novel, however, it may be helpful to look at a series of crime stories that were published some fifteen years later and whose appearance may have prompted the 1912 reissue of Nagiel's novel. Although much less sophisticated than Nagiel's work, these works exhibit in crude outline the problems of family succession and continuity that other immigrant crime and detective novels treat as explicitly ethnic issues.

These were truly "pulps," printed on cheap newsprint in the form of five-by-seven-inch pamphlets of about fifty pages each. The adventures of Bronisław Sęp and of Zofia Jastrzębska, contained in a dozen or so short works written anonymously and appearing between 1911 and 1916, form the Polish-American counterpart to the American dime novels Michael Denning describes as "an essentially anonymous, 'unauthored' discourse" in which the commodity is not the author but the hero.[1] They include the Sęp adventures *Ofiara hypnotyzmu* (A victim of hypnotism), *Ograbiacze trupów* (The corpse robbers),[2] *Spisek zbrodniarzy* (The criminals' plot), and *Widmo w zbroi* (The phantom in armor); and, featuring Jastrzębska, *Człowiek w żelaznej klatce* (The man in the iron cage), *Krwawe róże* (Bloody roses), *Lekarka obłąkanych zbrodniarką* (The criminal asylum keeper), *Mężobójczyni* (The husband killers), *Mord w wagonie* (Murder on the train), *Piekielny zegar* (The hellish clock), *Tajemniczy mnich* (The mysterious monk), *Włamywacze* (The burglars), and *Wróg ludzi* (Enemy of the people).

Bibliographical information about these works is difficult to verify and the evidence is contradictory. Not only are authors and sources of origin undocumented, but their publishing history is also difficult to trace. Like many other Polish-American imprints of this period, most of the detective novels indicate a year of publication but do not identify the publisher, which can be deduced only from other evidence, such as the company catalogues that ran in newspapers, almanacs, and in the back pages of other books. Even these sources are not completely reliable, however. Wojciech Chojnacki notes that both Dyniewicz and Paryski catalogues were sometimes misleading as to which items were their own original publications and which imported.[3] There is also some evidence that more than one publisher released the same novel. For instance, *The Hellish Clock*, published by Chicago's Polish American Publishing Company (without a date), is also listed in Paryski company catalogues beginning in 1911. Paryski also lists *Murder on the Train*, though it also appears to have been published by Dyniewicz. Similar cases exist among other

Cover of *A Victim of Hypnotism* (1911), featuring the Polish-American detective Bronisław Sęp.

types of publications as well, particularly involving the Dyniewicz and Paryski firms. The competitive motive is obvious, but it is curious that both Paryski and Dyniewicz seem to have first published this novel in the same year. A publisher might be expected to pirate another's proven seller, but since this does not seem to have been the case it is more likely that this novel was reprinted from a European import that came into possession of both companies around the same time. No proof of this origin has surfaced, however.

Further evidence for attributing publication can come from the design of the volume itself. But since Dyniewicz and Paryski often used the same typefaces, border designs, and layout, these clues are more useful in distinguishing their publications from those of other companies. Cover illustrations can be helpful, but also misleading. For instance, *Rabusie grobów* (The grave robbers), a detective novel known to be translated from an English-language original, features on its cover a crude drawing by Paryski illustrator Stanisław Śleszyński dated 1909. The discrepancy between year of publication, 1912, and the date of the drawing may indicate that the cover was done for an earlier printing of the novel, or for another work altogether. The cover of another detective novel of the same period, *The Corpse Robbers,* presents yet another odd discrepancy: the illustration shows two men walking down a dirt path, apparently in the tropics. One man is a well-dressed Westerner, while another is bearded, wearing a serape, short pants, and bandanna. But no such scene or characters appear in the novel, which takes place in New York City. Clearly, it will still take some detective work to sort out the true origins of these works.

The uncertainty of author and publisher, the history of book pirating by immigrant publishers, and certain idiosyncrasies of plot suggest that the Polish-American detective series, though set in the United States, may have originated in Europe rather than in the Polish-American community. Michael Denning has described a "world literature" of American and European cheap fiction that circulated beyond national boundaries, "borrowing" plots but using local particularities to appeal to the immigrant audiences for whom the works were translated.[4] Although Denning was referring to the Jewish and German communities, Polish-American publishers may well have followed this practice as well, translating English-, French-, or German-language pulps and transforming their heroes into Polish immigrants. An additional possibility exists that at least some of these novels were not reworkings of continental or American publications at all, but simply pirated reprints of European works that had originally appeared in Polish with American settings. Jeffrey Brooks's study of Russian popular literature describes cheap fiction based loosely on American and European detective heroes like Sherlock Holmes and Nat Pinkerton and "adapted from or inspired by foreign originals."[5] These appeared on the Russian market only a few years before the Polish-American crime pulps and, like them, used perfunctorily American settings and social conditions.

A comparable Polish-language genre may have developed in Europe and been transplanted here. So far, however, no correspondence has surfaced

Cover of *The Grave Robbers* (1912), pirated from an English-language original.

between specific texts. Neither Karol Estreicher's *Bibliografia polska dziewiętnastego stulecia* (Bibliography of nineteenth-century Polish publications) nor his grandson Karol Estreicher's unfinished second edition of the same work lists these Polish-American detective titles. Of course, the titles may have been altered for American editions. But, more likely, these novels would have appeared after Estreicher's 1899 cut-off date. (Unfortunately, a bibliography of Polish-language publications between 1900 and 1939 is incomplete.)[6] Within the texts themselves, the action takes place between the late 1890s and the first several years of the twentieth century. And as we have seen, these novels did not appear in America before 1910. Chojnacki mentions the appearance of sensationalistic novels in late-nineteenth-century Poland and the reprinting of crime novels by Polish-American publishers, but he was probably referring to the works of Eugène Sue, Edgar Allan Poe, Arthur Conan Doyle, and other Western writers, which Paryski and Dyniewicz also pirated around the same time.[7] Finally, authorial anonymity, the lack of a designated publisher, and discrepancies in publishing dates may well have been calculated measures of protection against copyright prosecution.

But the source of the material, intriguing as it is, may be less important for our purposes than the uses Polish-American detective novels served and the readings of America and of Polishness they encouraged among ethnic readers. The purpose of this examination is to interrogate these novels for the meanings their immigrant audience may have given them. Not only are we asking what relation these works have to their American and European counterparts, but we are asking what makes their appearance among an immigrant audience significant, and what they are likely to have suggested to that audience.

Probably most striking about Polonia's pre–World War I detective series is their apparent disengagement with the debates of the day and the paradigms of immigrant fiction: with place, language, religion, work, immigrant institutions, family life, and customs—in short, the lack of identifiably ethnic elements. Trying to read these novels for such qualities will only disappoint and puzzle. They are neither self-conscious examinations of immigrant reality nor explications of proper Polishness or Polish-Americanness. Nevertheless, imbedded in their themes are some of the issues that other ethnic forms engage more explicitly.

The world the Polish-American detectives inhabit, though it is sometimes peopled by immigrants, is not an immigrant world. As in the Russian detective fiction Brooks describes, most of these narratives are set in New York, which by the early twentieth century had been surpassed in importance as a Polish settlement by industrial cities like Chicago and Buffalo. Still, while other Polonian novels have offered descriptions of New York that are nuanced with the historical and social details and perspectives of Polish immigrant life, the detective pulps, like their Russian counterparts, offer only the sketchiest of details. Although addresses and place names are sometimes noted with a journalistic specificity, nothing about the urban and suburban spaces of these works expressly grounds them in turn-of-the-century New York. And, with minor exceptions, the society in which they maneuver has nothing specifically Polish-American about it—none of the landmarks of ethnic community so prominent in other immigrant novels, not the cafés, churches, taverns, or boardinghouses through which the immigrant characters in other Polish-American novels move. The New York of the detective pulps could be any city, not necessarily an American one. In fact, despite the assigned setting, these works suggest a European social and material landscape, with a perfunctory American overlay. *The Phantom in Armor* even brings its immigrant protagonist to a Polish castle to solve a case. Like the Russian pulps, these too exhibit an apparent disregard for or ignorance of geography: Sęp and his assistant arrive in Poznań the day after being summoned from New York. In other novels, the middle class live in "villas" and even working-class characters live not in tenements but in modest suburban cottages.

The immigrant factor, when it is present at all, is detached and static. Where the new Polish-American bourgeoisie appears, it has replicated European social relations, forming a new gentry class. In *A Victim of Hypnotism,* for instance, the New York home of millionaire Jan Nagórski, a "noble-faced" brewer, gives "the impression of an ancient castle," complete with hunting room. It is staffed by a bevy of faithful servants, "almost all Poles," whom the police characterize as "good and honest people."[8] Despite an overlay of factual detail—the recitation of names, dates, and addresses, the quotation of newspaper reports, the enumeration of prison sentences—for these stories to be understood in ethnic terms they must be read not as primitive attempts at realism but as allegories. Only then can their meaning as Polish-American literature be explicated.

The treatment of language can also perplex the reader examining these narratives for their ethnic elements. While linguistic tensions are a common

Cover of *Enemy of the People* (1911), one of the Zofia Jastrzębska novels.

feature of immigrant works, including other Polish-American ones, these crime stories are rendered in an undifferentiated Polish, and linguistic boundaries simply disappear. The speech of criminals, common citizens, fresh immigrants, American police, and Polish private detectives is rendered unproblematically into simple, standard Polish. This may have served a useful purpose, easing readers into basic literacy while familiarizing them with standard Polish grammar, orthography, and vocabulary (or at least familiarizing them with a dozen different words for scoundrel). It may also have been the simple result of authorial indifference or lack of literary sophistication. But for immigrant readers and writers, language was rarely a matter of indifference; rather, it was a fundamental source of antagonism as well as of community consolidation.

If under the partitions the presence of Jews, Germans, Lithuanians, Russians, Byelorussians, Ukrainians, and Rusyns, not to mention the dialect-speaking Pomeranians, Górale, and Kashubians, made the use of Polish problematic as a denominator of common identity, the immigrant world was also linguistically mixed. Even when they had little contact with individual Americans, Polish immigrants confronted the English language in the realms of commerce, entertainment, and civic authority. Within immigrant neighborhoods Poles were likely to interact with other linguistic groups as well, particularly with those with whom they had shared territory in Europe and near whom they tended to settle in America. Assailed by various forces, particularly by the gradual inroads of Americanisms into Polish-American speech, by pressures to educate their children in English, and by a Church hierarchy that was often unsympathetic, if not openly hostile, to Polish parishes, language maintenance became a powerful issue in Polonia, as it was in partitioned Poland, where German and Russian authorities had enforced policies against the use of Polish within civic, social, educational, and religious institutions. Consequently, language retention was often invoked as a rallying point of Polish nationalism, on both sides of the ocean. "Language," according to Norman Davies, "even more than birth or religion, is the essential ingredient of Polish nationality."[9]

But language is so invisible an issue in the crime novels that even dialogues that must logically be taking place in English are rendered in unambiguous Polish, with no authorial explanation or change in style. In *A Victim of Hypnotism,* Sęp is questioning the murder victim's immigrant valet, presumably in Polish, when Police Inspector Connell interrupts to answer Sęp's question himself. The language of the crime narratives does not reflect immigrant linguistic experience; it does not reproduce the contested and defended Polish language(s) that immigrants spoke, nor replay the accommodations and adjustments inevitable in a multilingual society. Instead, these tales offer a world that is communicated and experienced through a prism of deproblematized Polish.

If the Polish is generally unmediated by English, the names of characters of unspecified ethnicity are sometimes hybridized, with such results as "Marta Smith" and "James Waldek." The preponderance of Anglo-Saxon names might support the claim that these are polonized English-language novels, but the compounds also signal issues of identity and linguistic power that must have had meaning for their immigrant readers, so often forced to modify their names for American tongues. However, all characters explicitly identified as Polish retain their names in full, including the detectives, whose rather difficult Polish names apparently give the American characters no problem.

While these Polish narratives seem to fit only uneasily into paradigms of ethnic literature, they do echo patterns common to the popular crime fiction of other languages, and these patterns offer clues to the significance of these works in an immigrant context. In particular, the crimes, usually perpetrated by members of the victim's own family, tend to turn on matters of inheritance. Leroy Panek dismisses the "inheritance plot," which dominated European cheap fiction, as the "most amenable to sentimental fiction because inheritances invariably mean missing heirs and other romance motifs."[10] But it must have had more immediate meanings, both personal and political, in novels marketed for immigrant audiences, reflecting an uncertainty about the proper ordering and transmission of familial values/valuables that is also encountered in more conventional immigrant and ethnic novels. Casting the crime in familial terms, these novels are less about the violation of law than of blood, less about the usurpation of property rights than the betrayal of kinship. Rather than indicating a less sophisticated literature, as Panek suggests, these themes root the works in deeply felt anxieties about the meanings and obligations of family and generational succession, anxieties that had literal and metaphoric significance for Poles in Europe and in America.

Like the German-language reprints examined by Brooks, the origin of these pulps is less important than the stories they articulated to their Polish immigrant readers. Their overarching concern with family legacy and continuity has material as well as symbolic meaning. The inheritance plot must have struck a chord among peasant immigrants, for whom family and property were intertwined values that could unite and estrange relatives on both sides of the ocean, just as they do in the detective narratives. The very act of migration was often weighted with these concerns, as immigrants left their villages because family land had been subdivided beyond tenability, and as sojourners arrived with the intention of earning money to expand holdings in Europe. The immigrant letter writers of William Thomas and Florian Znaniecki's *Polish Peasant in Europe and America* express their continued engagement with issues of family property, readable in the common descriptions of old-country weather and crop conditions, details of land disputes, and explicit directions for buying more property with remittances from America. These letters indicate a sophisticated understanding of the intricacies of property rights and inheritance, an urgency over the proper distribution of family holdings, and a conviction of the connection between the integrity of family and of property.[11]

And these are also issues that have wider political significance in the context of carved-up Poland, where branches of the national polity had been severed and literature offered a voice of resistance. Metaphor was not simply a literary device but a language of opposition, which Poles were adept at reading. Thus Poland and Polonia's shared preoccupation with issues of common peoplehood and group loyalty become readable in the recurring metaphors of family treachery and threats to generational continuity upon which most of the detective plots depend. These themes conflate the political and the familial, and the crimes are so shockingly sensational precisely because they betray codes of group loyalty and threaten group continuity.

In all but one of the Bronisław Sęp crime novels, the plot turns on threats to familial order, reconfiguring the same basic anxieties over reproducing the line of descent, maintaining group unity, and transmitting an ancestral legacy. These are threatened by failure and betrayal from within the family itself, when some aberration or disruption of the normal line of descent, such as marriage across social or international borders, or a sexless or childless marriage, divides the family and pits brother against brother, son against father, nephew against uncle in competition for family resources. These intrafamilial plots are played on an international field: in all these stories, immigration becomes a way out of unhappy circumstances at home.

Whether these novels take place in Poland or New York, the troubled family is haunted—sometimes literally—by itself, by the legacy of a more glorious past, of a birthright denied, threatened by complicity with outside enemies and by betrayal from within. In *A Victim of Hypnotism,* for instance, an orphaned brother induces his innocent sister to commit murder so that he can collect the inheritance willed to her by her adoptive family. In *The Corpse Robbers,* two profligate nephews, the offspring of an inappropriate marriage, steal what they consider their rightful legacy from the grave of their uncle. And in *The Phantom in Armor,* set in Poland's Kruszwicki Castle, a disinherited brother kidnaps his brother's wife and haunts his bedroom with ghostly simulations of their ancestors. (Any reading of this last novel was likely to be nuanced by familiarity with the well-known legend of the castle's proprietor, King Popiel, who, under the influence of his debauched German wife, mistreated his subjects, ran his country into ruin, and poisoned his own uncles, only to be eaten by mice.)[12]

The converging themes of inheritance and family continuity do not determine one straightforward "immigrant" reading of these stories, a metatext of unambiguous moral unity. The formula of style, plot, and theme does not translate into a recipe for the (re)unification of divided families or nations. Rather, these works wrangle with the pitfalls of creating, maintaining, and reproducing internal coherence and cohesion, without offering the means to do so. This becomes especially clear when we turn to tales of the woman detective Zofia Jastrzębska. The crimes described in these works are not only more gruesome and disturbing than those in the Sęp adventures, but the outcome is more ambiguous, despite the fact that the crime is invariably solved and the criminals punished.

Besides reflecting familiar tensions over inheritance and progeny, these Jastrzębska stories tend to portray children, the future generation, as particularly under threat, and to equivocate over the ability of women to act as independent "agents." Kathleen Gregory Klein demonstrates the way American and British detective fiction undermine the position of women detectives by portraying them as either "inadequate women or inadequate detectives."[13] Although the English-language works she discusses seem to address gender and sexuality much more directly than the Polish-American ones do, the result is similar. While Jastrzębska is hailed as a famous detective, admired by male colleagues and feared by criminals, her cases leave questions about her competence, since a male sidekick must invariably snatch her again and again from danger. Without him, no crime would be solved. But even with the criminal behind bars, the family line, rather than being restored or repaired through the detective's efforts, is left in disarray.

In *The Hellish Clock,* for instance, Jastrzębska is thwarted by a simple door lock from saving the life of an heiress, and though the criminals are captured, the fortune goes to surviving distant relatives. In *Enemy of the People* Jastrzębska's (male) assistant must rescue his mentor from child killer William Pinkerton, whose basement is full of vivisected children.[14] The villain is finally imprisoned, but all the children are dead. In *Murder on the Train,* Jastrzębska cannot prevent an American husband from murdering his Polish wife for her fortune, although the family jewels are ultimately recovered. The convergence of gender patterns within these Jastrzębska stories with those of other crime pulps involving women detectives suggests, first of all, that all these works—whatever their origin—are products of similar trends in popular literature and shared concerns over women's autonomy. But within the Polish context, readings of both the Sęp and Jastrzębska novels take on additional colorings.

Rather than mere throwbacks to an earlier "sentimental" plot, as Panek and other historians of detective fiction charge, these formulaic stories must have echoed with meaning for their readers, simultaneously rearticulating their own anxieties about internal and external threats to family and ethnic continuity, and finally offering only an ambiguous catharsis. Despite the missing explicit engagement with immigrant social reality, these works reflect the concerns of immigrants at multiple levels, touching simultaneously on personal issues of inheritance and property, on metaphorical concerns about family loyalty and ethnic continuity, and on powerful historical conceptions of a divided Poland betrayed from within, by its allies and its own people. In addition, the Jastrzębska novels suggest evolving sources of these threats and anxieties, both in the modern world of science unchecked by morality and family feeling and in a disrupted hierarchy of gender in which women act autonomously and assume power over men. These are themes that will reemerge throughout the literature in this study.

However, an earlier Polonian crime novel that engages these issues explicitly while using many of the same plot devices can help illustrate the continuing utility of these metaphors. After eight years in the United States,

Henryk Nagiel returned to Poland in 1896, the same year he published *God's Punishment Crosses the Ocean.* Over seven hundred pages long, it bears all the marks of a sensational novel written for serialization: it is an episodic cliff-hanger spanning twenty years and following its host of characters through several countries and a score of American cities, its twisting plot full of romance, kidnapping, torture, treachery, robbery, near rape, adultery, and murder. Oskar Czarnik calls it a "criminal-adventure novel in the Eugène Sue tradition." Wacław Kruszka accused Nagiel of being "concerned only with sensation."[15] But Nagiel, an experienced journalist, sprinkled his work with engaging descriptions of Polonia's nineteenth-century social and civic life, utilizing the familial and superfamilial issues that mark the other crime narratives, but in the explicitly Polish-American context that the pulps lack.[16]

It is impossible to do justice to Nagiel's sweeping novel in a brief summary. The story concerns an exile of the 1863 insurrection reportedly executed for a New Orleans murder. When his daughter Jadwiga (Jadzia for short) learns this family secret many years later from Baron von Felsenstein, the father of her German-Polish fiancé, she breaks the engagement and goes to America to find out the truth. Like Jastrzębska, Jadzia is a failure as a sleuth. She may be called Wise Jadzia and speak a handful of languages, but her search for the facts about her father, of whose innocence she is convinced, leads her nowhere. Trailed and thwarted by an assortment of conspirators, she must be rescued from danger over and over by Szczepan, a young man she meets aboard ship, who has fallen in love with her.

Familiar immigrant networks facilitate Szczepan's progress in America: "Everyone advised Szczepan what to do, where and how to look for work, where to live, how to live. . . . Three boarders immediately offered to share a bed with him for the night. In a word there was nothing to worry about—just drink and enjoy himself."[17] These networks are not available to Jadzia, however. Like Szczepan, she has no family to help her in America, but she also, as Helena Staś had lamented, has no friendly saloon where she can be oriented to American conditions. Following the trail of her father's misfortune to Cleveland, she must go to the English-language newspaper simply to find out where the Polish neighborhood is located. In fact, it is an American reporter who mediates between Jadzia and her immigrant countrymen, and who is Szczepan's rival for her affections. But it will be Szczepan who ultimately solves the mystery of her father's fate.

While utilizing such well-tried formulas as the hapless and endangered female detective, *God's Punishment* contextualizes the very issues for which one must read between the lines in the crime pulps. It introduces all the signposts of locale, personality, and social dynamic that these lack. With the eye and ear of a reporter Nagiel is in his element when he describes, for instance, the escapades of New York's immigrant intelligentsia. Here he enumerates the clientele of a Polish café:

> Bankrupt counts knocked elbows with clerks, whose "records" left much to be desired; the crazy inventor of a perpetual motion machine drank to the health of the artist-painter, whose expectations, never great, were now unfortunately sinking in a delirium tremens; the doctor of law from Galicia rubbed shoulders with the cabby from Warsaw; here were former cashiers and poets with their clothes full of holes; honest butchers next to the worst breed of gallows bird; there was also the fair sex, naturally of a very emancipated shade. This varicolored group had one trait in common. Except maybe for the transients looking in out of curiosity, almost every one of them had some stain on his past—a deep pain, a bad habit, some guilt, an incompetence at life's practicalities, some heavy mistake, and sometimes (though rarely) even a crime. (95–96)[18]

In contrast to the undifferentiated Polish of the anonymous pulps, Nagiel uses language to establish character, delineate social hierarchies, and orient his readers to Polish-American conditions. Characters drink a "pajnt" of beer while discussing "byznes." Sprinkled throughout are common English expressions likely to be understood by readers, and meant to characterize turn-of-the-century America's urban, industrial, and commercial culture, rendered in italics but untranslated: "yes, sir," "all right," "ladies and gentlemen," "time is money." As readers are guided through transformations in the immigrant linguistic terrain, standard Polish terms are given their phonetic Polish-American equivalents: "Irlandczycy (Ayrysze)," and Polish-Americanisms are translated into textbook Polish: "I'm a 'sytyzen' (obywatel), I'm a 'voter' (wyborca), and what are you. . . . 'Beggars' (żebraki)" (167). In this last instance, the speaker appropriates English terminology in order to assert power over the immigrant uninitiated.

While Polish names in the detective series are treated ambiguously, Nagiel pays a great deal of attention to the meaning of names, to the Americanization of Polish names, and to the rendering of ethnic names into other languages. Jadwiga Śląska becomes in English Hedwig Slaski, with the feminine -ska form of her surname given the masculine -ski ending customary in America. Sarenka Morska (lit., Sea Doe) goes by the decidedly more prosaic Ethel Morse. Characters use a variety of names and aliases, often a sign of illegal activity. Morski becomes the criminal Miller, and his mercenary cousin Bogusz is also "in Lithuanian Buguszas, and for foreigners with whom he had business, Bogge" (127). By *foreigners,* of course, Nagiel means Americans. Villain Bolo L. Kaliski, a smooth-talking con man, is also known as Henry B. Smith and John Dix, before finally posing as an African-American doctor!

Throughout, Nagiel shows a sensitivity to names as ethnic signifiers, with characters at their best when they go by their original Polish names. But naming sometimes has historical and patriotic precedent as well. In "Jadwiga Śląska," for instance, Nagiel signifies a greater Poland stretching from northeast to southwest: the name Jadwiga calls to mind Poland's most beloved queen, whose marriage united the Polish and Lithuanian kingdoms into the vast Polish-Lithuanian Commonwealth, while Śląsk refers to Silesia, the often contested, ethnically mixed region now forming Poland's southwestern border. Just as full of meaning is the name of Jadzia's former fiancé, Konrad, which had such powerful significance for patriotic Poles in the nineteenth century that it became an act of defiance to bestow the name on one's son.[19] The name draws its significance from Romantic poet Adam Mickiewicz's patriotic martyr Konrad Wallenrod, which also gave birth to the Polish term *wallenrodyzm,* referring to an "apparent servility towards an enemy whom one intends to betray and destroy."[20] Mickiewicz's fictional Konrad is kidnapped as a child by Teutonic Knights and grows to be their commander, then deliberately leads the Knights to destruction by Lithuanian forces, sacrificing himself for the good of greater Poland. Nagiel's Konrad will also be forced to choose between Polish and Prussian family loyalties, and his decision will bring his own father to ruin.

Poland's political dismemberment is symbolized by the characters that people *God's Punishment.* Poland's Prussian rulers are personified in the haughty Baron von Felsenstein, who married a Polish woman not for love but money. Regretting this loveless marriage to a German, Konrad's mother makes amends by raising her son to be a Polish patriot. And after a crisis of conscience, Konrad reveals his father's crimes to the authorities. This tragic family drama raises the suggestion made elsewhere in Polonian literature (and discussed more fully in chapter 6) that Polish elements, foolishly and naively drawn to the nation's powerful neighbors, may have been complicitous in its exploitation and dissolution. In particular, the accusation that Polonia harbored Prussian sympathizers was bandied about with increasing frequency in the years approaching the First World War, by political strategists who saw the best hope for a restored Polish state in an alliance with Russia.[21]

Others argued with equal passion that the greater danger lay in the empire to the east. While the more benign Austro-Hungarian presence is only lightly touched upon, Nagiel personifies Poland's Russian oppressor in the despicable Aleksiej Iwanowicz, who had seduced and abandoned a poor Lithuanian girl. His socialist agitation sows dissension in the American immigrant colonies and ultimately serves not the exploited workers but the imperial powers of Europe. Other works repeat this characterization of Russianness as the archetype of cynical hypocrisy, which seduces with the power of fanatical idealism, only to betray and abandon even its own servants:

> In these Pennsylvania settlements, in the depths of the valleys, there resided so many subjects from under the various scepters of the czars that the imperial governments had long ago started to disrupt and occupy them. The banner of Polishness, the Rusyn national ideal, the Lithuanian spirit, here developed next to each other. Temples arose—and the people learned freedom. Wouldn't it have occurred to certain governments to suppress all the seeds of liberty, fearing they would sprout in this foreign country and be carried back to the homeland? . . . Oh, it occurred to them, all right. And so first they tried to convert the people and then stir them up. To render the name of Poles, Rusyns, and Lithuanians so loathsome and degraded in America that they would be excluded from social dealings and advantages, so that they would be considered dangerous hooligans, unworthy to work in industry. What a pretty goal for their ancient enemies, . . . to suppress the idea and spirit of freedom among them and turn them into slaves, ignorant and brutal.[22]

As in much of the prewar fiction, threats to Polishness on both sides of the ocean are essentially intertwined, with the dangers often coming as much from issues of old-world social and political domination as from Americanization. In a social universe perceived to be so treacherous, defining and supporting "one's own" became a byword and rallying point, and often a code word for anti-Semitism. This brings us to the mutable character of Bolo L. Kaliski. Szczepan calls him "a villain from under a dark star": "Under the elegant skin of an effeminate aristocrat is concealed a bandit of the worst sort. He's a man without nationality, a Polish or Russian Jew, half Germanized, half Americanized. He has no national ideals, not to mention morality. It's enough to add that he belongs to the pack of political spies with which the Muscovites bless the whole world" (234–35).

Kaliski contains within himself the catalog of commonly perceived threats to Polishness: religious, national, social, sexual, moral, ideological. These dangers transported from Europe find new fields of expression under American conditions. Rich and powerful factory owners like the immigrant steel magnate Mallory, loosely modeled on Andrew Carnegie, not only exploit their workers, but form part of a worldwide conspiracy with European imperialists. While men like Mallory may occasionally facilitate the progress of an immigrant worker like Szczepan, they may also order the cold-blooded murder of hundreds of others if it will quell the insurrections in their own private empires of capital. In a dramatically described labor dispute clearly based on the 1892 Homestead strike, Szczepan, a skilled electrician, must choose between the employer who has favored him and the striking workers, who are his neighbors and countrymen. Just as the Jastrzębska villain William Pinkerton dismembered children in his basement laboratory, Mallory's "Winkertons" are ordered to blow up immigrant husbands and fathers. There is finally no question where Szczepan's loyalties must lie. Even as Konrad betrays his morally decayed Prussian father, Szczepan rejects his Machiavellian American mentor. Nagiel places morality squarely within the boundaries of Polishness.

As the villains are politicized, so are the allies. Among Nagiel's minor characters are two cousins, Mania from Warsaw and her Lithuanian cousin Jan, who are traveling to Pennsylvania to claim an inheritance. As in several other novels, Polish and Lithuanian interests are depicted in common, a reflection of the former Polish-Lithuanian Commonwealth, and Poles and Lithuanians, while not part of the same immediate family, are shown as related to each other by ties of blood and desire. It is fitting, then, that although Jan and Mania are cheated out of their money by a distant relative, they marry each other, have many children, and eventually regain their inheritance. The dream of a restored nation is played out in the drama of their shared struggle to regain their rightful legacy. And the novel ends with justice reasserted for Jadzia and Szczepan as well. It is discovered that the decades-old charge of murder against Jadzia's father was orchestrated by Morski, Mallory, and Felsenstein—the forces of capital and imperial power facilitated by Polish collusion—but that at the last minute the old revolutionary's death sentence was commuted to life in prison (thanks to the intercession of the governor's Catholic wife). When all these villains are punished and Jadzia's father is at last released, the way is clear for a future life in Poland: Jadzia and Szczepan return with her father to Poznań and marry there.

These intricacies of plot reinforce what is an underlying subtext to *God's Punishment,* the examination of Polish political identity within the framework of the crime-romance. Polish and Polish-American issues intertwine, as they do in other works of Polonian literature, as journalist-novelists elucidate Poland's political and cultural oppression under the partitions, encourage and shape the development and perpetuation of a Polish identity (augmented or not by an American experience), and illustrate proper responses to threats to ethnic solidarity. Just as the Polish patriot's aim was the reunification of the Polish nation, *God's Punishment* and other Polonian crime novels are informed by the national metaphor of family unification and the restoration of family property. Nagiel's novel must be, and certainly was, read on several levels: as an action-adventure thriller, as a family melodrama, as an immigrant saga, as a romance, as a social exposé, and as a political allegory. His simultaneous engagement of these issues of loyalty and identity on familial, ethnic, and political levels offers a clue to the meanings submerged within other crime narratives and suggests ways to read other Polonian works as well. Whatever the categories of communal identity, no matter who is allowed into the family, the same essential sets of intertwining and multilevel issues are replayed.

In the late 1920s, following World War I and Poland's rebirth as a nation, the genre reemerged, modified in literary form and style. Buffalo's *Dziennik dla wszystkich* began serializing turn-of-the-century Nat Pinkerton and Sherlock Holmes detective stories along with contemporary Polish potboilers like those by Antoni Marczyński. But the paper also ran the anonymous "Przygody polskiego detektywa" (Adventures of a Polish detective), set in Buffalo's Polonia.[23] Soon after, the Stevens Point, Wisconsin, literary monthly *Jaskółka* printed two contemporary crime novels, "John Neewen" and "Szumowiny" (The scum), by its editor, Bronisław Wrotnowski, writing under pseudonym. *Dziennik chicagoski* even rereleased Nagiel's *God's Punishment*

Cover of *In Iron Pincers* (1915), a political crime novel based on a real case of Prussian espionage and sabotage against the United States, by Józef Orłowski.

Crosses the Ocean, to some fanfare.[24] This new wave of interest in crime novels may reflect a confluence of Polish and American issues, as well as the concurrent development of a new American detective genre. While Polonia shared America's general preoccupation with Prohibition-era gangsters and their crimes, it was also struggling to forge a new relationship to the restored homeland. Now that it was indeed possible to "go home again," immigrants had to consider where their familial loyalties truly rested, activists were faced with hard questions about the intersection between their political ideals and their personal lives, and institutional Polonia was finding it increasingly necessary to assert its autonomy in the face of Polish attempts at control. As conceptions of the relationships between Polonia and America at large, and between American Polonia and the resurrected Poland, rapidly changed, the detective novel again expressed the conflict over and longing for family solidarity.

Less formulaic than the Sęp and Jastrzębska stories, these later full-length novels are more sophisticated in plot and character development while still working with elements common to the earlier narratives. The themes of family unity and inheritance are now interwoven within an expanded social universe that engages Polonia in complex and conscious relations with the world outside the ethnic enclave. Part of the intricate threat to a Polish legacy now comes increasingly from outside Polonia. The solution, however, is still a drawing in of the ethnic family circle, but in ways that recognize and attempt to creatively engage changing social and political realities.

These novels are linked thematically by a concern with reassembling the family, particularly with uniting earlier and later generations and making proper alliances for its perpetuation. Both Wrotnowski novels, like Nagiel's, are concerned with undoing the personal and familial disorder resulting from the false accusation of crime—that is, with recovering one's good name, reclaiming an honorable past, and so restoring the promise of a future. In *The Scum,* a Polish immigrant is led to believe that he has committed a murder; he flees to South America, leaving his young daughter behind. The rest of the novel concerns his efforts to clear his name and reclaim his daughter.

"John Neewen," on the other hand, plays upon the reconciliation of multiple assumed identities. John Martin, a clerk framed for robbery by the degenerate son of the bank president under whom he works, has created three new identities for himself: a businessman, the leader of a band of thieves, and the owner of a speakeasy. Though Martin exists as three separate people, in essence he has ceased to exist at all, until his name is finally cleared and he once again becomes a man with a past and future, thanks to the help of his Polish-American sweetheart. The values of authenticity and honor are grounded in her, even as she worries her parents with her American ways—speaking English, carrying on a secret romance, and finally marrying an American.

"John Neewen" is a strange novel that complicates the ideas of name, identity, and belonging by exploring community perceptions of the faces that characters assume and through which they represent and refashion their identities, and by trying to work toward some sense of a unified self. The consolidation of alternative identities, however, results not in acceptance into the community but in removal from it: not in a return to one's old identity but the creation of something new, as the vindicated Neewen and his Polish-American bride (and their Japanese servant) set off for a new life in South America. Still, even this presumably happy ending is offset by the warm picture Wrotnowski has offered of Polish-American community and family life, a world from which the second-generation heroine is willing to emigrate without apparent regret.

This element of intermarriage is a common plot device of post–World War I Polonian literature, with clear implications for familial and ethnic continuity, and will be explored in depth in chapter 6. It is also a factor in the richest of the later crime novels, "Adventures of a Polish Detective," making wide use of local social and cultural conditions. As in the other novels of the period, the world it represents is multiethnic. Polish-American policeman Drabczyk is pitted against a Chinese tong operating in secret tunnels under the streets of Buffalo, as well as against criminals with names like Polak Joe, Dago Frank, Cherokee Al, and Black Jack. If the Italians are portrayed as violent and cowardly, the Chinese as clannish and secretive, and the Native Americans as noble and stoic, if the Americans are factory owners and the Jews moneylenders, these ethnic stereotypes, rather than simply encoding prejudice, also elucidate Polonia's attempt to position itself as part of a many-faceted American society. But this search for a collective place within and stance toward a culturally varied America is inseparable from the legacy of an ongoing relationship to the homeland.

By way of a legend that Buffalo was founded by a Polish nobleman-turned-fur trader who settled among and was adopted by the local Indians, the novel links Poles with Native Americans, and Poland with America. This is the only Polonian novel to include the element of intermarriage with a Native American, the purpose of which, Mary Dearborn has theorized, is to legitimate the immigrant group's connection to America. Certainly the legend that this rich trader buried a treasure in family jewels on what is now an Indian reservation suggests that America is a land that Poles can also rightfully inherit. But Dearborn's basic reading misses additional implications for Poles. There is something more at work in the story of "The Great White Friend of the Red Skins" than simple sentimentalizing and rationalization. This union of red and white evokes the image of Poland's national flag, and the invocation of ancient leader Grey Eagle is reminiscent of Poland's own national symbol, the white eagle. Besides lending a historical prerogative to Poland's presence in the United States, the legend claims a "natural nobility" for both Poles and Native Americans, "the true lords of the country."[25] More than that, it suggests a shared experience of exploitation and disinheritance, with Poles relegated to their own "reservations" overseas by the appropriation of their native European lands.

That history of subjugation also manifests itself through Polonia's internal social codes, enforced through neighborhood gossip. This informal system of control may have reinforced group cohesiveness in the old country, but it contributes to disunity in America. Drabczyk is not only acutely conscious of his position as a Polish representative for those with whom he comes into professional contact, but of the mixed reactions he evokes within Polonia itself (*drab* can mean both strong fellow and scoundrel, and the derivative *drabant* refers to a king's guardian). For many, he is a traitor to the community because he is an agent of the law, of a system that makes a crime out of drinking and of the internal settling of disputes, and that places him in a position of authority over his neighbors. That authority, rather than emerging from the community's own values and structures, has been imposed from without, provoking bitter association. The reaction of one neighbor is typical: "Like every average man in the foreign neighborhood, he had an inborn fear of and aversion for the police. Why? Certainly from age-old tradition, when in the old country our ancestors rightly considered the Russian, German, and Austrian police as their enemies and oppressors." This mistrust is replicated in America, where "in minor quarrels over trade or between neighbors, the policeman, not understanding the Polish housewife's explanations, often took the side of the better-speaking Irishwoman."[26]

Drabczyk's position is also outside the scope of the working-class community: "These good people couldn't figure out how a Pole could be certain of his future here if he wasn't a 'professional' like a doctor, lawyer, priest, or at least a grocer, or if he didn't work hard in a factory. Aside from hard physical labor everything seemed unstable to them."[27] This professional nonconformity carries Drabczyk out of the community fold—he is taken to be an American, that is, a non-Pole, and is accused of not reading the Polish papers, and of giving up Polish sausage in favor of chop suey.

In these later crime novels, while the specter of the partitions remains, continuing challenges to the legacy of Polishness emerge from some new sources, particularly from wider contact with a varied American social landscape, in which *American* comes to mean anything non-Polish. At the same time, America continues to be claimed as a Polish outpost, as expanding social and economic horizons stretch Polonia's boundaries beyond the enclave and its own networks of power and control, and as the reality of a resurrected Polish state demands a newly negotiated relationship between Poland and Polonia. The resurgence of interest in crime and detective stories and the persistent reliance on inheritance motifs, woven into increasingly intricate plots, suggest the continued salience of issues of generation, descent, and family legacy. Family bonds and obligations, their maintenance and their disintegration, extrapolate to the ethnic community and the Polish state, encouraging a politicized reading of even the most sensational crime story.

The criteria and obligations of group identity that became consuming issues in Polish territory and in American Polonia found particular potency in the metaphor of betrayal from within the circle of family and community that the detective and crime narratives articulated. But Polonian authors also used this metaphor to explore ways of defining communal identity and its obligations. The migration sagas to which we turn in chapter 4 reconstruct the passage away from Poland in order to map out the boundaries of Polishness and to point the way back home.

4 ||| Crossings and Double-Crossings

Family Ties

In Alfons Chrostowski's "Niewolnik polski" (The Polish slave), serialized in 1893–94, a young man fleeing Prussian army service bribes his way past the border guards. Suddenly, he retraces his steps and crosses back onto Polish soil:

> He knelt and kissed the cold, hard ground. It was his farewell to the country of his fathers, to his poor mother—the land. She was truly poor. Concealed in her womb was the dust of his forefathers, once wealthy and free. But, unfortunately, she was not in a position to gladden the grandsons stumbling about in her borderless spaces—today's Polish slaves. They were compelled to look for their bread in the wide and foreign world.[1]

Chrostowski's passage, full of conflicting imagery of liberating enclosure and repressive boundlessness, lays out the ambiguities of Polish immigration under the partitions. In a Poland whose borders have been dissolved, Poles are compelled to carry their nation within, internalizing the criteria by which they distinguish themselves. If this realm marked only by historical memory and maintained by personal conviction is strengthened by belief, it can also be endangered by it, and so ideological battles signify more than petty infighting—they are the border disputes that give form to an idea of peoplehood.[2] In such a configuration, emancipation will come through the cultivation of ideological boundaries, even as one wanders across the geographic borders imposed by others. And the eventual goal is repatriation—symbolic and material, individual and geopolitical.

The novels and short stories through which these issues will be considered will be of a type familiar to students of immigrant and ethnic literature.

They fall loosely into the category of immigrant saga; that is, they chronicle the physical, psychological, and cultural process of emigration, from the decision to leave the homeland through the initial period of adjustment to life in a new country. All deal to some degree with the immigrant response to new experiences and circumstances, and with the relationship to the Old and New Worlds that these responses forge.

But these works also compromise any rigid definition of the act of immigration by treating it as a process, a continuing engagement with varied sets of boundaries and lines of demarcation: physical, emotional, historical, ideological, and theological. What is more, this process of passage is often envisioned as circular, ending not in assimilation and comfortable success in America, but in the return to, and of, Poland. The authors of these narratives reconstruct the immigrant journey in order to provide their readers with moral and ideological maps by which they can trace the paths that led them from Europe, orient themselves in American Polonia, and, ultimately, find their way back again to Poland.

By looking at ways these works treat the social and cultural pressures that resulted in and from immigration, we can not only position them within the context of an immigration saga genre but also identify ways in which they delineate sets of specifically Polish concerns. The discussion of these narratives will highlight their engagement with the boundaries of family, community, and nation, and with the literal and figurative crossing and recrossing of these boundaries. Like the immigrant tales of other ethnic groups, these works treat the old-world contexts that spurred migration, as well as immigrant community issues like language maintenance, religion, family relations, the work experience, interaction with other groups, and continued ties to the old country. But their treatment of these concerns is also colored by Poland's unique situation under partition and, later, as a newly restored nation. In particular, Polish immigrant literature is preoccupied with the issue of double-crossing, of treasons against Polishness facilitated by disputed ethnicity.

Themes familiar in the detective stories resurface, as the rubric of family is expanded and politicized to encompass community and national identity. This widening of the family romance beyond the home suggests webs of significance with which the movement across geographic and conceptual boundaries was weighted, and ways in which national and ethnic identities were

Cover of *From a Pennsylvania Hell* (1909), a novel about immigrant miners, by Stanisław Osada.

molded through the re-visioning of a collectivized experience of migration. Although the immigrant audience was of mostly peasant origin, these narratives often reflect the perspectives of their urbanized, politicized journalist-authors, encouraging immigrants to read their flight from Poland in the context of political oppression and to form alliances in America based on national ideologies. Authors were sometimes accused of failing to fulfill their obligations as educated Poles to enlighten and guide the immigrant community, something that could only be accomplished, it was argued, by offering literature that reflected the peasant immigrant experience. Undeniably, some works strive to this purpose. However, even those that chronicle the passage of young professionals and petty nobility offered readings of national identity that were charged with implications for the whole community.

The narrative frames through which authors created and readers perceived these stories should be considered as components of a rhetorical strategy rather than as signals of an undeveloped literary method. They reflect the continuing relevance and utility of literary devices like the folktale and epistolary fiction, which were based on community and village models of communication, alongside the novelistic form. Rather than demonstrating a developmental progression beginning with letters and diaries and ending with prose fiction, Polish immigrant writing exhibited these forms simultaneously and in creative combination and reshaped traditional forms to meet new cultural challenges.[3]

Thus Chrostowski's "The Polish Slave" is more than the literary enactment of an experience of Polish immigration. Like other Polish-language fiction of the Great Wave immigrants, its purpose is as much polemical as it is literary, encouraging a political reading of migration which has as its moral touchstone the reestablishment of Polish sovereignty and the affirmation of Polish identity. Even as these works shift their focus to events in America, conditions in Europe continue to supply the terms of negotiation and struggle and to shape the creative impulse. Familiar literary conventions are adapted to new conditions and opportunities. And familiar religious, political, and social points of tension in the continuing debate over the criteria of Polishness find new realms of expression.

That these immigrant crossings are often facilitated by Jews may reflect not just a more or less general characterization of Jews as outsiders, but some of the particularities of Jewish-Polish relations at the end of the nineteenth and in the first quarter of the twentieth century. Jews serve as common literal and figurative agents of passage, whether by guiding the traveler through unfamiliar territory, by arranging an illegal border crossing, by inspiring the courage to break free from social norms, or by providing an example of success and solidarity.

Of all the Polish Others against whom identity was most commonly measured—Russians, Prussians, Americans, Irish—Jews are the most ambiguously treated: the objects of admiration and resentment, of affection and suspicion, sometimes countrymen and comrades, sometimes aliens and betrayers. The liminality of Jews everywhere, but particularly their position simultaneously inside and outside Polish society, the unresolved questions over Jewish inclusion in the Polish body politic, the economic niche that brought them into contact with a world outside the village, as well as the Jewish lack of a religious homeland, made them apt symbolic middlemen to the Polish immigrants' pilgrimage.

The instructive purpose of the immigrant narrative is easily readable in many newspaper short stories.[4] Generally, these exempla deal not so much with the process of moving across borders as with the shift in values necessitated by these new circumstances. They act out the potentially disastrous results, for the individual but more importantly for the family, of the refusal to adapt—to embrace education, to respect the law, to accept personal responsibility, to persevere despite difficulties.

Through the example of a Jewish pattern of immigrant self-help and solidarity, *Przygody Lejbusia w Ameryce* (Leybus's adventures in America) offers a model of family solidarity meant to foster independence and personal ambition, values generally viewed with suspicion among peasants. Leybus, a Polish Jew, remembers how his own relatives put him to work as soon as he arrived in America, how they charged him for room and board, with interest, how they made him save his money, gave him his start in business, and advised him at every step. Leybus offers the same advice to a Polish Catholic newcomer:

> When our Poles arrive as "grinors" from the old country they don't look for work first thing, but get a gallon of "wiski," and a whole keg of beer, maybe more. That brother or brother-in-law to whom the grinor comes stops going to work and they start to drink. . . . Two, three days, and sometimes all week. Then they both start to look for work. Sometimes they look

> for a whole week, and sometimes for a month, and when they finally find it, it's every night straight from work to the "saloon." There this grinor begins to learn what's better, wiski or "brendy," and to honor the one who can drink up the most beer. But if that grinor learned to subscribe to a good Polish paper and read it, if he would start to go to "najt skol," if he would buy himself a Polish-English dictionary, if he would start to learn to read and write English—but oh, no! God forbid! He would never think of that at all. . . . They say, "Ah! In America the good life is just for Jews. They get all the business in their hands, and we Poles have to work in the factories." . . . [But] Jews help one another, while Poles swindle each other.[5]

That the *gawęda*, "a loose, chatty form of fiction . . . in highly stylized, personal language," remained popular in the United States is evidenced by the reprinting of European stories.[6] It was also well suited to immigrant storytelling: compact, entertaining but exemplary, and familiar to all strata of Polonian society. Its adaptation to immigrant experience helped link Polonian with Polish popular cultural expression, and refocused village codes of values within an urban-village framework. When the gawęda's instructional tendency was turned to social critique (and, inevitably, advertisement), it could challenge the institutional basis of Polonian life while still underscoring the importance of group loyalty, calling on the primacy of community relationships to reorder the sources of power and authority.[7]

Immigrant gawędy use the form's lightly humorous tone to dramatize the ironies in Polonian society and to demonstrate the value of group solidarity. Jan Niemir's *Jak się zemścił borowy Zielonka nad Wojtkiem Bruchyłą* (How Greenie the gamekeeper got revenge on Wojtek Bruchyła), the earliest identifiable Polish-American narrative, establishes the interconnectedness of village life in Poland and America. Niemir's 1880 tale must have been popular, because a new edition was released in 1890, still an early date for such fiction. This may account for its subtitle: "A Poznań-American Folk Novel," which reflects 1880 Polonia's mainly Prussian makeup, when emigration from Russia and Galicia had barely begun. Later works also take note of regional identities, sometimes stressing the divisions they reflected and encouraged in the Polish-American community, but none endorse regional distinctions in this unquestioning way.

In Niemir's story, a group of villagers from the Poznań area of western Poland conspire to save the wayward soul of a thief, using the common folktale

Cover of *The Interesting Tales of Matt Seedbed.* A "doctor of enlightenment" instructs an immigrant on the importance of reading.

device of the supernatural to trick him into reforming. Village life, the narrator tells us, has already long been disrupted by revolution and social upheaval, with bands of peasants taking advantage of the general confusion to pilfer the manor forest of wood, which in addition to burning for themselves they can sell to the new German settlers. The most notorious of these raiders is Wojtek Bruchyła, who has lost his land through hooliganism and "double-dealing with Jews" (19). More to save Bruchyła's soul than to spare the forest, the gamekeeper and other men of the village trick him into digging for treasure in an abandoned well until the village has a renewed source of water. When Bruchyła realizes the error of his ways the men decide to emigrate together, but only after a returnee from America assures them that there are Polish Catholic churches over the ocean. Though some of the men temporarily go their own way in the United States, as soon as they can they reestablish ties with the land and with each other. Bruchyła digs in the dirt of Zielonka's brother's farm until he and another immigrant are able to buy adjoining land of their own. They even send money back to the village fortune-teller. And Zielonka, whose name means Greenie, opens a beer hall in Chicago, "where he certainly was visited often by his [village] friends when they arrived at the market with their produce" (72).

Structurally, *Zielonka the Gamekeeper* contains two stories, only perfunctorily connected. The American episode functions as a kind of epilogue, and the book could easily have ended with the thief's reformation (as perhaps it did in an even earlier version). But there is a thematic connection: on both sides of the ocean the villagers' connections to the land, to each other, and to their home village are reordered and ultimately reconfirmed and revitalized in the face of economic and social pressures. While it is not quite possible to recreate the village of Mieczewo in America, village ties and cultural values can be reconfigured even in the heart of an American city.

The gawęda form encouraged an emblematic reading of the immigrant hero's experiences and invited a comparison with the reader's own. This is certainly the purpose behind Kazimierz Neuman's weekly columns for *Dziennik chicagoski.* The stories Neuman tells use the cultural symbols and values of the common folk in order to bring them a lesson about their own society. His humorous sketches from the streets of Chicago's "Polish downtown" cast an ironic spotlight on issues of immigrant cultural loyalties and identity. The following episode about Polish names, for instance, plays on the difficulties of

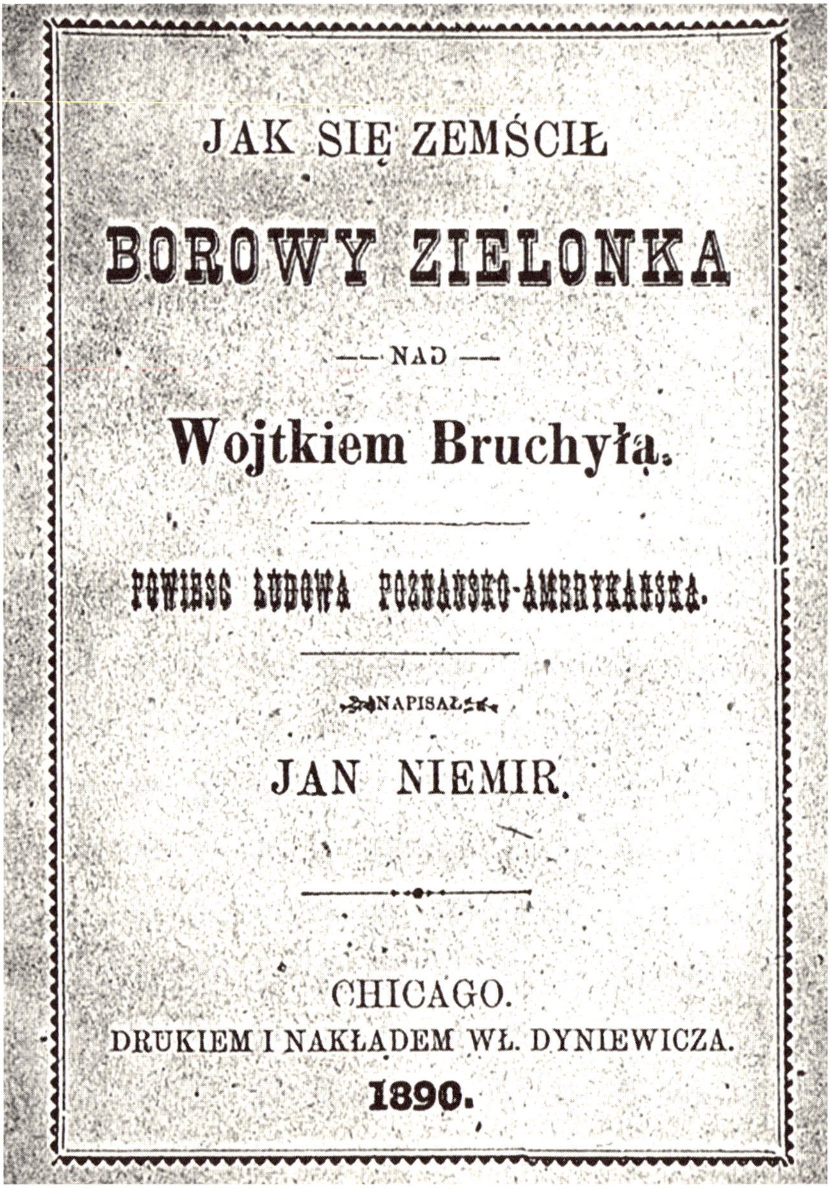
JAK SIĘ ZEMŚCIŁ

BOROWY ZIELONKA

NAD

Wojtkiem Bruchyłą.

POWIESC LUDOWA POZNANSKO-AMERYKANSKA.

NAPISAŁ

JAN NIEMIR.

CHICAGO.

DRUKIEM I NAKŁADEM WŁ. DYNIEWICZA.

1890.

Title page of Jan Niemir's *Zielonka the Gamekeeper.* The first known Polish immigrant novel published in the United States. Only the second edition (1890) is known to be extant. Courtesy Polish Museum of America, Chicago

reading the signs of Polishness, which can be variously interpreted as expanded, appropriated, or shared. Here Neuman's fictionalized newspaper editor explains to a newcomer from Galicia that "a Polish name doesn't mean someone is a Pole." The newcomer noisily agrees, since of the businessmen he encountered, "One was an Americanized German Czech, and the other, damn it, a pure-blooded Jew from the depths of Russia. Each of them argued that he's a born Pole." Not only does the editor insist that these businessmen do indeed help maintain Polishness in America, but under his breath he calls the newcomer a "grynhorn" for not understanding this country's situationally malleable and commercially utilitarian ethnicity.[8]

However, Neuman's ironic voice and sometimes unreliable narrator destabilize any straightforward reading of his position, and our sympathies are brought closer to those of the confused Galician immigrant than to those of the jaded editor. Our reading of all this is also complicated by the fact that Neuman must have been especially sensitive to the question of ethnic identity. His name is German, of course, and although the *Dziennik chicagoski*, for which he wrote, was a firmly Catholic paper, several years earlier Neuman had been accused of hiding the fact that he was really a Galician Jew.[9] This was a common charge against public figures whose names were not identifiably Slavic, part of ongoing arguments over the intertwined linguistic, religious, social, and ideological criteria of Polishness foregrounded by political disagreements, professional rivalries, and personal jealousies.[10]

A more familiar issue in immigrant literature is the changing of original names to Anglo-Saxon ones, and there are many instances in Polonian literature in which this tendency is treated, always critically. In Julian Czupka's short story "Irlandczyk z Smorgonii" (The Irishman from Smorgonia), for instance, a Montana innkeeper named Mac Adlo (that is, Jan Macadło) weeps at the first sound of Polish he has heard in twenty years.[11] The immigrant in "Listy Wojtka do starego kraju" (Wojtek's letters to the old country) hints at the class component of ethnolinguistic identity: "If he was called Jaśko in the old country, here he's Dżan [John]; if Franek, here he's Frenk; if Stach, here he's Stenli; and if Józkiem—here he's Dżo. The fellows here want to call me Albert, because they say that Wojtek is the peasant way."[12] The larger collectivity of which these men consider themselves a part, and which they seek to escape, is an unnationalized peasantry. Wojtek himself, who has been reading the Polonian papers and learning something (in his own confused way) about

Polishness, sees his name not as a sign of inferior social status, but of a God-given identity with attendant obligations and honor.

As the above examples suggest, the crossing of geographic borders can disengage the self from its grounding in the reinforcing networks of the community. When immigrants manipulate this confusing multiplicity to their own advantage, the result is a certain difficulty in properly reading ethnic signs and the possibility of dissembling and "passing." Julian Czupka's short tale "Tyrolczyk" (The Tyrolean) is a study in ethnic tricksterism and the strategy of identity; an immigrant plans to earn his living by dressing up like an Austrian and yodeling in American saloons. At an "Arabian bazaar" he buys a Hungarian waistcoat from a Jewish shopkeeper who is posing as an Arab and wearing a Polish priest's hat. "Ich bin ein Jaegersmann," the hero shouts, and makes a living passing off Polish drinking songs as Italian opera.[13] The message of this amusing story, however, is not that the immigrant can reinvent himself in a wide-open America. While such strategies may be temporarily necessary, they take an internal toll. Czupka's singer shudders all the while at his duplicity, and finally settles down with a Polish wife in a properly Polish home, hanging his Tyrolean costume on the wall as a reminder of his foray into an assumed self and his successful return to authenticity.

Czupka's insistence on his lack of literary pretensions and on the veracity of his tales positions him as a community storyteller, the preserver and presenter of the Polonian chronicle. Complete with names and addresses (he tells us, for instance, that "the road to America leads through Wiśniewski's saloon"),[14] these sardonic sketches provide something of a guide to new immigrants but more pointedly, Czupka tells us, they should serve as a warning, "to diffuse and restrain the desire to emigrate . . . among our young educated people, who after landing in America are exposed to so many disappointments, experiences, and disillusions that the poorest existence in Poland is a real paradise."[15] Almost all these tales involve some destabilization of identity, some loss of place and of self: an artist is forced to earn a living as a housepainter; a young gentleman becomes a tramp. According to Czupka, the surest way to reorder this world and regain one's bearings is to return to Poland.[16]

Czupka meant his work as a counterpoint to the letters from America that were passed around so eagerly in Polish villages and towns and that spurred so many new immigrants to follow their predecessors. Given the

Julian Czupka, journalist and author of immigrant short stories. Source: Waldo, *Sokolstwo.* Courtesy Polish Falcons of America

importance of these letters, it is not surprising that authors found the epistolary form particularly suited to the circumstances of immigrant literary creation, to the expression of immigrant experience, and to the understanding of the immigrant audience for which they wrote. Especially for writers publishing their works serially in newspapers, the inherently episodic epistolary frame made sense. The immediacy of journalism also allowed specific individuals, organizations, and events to be targeted along with more general issues. Through the juxtaposition of fictional letters between the immigrant and those left behind in the old country, authors contrasted conditions and experiences in both countries and demonstrated immigration's power to transform the individual and the culture. Often this juxtaposition provided an ironic, sometimes comic, comment on both societies.

Perhaps the most important aspect of the immigrant epistolary, however, is its reflection of a mode of communication that the immigrants themselves utilized, understood, and valued. Immigrant letter writing was a convention in which social and familial relations were honored within a codified system that nevertheless allowed for individual expression of intimate feeling and experience. Like immigrant journalism and gawędy, it bridged oral and written forms and reinforced a sense of shared community. Both newspapers and letters were meant to be passed along to others and to be read aloud; in essence they were community property. The specific conventions of the peasant immigrant letter, as Thomas and Znaniecki point out, had literal and symbolic meanings that all immigrants were likely to comprehend and that consequently provided an immediate window of understanding for readers of the epistolary novel. Violations of those codes could also illustrate points of cultural contention and change.

Listy Bazylego Szturkajły do żony w starym kraju i jej odpowiedzi (Basil Poker's letters to his wife in the old country and her replies), by "A. K.," is a typical example of the immigrant epistolary. Following peasant oral and written conventions, each letter from Katarzyna to her husband begins with the greeting, "Let Jesus Christ Be Praised!" and his to her with the response, "For ever and ever, Amen!" With the grammatical and spelling mistakes typical of the poorly educated peasant, as well as a sense of the vital community and family function of the letter, a typical letter from Bazyli ends, "Now I greet and bow to you one hundred thousand times. . . . Bow also to my godfather and godmother, and tell our neighbor Karaś to wait till I send the papers to buy the meadow. [Signed] Your eternally loving husband."[17]

The epistolary form is a reenactment of the national dialogue on a familial stage, reinforcing relationships but also reconfiguring them. The basic source of comic irony in the epistolaries is their transoceanic misunderstandings—the greenhorn tries to enlighten the peasants back home, but his knowledge is revealed to be superficial and misinformed. Likewise, the peasant's narrow understanding and ignorance of alternative systems of language, value, and experience are exposed through a wider American context. The immigrant readers, by implication, are no longer greenhorns but have already learned the lessons that allow them to laugh at this replaying of an earlier, more naive, self. Individual change and growth are acknowledged and valued, but so also is a continued identification with and attachment to the old country.

"Wojtek's Letters to the Old Country," printed anonymously in the Resurrectionist *Dziennik chicagoski*,[18] illustrates the episodic and topical possibilities of the epistolary form, using immigrant letter-writing conventions to feature and comment on current issues like the Lattimer massacre and trial, Jan Rybakowski's Coxey-inspired march of the immigrant unemployed,[19] local church wars, and the Spanish-Cuban-American War, in which Wojtek, like many other Polish immigrants, finally enlists to fight ("In

Cuba, Negroes live, and other people, and they're under the Spanish, like the old country is under the Muscovites and the Germans," Wojtek writes).[20]

A recurring source of comedy and social criticism in the epistolaries, as in the gawędy, are the misunderstandings resulting from the Americanization of the Polish language. This attention to linguistic transformation is not merely disapproving but illustrative of new concerns, values, and meanings that defied the understanding of readers back home. In answer to his parents' complaints about his unintelligible Polish-Americanisms, Wojtek attempts to map out a new linguistic geography: "*Orejt,* I have a little time today so I'll explain to you. A *sztryta* is a road along which the *treki* lie, and the *kara* runs on them, either electric or *kebel.* . . . In the *hauzach* [houses] there are *sztory, buczernic, grosernie, zaluny,* Jewish *kloting sztory, cygar sztory,* and others. Every *sztryta* has a different name, and every *hauz* a number so you can find a person."[21]

Such comical uses of Americanized Polish, Barbara Szydłowska-Cegłowa argues, lend realism by signaling "geographical-cultural singularity."[22] This language, which, particularly for readers in Europe, is a class marker carrying negative connotations, may work positively within Polonia, she argues, by "shading [the work] with sentimentality and atmosphere, which allows one to burst with laughter in a climate of intimacy, of familiarity, of the feeling of being an insider that that environment unites, consolidates, and identifies" (203).

Although in the long run Polish-Americanisms may have functioned as a unifying element in the community at large, most writers and activists at the time tended to see them as a signal of the deterioration of Polishness in the emigrant community, of the breakdown of distinctions that carry a moral imperative. The hero of Wojciech Morawski's *Na dwóch półkulach* (On two continents) warns against Polish-Americanisms: "Fear God, my countrymen! Isn't the wonderful language of our fathers rich enough, beautiful enough that you don't have to deform and offend it with such foreign borrowings?"[23] The laughter that greets this outraged defender of linguistic purity places him clearly outside Szydłowska-Cegłowa's "climate of intimacy" and points to the growing distinctness of American-Polonian culture. This culture, some authors argued, carried its own legitimacy: "The language is broken American," the heroine of Helena Staś's *In the Human Market* asserts, "but the heart and soul are Polish."[24] The Americanized immigrant of Telesfor Chełchowski's "Legjonista 'Dzioł'" (Legionnaire Joe) speaks "pure Polish-American, which

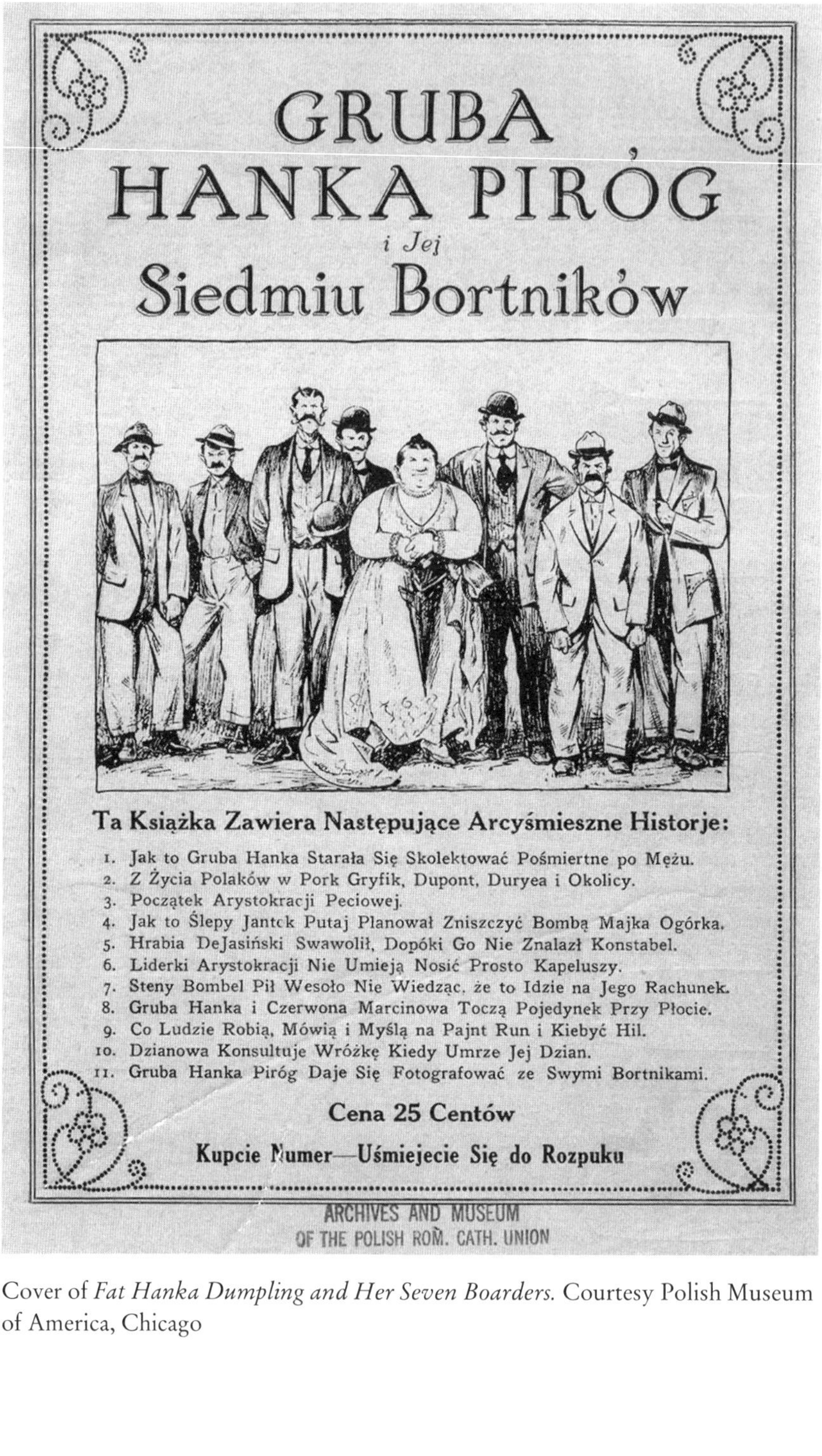

Cover of *Fat Hanka Dumpling and Her Seven Boarders.* Courtesy Polish Museum of America, Chicago

only a 'Polish-American' can understand,"[25] but at the first sign of war he runs away to Poland to fight. Even though his fellow soldiers can barely understand him, Joe is a Polish patriot. When he is awarded a medal for single-handedly capturing a group of Russian soldiers, he answers in "Polish-American," "Aj donkier o tytuły i medale! . . . Robiłem to, co trzeba było robić, bo służba ojczyźnie, to nie 'fon' żaden!": "I don't care about titles and medals! I did what had to be done, because you don't serve your country for the fun of it!" (35).

Wojtek's letters demonstrate the immigrant's attempt to reconstruct a social order, to find his way under changing and ambiguous conditions. His neighborhood, Wojtek explains, is Stanisławowo, where everyone is a good Pole and a Catholic, not like the schismatics in the neighboring parish.[26] In the peasant village, where everyone occupies a defined and understood place, knowledge of which is part of the inseparable past and present of community life, such explanations are unnecessary. But in America, a multiplicity of directions and possibilities can bewilder and disorient, and the juxtaposition of Polish with other cultural strands, rather than awakening and consolidating ethnic consciousness under a general rubric of Polishness, dilutes ethnicity and lessens its imperative:

> The same street presents itself as both wonderful and horrible. Twenty-story iron-faced buildings neighbor on little wooden houses glued together out of sticks. Here you have glistening-clean asphalt pavement, and on the next street dirt and mud. On another street there's no pavement at all.
>
> Here there are a thousand temples, and next door ten thousand taverns dispensing drunkenness and debauchery. The central city is filled with factories, lumber warehouses, combustible materials, and yards housing thousands of cars of the forty different railway lines.
>
> The Polish neighborhood is worse. The sound of a foreign language beats incessantly on Polish ears. The Polish Catholic church finds itself next to the temples of other denominations, and what's more, it belongs to non-Polish bishops. Polish habits are lost in the chaos of cosmopolitan customs, supported by the Pan-American flag. The lack of a system of persecution, and religious and national tolerance, work to pinch off the feeling of our group separateness.[27]

If any patterns emerge, it may be the repeated grappling, successful or not, with the need to determine the limits of kinship, define the boundaries of community, and solidify the resulting moral obligations. The episodic, topical, and dialogic possibilities of this narrative form may make it especially appropriate for juxtaposing the shifting and contradictory claims of emerging ethnicity and for leading readers through the confusion, if not exactly clearing it up, with lines of demarcation marked by language, religion, political ideology, and social class.

The epistolary novel, gawęda, instructional tale, and other forms of early immigrant fiction should not be viewed as evidence of Polonia's rudimentary literary development but rather as the consequence of artistic and political strategies emerging from very particular circumstances within the immigrant community. In short, these forms of expression bridged the oral and written word, and offered authors a way to conduct a highly nuanced conversation over proper Polishness that could speak to an audience of poorly educated readers.

When writers turned to the realistic, full-length novel, they not only framed their stories differently but they often enacted different stories, focusing on the educated Polish city dweller rather than on the peasant. This is partly, perhaps, a matter of audience: these more sustained works were probably perceived as appealing to more-educated readers. In part, it may also be a product of historical influences in the development of the novelistic form, and to the class-based perspectives of predominantly well educated writers. Class is one of the issues that these writers tended to underscore in their literary treatment of the pre-emigration experience, conflating the crossing of national and social boundaries.

A stifling social hierarchy and political oppression motivates the well-educated young immigrants of Bronisław Wrotnowski's "Szlakiem dolara" (On the trail of the dollar), in which well-educated young men who see no opportunities for personal fulfillment and career advancement in partitioned Poland look to America for fortune and a sense of purpose. Similarly, failed exams, boring jobs, and work assignments in foreign posts are the factors that propel the immigrants in Neuman's "Moi trzej przyjaciele" (My three friends), who find their success in Poland blocked for political reasons and themselves "wanderers among their countrymen, without a tomorrow, without a past."[28]

Each achieves some level of success and social power in American Polonia, but Neuman juxtaposes their separate paths in order to demonstrate the proper one. It's not enough, he shows, to have a prosperous business and a strong family life, like the bartender whose home is decorated with prints of Kościuszko and Lincoln, the two great champions of liberation from bondage. Neuman's heroic model is a poverty-stricken priest, who preaches

Cover of *My First Thanksgiving Day* (1908), a story about immigrant adjustment by humorist Henryk Szczutowski.

education and Polish patriotism from an immigrant mining town. The three friends of Neuman's tale articulate the bases of Polonian power and, for Neuman, the emptiness of any model of Polishness that does not include Catholicism, education, and the Polish language.

Neuman's young fortune seekers may blame their fate on government retaliation for their revolutionary agitation, but at least a partial explanation lies in their own personal failings. While some writers, particularly Helena Staś, criticized the intelligentsia's attempts to transplant their cultural authority over their fellow immigrants from the peasantry, like "My Three Friends," many displaced gentry may have seen emigration as a way of reestablishing their lost potential for power and influence: "A mass of working people is crossing the ocean. What will those people do without the intelligentsia? They'll denationalize and sink in a sea of Americanization. This destruction of the Polish masses has to be prevented. The Polish emigration needs help to hold onto its nationality, to preserve its group identity, to give it equal intellectual rank with the Irish, Germans, Swedes, and the French."[29]

Piotr Yolles's "Trzy matki" (Three mothers), serialized in *Nowy świat*, the New York daily that Yolles edited during the 1930s, posits immigration as a passage not just across political or geographic boundaries, but across social and conceptual ones as well. Printed under the pseudonym Włóczęga (Wanderer), "Three Mothers" concerns a young lawyer whose disastrous love affair with his family's housemaid results in his resolve to flee his past and go to America. It is the example of his Jewish employer's marriage to a gentile that inspires Władek to seek his own happiness beyond the obligations of family and social position. "Three Mothers" encourages the transcendence of class and religious barriers and looks to America as the site of individual fulfillment and natural alliances based on personal feeling, an issue that will be explored in chapter 6.[30]

For Jan, the aristocratic hero of Chrostowski's "Niewolnik polski" (The Polish slave), the immigrant passage to America offers not a series of ever widening opportunities, but rather disillusionments and assaults against his social position.[31] Tricked by Polish shipping agents in Germany, he finds himself in an emigrant hotel in Hamburg, where for the first time in his life he sleeps with a woman, the Polish maid whose job it is to entice him into spending money on overpriced food and wine. In this several-layered rite of passage, Jan must first overcome his internalized sense of the social distance between himself and this common maidservant (who has herself fled a romance with the son of the Berlin family for whom she had been working.) As in Yolles's novel, the hero's loss of virginity signals the movement (however short-lived) away from blind acceptance of old-world social hierarchies.

This chipping away at Jan's sense of social entitlement is reinforced when he is led lower and lower into the steerage quarter of the emigrant ship:

> He recognized it immediately. He recognized it by the unpleasant smell bombarding his senses, by the dark, dirty ceilings set against the splendor he had glimpsed one level above. He recognized it finally by the faces of those who populated this place. By the emaciated and terrified faces on which misery had engraved its stamp. He belonged to them. He was a member of that great family, or rather that tribe, peopling the whole world, that is united in the unravelable knot of misery, that wanders from corner to corner, from country to country, like the eternally wandering Jew, and looks for bread. Jan felt that this crowd of people here on the "zwishendek"—women, men gathered from various corners of the world, Germans, Italians, Jews, Czechs—they were his brothers and sisters! United in one common unbroken chain of the distress of misery, stronger than the bonds of blood or love, they all had come to seek work, shelter, and bread.[32]

It is poverty, not Polishness, that binds him to his fellow steerage passengers, and it is his poverty by which he is judged by others: among the poor, all national distinctions are subsumed in an undifferentiated experience of mass misery. But for Jan, the shock of his social descent brings the realization that old boundaries have become invisible and old privileges meaningless. The new hierarchy, the new respectability, is based solely on capital: "The human and religious commandments are different for the poor than they are for the rich."[33]

Chrostowski, a socialist and religious schismatic, here exemplifies one of the alternative collective identities that widening horizons and the breakdown of social barriers could create: one based on class, rather than on ethnic or national identity. Most Polish immigrant socialists tried to combine these commitments, retreating from the internationalism that denied Poland's national struggle. In general, writers tried to link social and economic exploitation in America with the oppression of Poles under the partitions, refocusing any developing class consciousness on a sense of ethnic solidarity and transferring peasant resentment against the Polish nobility to resentment against non-Polish sources of power on both sides of the ocean.

Morawski's *On Two Continents* also represents the passage to America in terms of undifferentiated misery, imprisonment, and exploitation, but it encourages readers to see their experience as emigrants as a continuation of Poland's national exploitation under the partitions:

> He well remembered that ship, crammed with emigrants fleeing their homeland in the face of injury and misery, that ship-prison in which the German sailors treated the poor Polish peasant like a dog, where these peasants were fed on scraps and suffocated in airless, stinking chambers under the deck. That these people didn't die from misery and oppression on that ship was perhaps only because they were comforted by the hope of a better future, because they promised themselves that they would find a paradise in the unknown country to which fate was carrying them.[34]

The hero of *On Two Continents* is Jan Krzysiak, a young Polish escapee from the Russian army who is rescued by a Ukrainian freedom fighter. Krzysiak is passed along a kind of underground railroad of peasant- and student-patriots and with the help of a Jewish innkeeper is able to escape to America. Morawski unites a Polish desire for freedom with that of other nations, recognizing them as independently legitimate struggles.

But his sympathy for the downtrodden, though it may extend to others, is specifically Polish, and his novel is dedicated "to the Polish laborers in America." (In contrast, one of Wojtek's "letters from the old country" warns against labor activism: after all, "God didn't go on strike.")[35] Morawski polonizes and politicizes the exploitation of workers, who "were treated like cattle, as the Moscow gendarmes might treat them" (66). Much of the novel treats the immigrant protagonist's demeaning work experiences: as a bricklayer for an exploitative German employment agent, as a hotel janitor, a delivery driver, a coal miner's helper, and a factory operative. He is injured in a Pennsylvania mine explosion, the result of the lack of safety measures. "Thus," the narrator proclaims, "the capitalists in their monstrous greed played with the life of the worker" (82). In the furniture factory, his skill provokes his German coworkers. Economic and political oppression are conflated and intertwined:

> He was reminded of those throngs of Polish workers who came here by the thousands as to the promised land and were lost in this sea of American humanity. . . . At that thought Jan's heart seethed; he was in pain, because injustice acted so terribly upon these good people—the injustice of centuries-

> old ignorance, the injustice of eternal slavery that killed the mind and all its flights toward eminence. It was not their fault, not these poor folk, but the fault of those handicaps under which from the distant past up to the present day they yielded and cried out! And, thinking about this, Jan suffered very much. It seemed to him that he wasn't suffering alone, but together with the entire throng of his wronged countrymen—those who like himself had wandered here to this so-called promised land, and those across the immense ocean whose blood flowed under the lash of the wild Cossack. (90–91)

Morawski's novel attempts to unite Poles on both sides of the ocean in a struggle for political freedom that is not blind to the same impulse toward freedom and human dignity in others, and in a sense of peoplehood that is distinct but not chauvinistic—values that form the basis of honorable Polishness on two continents.

That Polonian writers continued to produce immigration narratives well into the 1930s, even as other novels were exposing abuses of entrenched institutional authority and exploring the manners and morals of the second generation, testifies to the continued potency of the issues these novels raised. One of these later immigrant sagas is Czesław Łukaszkiewicz's *Anioł stróż i djabeł stróż* (Guardian angel and guardian devil). Informed by the author's anticlericalism, *Guardian Angel and Guardian Devil* provides Polonia's most detailed fictional portrayal of peasant immigration. In particular, it treats immigration as a process of growing dissatisfaction, not just with economic pressures or social injustice but with village parochialism. As such, it is worth examining in some detail.

The story of Jacek Kondzioł's coming of age, of which his emigration is a crucial component, is framed by the competition between the two guardians of his mind, body, and soul. The impetus toward emigration is set in motion when the village priest orders the hungry boy severely beaten for stealing apples from his orchard. This act of trespassing is just the first. His guardian angel, Durniel (roughly, Dumb Ass), argues against Jacek's natural curiosity, the physical needs of his body, and his innate sense of justice. He terms Jacek's resulting theological skepticism blasphemy, but his guardian devil, Chudybub (Whippersnapper), calls it courage. The beating sets in motion a feud between the priest and Jacek's father that escalates until a letter from a villager who has settled in New York prompts several families to emigrate together. (In the enclosed wedding picture, Kaśka from the neighboring

Cover of *Guardian Angel and Guardian Devil* (1932), a detailed portrayal of an immigrant's internal transformation from village peasant to American Pole, by Czesław Łukaszkiewicz.

village is at first taken for an American heiress.) Durniel calls emigration a sin, a disruption of divine order:

> Oxen like these go to America, earn three dollars a day, and immediately get used to all the comforts, to extras, to clothes, but they only offend God with it. . . . They hardly earn it before they spend it on a six-room house, they put up a porch, they fix up a bathroom (pfe!) and at night instead of going to sleep and not offending the Lord God with sinful thoughts, these animals trudge out to the theatre. . . . But that's nothing. Many of them even feel like going to school.[36]

Łukaszkiewicz's lack of nostalgia makes the family's preparations to leave all the more poignant. They pack the holy pictures and a handful of garden dirt. Jacek's mother bids a tearful farewell to her cows, while his father silently smokes and spits. Both of their hearts are breaking. The last stop is the village church, where the priest begrudgingly blesses their voyage, sprinkling their wagons with holy water and admonishing them to expiate their sin by sending dollars back to the parish. If they aren't themselves returning, perhaps even better, their money is.

The author details each phase of the journey as it takes the emigrants farther and farther away from their parochial conception of the world. At every step there are new sights and experiences to assimilate, from drinking coffee at an inn, to crossing their first river, to negotiating the streets of Kraków, where Jacek is amazed by the statue of the poet Mickiewicz: he assumes all statues (including the Statue of Liberty) to be images of saints. He is taking his first steps into a secular world whose saints are icons of freedom, enlightenment, and national culture. On the train to Germany, the old folks recite their rosaries, but Chudybub tells Jacek to keep his eyes open, to remember everything so that one day he will be able to compare his past self with his future one.

The ocean voyage becomes a period of transition that carries Jacek further toward manhood and independence of soul. Released from responsibilities for the first time in his life, Jacek relishes the time he now has to think and read (both sins, according to Durniel). As their ship passes another headed back to Europe, the emigrants do not know whether to envy those on board or not. Already the sense of their firm place in a static world has been compromised. But they are not yet sure of where or how to maneuver on the still shaky ground on which they find themselves. They hesitate at the threshold of the new world. Jacek, who has been on the emigrant path ever since he first questioned the wrongheaded whisperings of his guardian angel, leads them into "Hameryka": "Follow me, people from Bysina!" He has, as Chudybub says, become "a real man" (185). But his transformation is not yet complete: in America, Jacek's mountaineer dialect is replaced by standard Polish. He joins the quasi-military Falcons, manages their library, and becomes a book agent. He becomes engaged to a cultured young widow, who is proud to kiss the hand of her peasant mother-in-law. And by the end of the novel, his road to maturity leads Jacek back to Poland, to fulfill his dying father's request to set things right with the villainous priest. He has crossed political borders and geographic obstacles, and transgressed against barriers to national consciousness and personal development. When he recrosses the ocean, it will be as a man, and as a Pole.

Jacek's passage to America and the confrontation with varied worldviews it has offered has resulted in a transformation of ethnic consciousness. Neuman worried that these contacts would dilute Polishness, while Fredrik Barth and his followers argue that this confrontation with the Other is a necessary factor in ethnogenesis, leading to the consolidation of a group identity in juxtaposition against other groups. For Jacek, these Others are not so much the Irish bishops or German foremen but his fellow Poles from different social, religious, and regional backgrounds. As he sees himself juxtaposed against these countrymen, he comes to see himself united with them. "Nationalism is best understood," writes Matthew Jacobson, "not as a political monolith, but as an idiom, a language capable of expressing a wide range of ideals."[37] And these varied ideologies unite under the banner of common national idealism that Jacek now carries back to Poland with him.

In the continuing process of immigration, alliances and identities, constantly in flux, were being formed, reformed, affirmed, and complicated. Family ties, stretched and challenged by emigration, were sometimes broken but might also be reevaluated and revalued. Through immigrant narratives that replayed these processes, Polonia's writers modeled a movement toward Polishness with which their readers were encouraged to identify. It was by the written word, through the exchange of letters (along with the remittances and the steamship tickets they often contained), that ties to the old country were honored and maintained. Literature attempted to affirm those relationships by replaying them through a national filter, by rearticulating the interchange between emigrant and old country in ways that encouraged sanctioned responses to experience and memory and a continuing and politicized relationship to the old country. The volatility of that politicization is expressed most strongly in the novels and short stories considered in the next chapter, which examines literature's engagement with issues of Polonian institutional authority. While authors used immigrant narratives to draw readers into an extended national polity, they aimed their literary polemics at its leaders.

5 ıIı Power Plays

A Family Squabble

If Polonian pre–World War II fiction was so often polemical, its polemics were largely directed within the immigrant community itself, focusing on issues of local power and alliance. But rather than demonstrating a merely parochial outlook, these often scathing condemnations derive from Polonia's transnationalism, reflecting the competing stances toward Polish identity and nationhood being played out in the churches, meeting halls, and kitchens of Poland's fourth partition. Circumstances grounded in the United States are refracted by Polish historical experience and contemporary European issues. Even when immigrant authors are exposing the pitilessness of the factory system or the arrogance of American chauvinism, it is most often to implicate their ideological rivals within the immigrant community in common patterns of old- and new-world injustice and exploitation.

With the moral touchstone firmly grounded in Polish soil, Polonia's journalist-authors focus their criticism on the immigrant leaders and institutions they accuse of complicity with outside sources of hostile power. The issues these authors engage, and the highly charged terms of their polemics, not only reveal the inner workings of the immigrant community and the sources of its day-to-day concerns and pressures, but expose the continued reliance on a European worldview in structuring what was to be an exiled *Polska zmniejszona,* "a miniature Poland."[1]

Despite this preoccupation with the issue of Polish independence, "the Polish question," a few notably idiosyncratic works do take aim at purely American institutions and conditions. Franciszek Iwanowski's "'Od nagłej, a niespodziewanej'" (From a sudden and unexpected)[2] equates the plight of the animals moving to their deaths in the Chicago stockyards with that of the expendable workers on the killing floor, suggesting that workers are dehumanized not only by their treatment within the factory system but by the nature of the murderous work they are compelled to do. But Iwanowski's focus, uncomplicated by the charged symbolism of Polishness, makes his story an anomaly in Polonian fiction.

Other short works also deal with labor issues, but rather than offering Iwanowski's systemic criticism, they concentrate on the challenges of labor unrest to the integrity of the individual, the home, and the ethnic community. The long-term strike in the story "Tchórz" (The coward), for example, published in the conservative *Dziennik chicagoski,* is less a contest between workers and owners than a contest between moderate and radical strikers. Their antagonisms are enacted on the streets and in the homes (and, by implication, in the bedrooms) of the suffering community, where the conciliatory hero is labeled a coward by his neighbors, his coworkers, and his more militant fiancée.[3] "Maszyna piekielna" (The hellish machine), published two months earlier in the same paper and probably written by the same anonymous author, warns against anarchy not only because, the story suggests, it sanctions wanton and cowardly murder but because it demands denationalization: "All your fairy tales about God and Country are fine for children," a misled anarchist argues, "but not for a man with a mind of his own. . . . Monarchies will buckle, churches will be destroyed, we'll exterminate the priests, and on the ruins of that uprising will arise one common fatherland."[4] For Poles struggling to bring about Poland's rebirth as a nation, internationalism could be nothing less than treason, and the international socialist a traitor to the Polish cause. However, appearing as these stories do in the Resurrectionist newspaper, it is likely that their real targets are Polonia's nationalist organizers, who in their opposition to the religionists were painted indiscriminately as Masons, anarchists, and atheists, who "recognize neither the aristocrat [nor] the slave, the Catholic nor the non-Catholic," but would "create an indifference among Poles by leveling all classes in society."[5]

Despite a handful of minor exceptions, then, the tendency among Polonian authors was to take on specifically immigrant institutions, personages, and power brokers, rather than outsiders. The villains are almost universally Poles, or those accused of posing as Poles either for their own gain or on behalf of larger forces working against Polish interests. Criticism centers around the failure to serve faithfully the immigrant community and the Polish national ideal, and two major targets emerge: the Polish-American clergy, and immigrant secular institutions and their administrators. The sites of these conflicts indicate divergent conceptions of the immigrant community's relation to America and to Poland, competing strategies for the construction and continuation of Polishness and for the reconstruction of a Polish state, and the continuing iconic power contained in the accusation of betrayal from within.

Given Polonia's often noted loyalty to its ethnic parishes, a surprising number of novels and stories are unstintingly critical of the immigrant clergy. While newspaper editorials attacked the German and Irish hierarchy within the Church in America, fiction writers focused in scandalous detail on the moral transgressions, cynicism, and venality of Polonian priests. Not unexpectedly, one subset of these critiques of the clergy is the handful of works produced by followers of the Polish National Catholic Church (PNCC), including several by its founder, Rev. Franciszek Hodur. His "The Pharisees and the Sadducees," "not a made-up, fantastical picture, but the sad and bitter reality," features a cabal of Satan-worshipping clerics in the pay of the factory owners and in collusion with the Germans, opposed by an idealistic young priest revealed to be none other than Christ himself.[6] Other Hodur plots, in "Ksiądz jednooki" (The one-eyed priest) and "Ksiądz-bandyta" (The bandit priest), follow a similar line, often relying on miracles and divine revelation to legitimate the controversial National Church by grounding it in the trinity of God, Poland, and the Common Man.[7]

So even those who agreed that the measure of morality was to be "a Pole and a Catholic" could dispute the meaning of both terms. The National Church called for a Catholicism that recognized Polish cultural and linguistic exceptionalism, and that addressed the struggles of immigrant Poles like the Pennsylvania mining families among whom the Church was most solidly established. Hodur's combination of populist and iconoclastic rhetoric united the spiritual and practical interests of thousands of working-class immigrants and linked economic exploitation with intellectual and spiritual oppression. Without questioning fundamental Roman Catholic dogma, National Catholics challenged its sources of power, both in the Vatican, in the predominantly Irish- and German-run American diocese, and in the rectories of the growing numbers of Polish-American parishes. Rather than as a repository for frustrated patriotism, PNCC fiction portrays Roman Catholicism as yet another foreign threat, questioning even the Polishness of the ethnic parish that functioned so often as the neighborhood's cultural anchor.

"Józef," the anonymous writer of *Dzielny Michałek sierotka* (Brave Mikey the little orphan), for instance, repeats the PNCC position favoring public over private parochial schooling. By discouraging immigrants from sending their children to the parish schools in which, it was argued, poorly trained Polish-American nuns denationalized their students by teaching them a bastardized Polish that no genuine Pole could understand, the National Church challenged the very foundations of institutional Polonia—its already consecrated history, the very geography of its daily life, and its most common blueprint for a future in America.[8] Educated in a public school and trained in Polish language and history by a PNCC priest, Mikey helps convert his "barbarian" stepmother from "a mad popish fanatic" into "a good-souled and prudent Pole—a Christian."[9] "I'm a Pole, my son is a Pole, and my husband's a Pole," she comes to understand, "so our place is there [in the PNCC], not in a foreign, hypocritical church" (46).

Ultimately, this story and others conclude, the place of the Pole, and the place of the PNCC itself, is in Poland. But in the meantime, for immigrant readers struggling with the pressures of the factory and the coal mine, National Catholic writers consistently took populist and pro-labor positions, in opposition to the "church of the rich and the capitalists" (45). This is illustrated in the recurring parable of the Roman Catholic priest who refuses to bury the dead of destitute families. In the anonymous "Chrystus przed sędzią pokoju" (Christ before the justice of the peace), for instance, a suffering father who has been arrested for illegally burying his child is condemned by the local Roman Catholic priest as "a patriot [and] a mason."[10] Subtitled "a legend based on a story told by the Polish people of Nanticoke," this tale introduces the multilayered symbol of resurrection as the dead child is brought back to life through the intercession of Christ, in the garb of a common coal miner. If Poland is the Christ of nations, in the PNCC cosmology its soul is represented not by priests and politicians but by poor folk.

While PNCC fiction was portraying its critics, and the Roman church in particular, as traders in immigrant flesh and traitors to Polishness, Roman Catholic writers were not neglecting the National Church. It was a frequent target of Kazimierz Neuman's humorous short fiction for the *Dziennik chicagoski.* In "Niezależne piekło" (An independent hell), a deceased PNCC follower discovers that neither St. Peter nor Satan has ever heard of "the Polish parish of the true patriots." The devil finally allots the exasperated fellow a corner in which to make his own sorry hell "with a bucket of pitch, a bucket of sulfur, and a pack of matches."[11]

But criticism of religious institutions was not limited to sparring between proponents of the Roman and the National Catholic Churches. Authors not openly affiliated with the PNCC also took on Roman Catholicism, particularly in the person of the "villain-priest." It is difficult to overestimate the power priests held in Polish villages and immigrant communities. However, the preponderance (and the apparent commercial success) of so many anticlerical novels also suggests that immigrants were not passive recipients of priestly authority but were active and conscious participants in a system whose imperfections and abuses they knew how to read in their daily lives.[12]

The most notorious and most gifted critic of the Polish-American clergy was political activist and journalist Czesław Łukaszkiewicz. Not long after his arrival in the United States around 1914, as an organizer for the Piłsudskiite Komitet Obrony Narodowy (KON, the National Defense Committee), Łukaszkiewicz began his long association with Antoni Paryski's *Ameryka-Echo.*[13] The popular *Księży chleb* (Priestly bread) was the first of a series of Łukaszkiewicz novels published by Paryski—including *Zakonny welon* (The nun's veil), *Ucieczka grzesznych* (Refuge of sinners), and *Listy Księdza Świeczki* (Father Candle's letters)—that focus on the scandalous misadventures of a band of immigrant priests. Karol Wachtl accuses the author of "unjust derision and mockery." Stanisław Osada calls Łukaszkiewicz "a very considerable talent, misapplied," and his novels "very funny, but malicious beyond measure."[14]

Łukaszkiewicz's priests not only take economic advantage of the simple faith of their parishioners but perform mass while drunk, seduce nuns, visit brothels, live openly with their "housekeeper" mistresses, father illegitimate children, and are even complicitous in murder.[15] Łukaszkiewicz accuses church leaders of willfully misleading their flocks, of betraying the spirit and law of Christianity, and, in the process, of betraying the Polish immigrant community that is placed in their hands. He attacks not so much the Church in general, nor the Irish and German priests who ruled in America (and who are portrayed as curbing the excesses of the Polish scoundrels). His targets are the cynical and hypocritical Polish-American priests whom

The Nun's Veil, one of a series of satirical, anticlerical novels by Czesław Łukaszkiewicz (1925 reprint of 1920 edition). Courtesy Alumni Memorial Library, St. Mary's College of Ave Maria University

he accuses of leading rich, sensual lives at the expense of their self-sacrificing immigrant parishioners.

A few examples will give the flavor and direction of Łukaszkiewicz's work. Falstaffian Father Świeczka, the hard-drinking womanizer of all Łukaszkiewicz's anticlerical novels, initiates the newly ordained and idealistic Father Banasik, who has just arrived from Poland, into the society of Polonian clerics. Steeling himself with drink in the sacristy before giving his Sunday sermon, Świeczka explains his position:

> "I don't play cards, so evenings are often long. Others would run around after girls, but I respect priestly dignity. Well, anyway, not completely, but I don't go crazy anymore. So, what's left? I sit myself in a chair, I drink to my own health, and I philosophize. Do you know, Father, how thoughts sometimes come into a person's head?! If someone wrote it all down, what a book that would be! Do you know what I've even thought about? What would happen to us chaplains of God if everything we taught people and everything we were taught were actually true . . ."[16]

Łukaszkiewicz's clergymen see Polish immigrants and their American-born children as peasants and themselves as transplanted aristocrats with a responsibility to enforce an increasingly besieged social hierarchy. After all, admits another priest during a night out on the town, the socialists who scoff at Church dogma are right: "'We all know it's a fairy tale.'"[17] The problem arises when the socialists spread this knowledge among the parishioners, on whom the clergy depend for their livelihood. "As long as the peasant stays stupid," another argues, "he's happy." Świeczka, who has been paid off by local factory owners to avert a strike in his parish, agrees: "In the past they worked twelve hours a day and it was fine. Now they only work ten hours, and already they want eight" (62). After all, he asks, what will a worker do with more free time: "He'll drag himself to the theatre, to the show [*siou*] or out to some ungodly association where they'll teach him to read and then he'll turn himself into a heathen. The way things are now is best for God's church. A peasant sleeps, works, prays, drinks, sleeps some more, works, and doesn't have time for nonsense" (79).

It is not only the parishioners whom the priests dupe, however. In *Refuge of Sinners,* Świeczka's cozy set-up (he has founded an orphanage for priests' children, including two fathered by the now thoroughly corrupted Fr. Banasik) is threatened when the Irish bishop tries to assign Polish-

American nuns, "she-devils, not women," to help him.[18] He tries to rid himself of the Felicians by getting them drunk, nearly starving them, assigning them physically tortuous penances, and finally by attempting to bribe the Irish bishop. When the Great War breaks out, he discourages his young male parishioners from enlisting in the Polish-American army, which will mean a loss of revenue for him. Using the rhetoric of Americanization, and enlisting the aid of the mine owners, who are reluctant to lose their most productive laborers, he preaches, "Love this free land of Washington and scrape in it to find black coal, because that's the way to serve all your people. . . . You know it's the hand of Providence that put you here in America, so that when others are dying, you will be the seed of a new generation" (215). When Polish recruiters arrive, Świeczka arranges their arrest. Łukaszkiewicz's novels argue that the Polish-American clergy are among the most active and powerful enemies of Polonia—oppressing, exploiting, and de-polonizing the generally honest and hard-working immigrant communities they serve and actively working against Polish interests.

Not all works fall into as neatly definable a niche as Łukaszkiewicz's anticlerical novels, however. Writers like Helena Staś, for instance, portray priests as neither consistently villains nor heroes: her works contain both, and religious authority in general is allowed a range of moral positions based more on individual propensity than on systemic corruption. When the seducer-priest appears, as he does in *In the Human Market,* the tragedy is played out in human terms with human victims, and the priesthood as an institution is not unequivocally implicated.[19]

Avowed Roman Catholic writer-activists like Stefania Laudyn also belie easy distinctions between religionists and nationalists. Her short story "Biały murzyn" (The white Negro) complicates this oversimplistic division through the situation of a poverty-stricken newspaper editor who is fired by the nationalists, then offered an editorship with the Resurrectionists. All he has to do is follow the clerical line (drinking, he's told, will make it easier). But if the religionists are unattractive, it is the nationalists who truly betray the editor: "It is they," Oleś tells his wife, "who would have stabbed and trampled me with greatest pleasure" (70). Exile from his beloved newspaper work is likened to "hard labor" in Siberia, meted out by those whom he served with naive idealism (73–74). Their denunciation that he is a swindler and a traitor, a "Moscow-lover," a "Russofile," must have had strong meaning for Laudyn, who under similar charges resigned (or, as she claimed, was dismissed) as editor of the Polish Women's Alliance's *Głos Polek.*[20] Because under the nationalist masthead Oleś has exposed Polonia's "parties, cliques, partisanship, [and] personal interests" (92), he is now forced to "play, as [the priests] direct," even if it means fighting against the nationalist cause, in which he still believes. A similar note is sounded in Laudyn's bitter story "Doktorka" (The woman doctor), in which the protagonist ruefully imagines sending to the Warsaw papers a photograph of her husband captioned "Polish philologist—raising cows in America."[21] The cause of his fall from position is not ruthless American capitalism but Polonia's own factious jealousies. And the site of arbitration and appeal is neither American nor Polonian but Polish.

If Polonian literature is so often consciously oppositional, the factions are contained within the community, and little thought is given to their relationship to American politics and policies. This blindness to the American position could have serious implications, as it did during the First World War. Poland's political situation, with territory on both sides of the conflict, heightened and complicated the already existing divisions within Polonia and brought the Polish-American left—Łukaszkiewicz among them—into direct opposition with American policy. For patriots whose primary goal was Polish independence, the question was not with which side America was allied but which side's victory was most likely to result in a Polish state. Thus for Łukaszkiewicz's fictional Polish-American recruits, fed by decades of Polonia's nationalist rhetoric, the war is not between the Central Powers and the Allied Powers, but between Poland's defenders and its enemies. When for inspiration the well-meaning soldiers sing anti-Moscow songs from the last century's uprisings—no doubt learned in the United States—they are hurriedly instructed not to show "any anti-Slavic tendencies." After all, the commander informs them, "we're going to be next to them, fighting the Teutonic horde. We have to get rid of all references against our Slavic brothers, with whom we'll be united under one scepter, with freedom of religion and language."[22] The irony is, of course, that part of Poland was already under the scepter of the czar, but without the promised freedoms. When Polish Legionnaires agitate for an independent Polish effort against Russia, the right accuses them of "collusion with the Swabians" (223) and finally, when all else fails, of Jewishness.

Łukaszkiewicz's own politics fall into this complicated configuration.

Stefania Laudyn, before emigrating to the United States. Courtesy Aurelia Sobczyk

As a KON activist, the author placed his hopes for an independent Poland on an alliance with Austria-Hungary against Russia. Denounced by Polonian priests and opposed by activists like Stanisław Osada and Stefania Laudyn, Łukaszkiewicz was imprisoned for six months by the xenophobic American government as a Prussian sympathizer. This experience no doubt contributed to the animosity of his anticlerical novels.[23] But they also reflect Polonia's unavoidable difficulties in negotiating world politics from the United States, where American leaders had little interest in or understanding of Poland's historical situation and of Polish America's complex and contradictory interests in the war.

Opposing leftists like Łukaszkiewicz was Józef Orłowski, whose position against the Prussians was less likely to draw unfavorable attention from American authorities. A political activist and friend of Paderewski, Orłowski used his 1915 novel *W żelaznych kleszczach* (In iron pincers) to accuse the Polonian left of unwitting collusion with Prussian attachés, German-American businessmen, and Irish-American politicians plotting Poland's demise. Orłowski charged that KON's support for the Central Powers and its dispatching of funds to Galicia for a Polish army under the flag of Austria-Hungary were being carefully manipulated by these enemies: "All the money the Poles collect for the fight against Russia, they collect for their own expropriation," a diplomat chuckles.[24] When a meeting of New York KON supporters (including a fictionalized Łukaszkiewicz) degenerates into a near brawl, the Polish and Polish-American left merely acts out gleeful Prussian predictions. (And as for the socialists, they are completely ineffectual, being unable to agree to support Poland's national aspirations at all). Although Orłowski's novel is set in America, the worldview is European, and no clear distinctions are made between Prussians and German-Americans, or between Poles and Polish immigrants. Polonian and Polish interests are the same, with the relevant differences arising from political ideologies born in Europe. Finally, despite Orłowski's unmistakable partisanship, he criticizes the contentiousness that renders the efforts of all factions ineffectual: "For us," the observation is made, "anyone with whom we don't see eye to eye is a traitor" (223). It goes without saying that one can only be a traitor to Poland. The possibility of being a traitor to America is barely considered (hence Łukaszkiewicz's troubles).

In a rare example of Polonian literary intertextuality, one of the participants in Orłowski's debate is the self-styled general Tabaka. This fictional leader of a Polish army in the "Junajted Stejts" was originally born of the pen of leftist Telesfor Chełchowski, whose satirical *Baczność! Jenerał Tabaka ma głos!* (Attention! General Tobacco has the floor!) points out the discrepancies between European political realities and Polonia's deliberately idealized Polishness. Tabaka's motto, "Whiskey, Poland, God!" is taken from the traditional "God, Honor, Fatherland," and his sorry army spoofs Polonia's numerous patriotic paramilitary organizations, complete with uniforms, drills, and elaborate drinking rituals.[25] Tabaka's army gathers in saloons and defends priests from cuckolded husbands.

The internal enemies whom Tabaka urges Polonia to resist include socialists and reformers who would disrupt the God-given order by leveling social hierarchies and voting corrupt officials out of office, as well as educators who would damn a Christian's soul by encouraging the reading of books. And despite its preoccupation with Polish independence, Polonia's ignorance of conditions in Europe is revealed when Tabaka sneaks into Poland to make contact with the right-wing Dmowski. Not only has that leader never heard of Tabaka and his eleven "knights," but a peasant nearly laughs Tabaka out of the country when he hears of his plan to instigate an uprising;

instead of throwing down his scythe and joining the patriots, the farmer chases Tabaka off his land with loud assurances that "the Emperor of All Russia" is good to the Poles. When he's also beaten up by Prussian border guards, Tabaka has had enough of this ungrateful Poland: "We'll muster in saloons and bars and nowhere else" (61).

Tabaka's repeated appeal to his "countrymen, faithful Christians" also reemerges more than a decade later in Łukaszkiewicz's *Przygody Głupkowiaka z Mędrkowiakiem* (The adventures of Blockhead and Half-Wit), a satirical account of the upheaval at the 1927 Polish National Alliance convention, in which "old-guard" conservatives were supplanted by followers of Piłsudski. The popular adventures of Majk Głupkowiak ("Mike Blockhead"), "old warrior and swordsman," were begun as a newspaper column in the early 1920s and continued in *Ameryka-Echo* until the author's death in 1945. Głupkowiak spends his time politicking around the barstools of every Polish neighborhood, developing elaborate drinking rituals ("po Hamtramcku," "po Detroicku," "po Krakowsku"; that is, Hamtramck-, Detroit-, or Kraków-style), cheating other immigrants in real estate deals and raising money for patriotic causes that he knows will never come to fruition. Every episode ends with Głupkowiak, outraged at some example of honest dealing or principled action, proclaiming, "*Maj Gad! Maj Gad!* And this is supposed to be Poland!" This lament signals—beyond the author's distaste for Polonia's leadership—the distance between an unrealistically static ideal of an imagined Poland and the dynamics of a developing ethnic consciousness. To say in America, even satirically, "But this is supposed to be Poland!" suggests the general hope that, if Poland could not exist as a state (and later, if it could not exist as a democratic state), it could live as an ideal, as a moral category against which action and belief could be measured, and fall short. It reflects the conviction that democratic America, with its millions of Polish immigrants and their descendants, could be the geographic home of that ideal. The fact that these lines were written *after* Poland regained its independence in 1919 points to the development of American Polonia as its own cultural entity, separate from Europe—to an independent and evolving identity as Polish in America. And finally, by implying that this American Poland was the real nation, it also hints at a growing disillusion with and distancing from the Polish government in Poland, when it didn't conform to Polonia's expectations.[26]

The shady Głupkowiak, who seems oblivious to his own immorality or

Collection of sketches by Telesfor Chełchowski (1913), satirizing Polonia's patriotic-military organizations. Behind the bar is written "Czołem" (the standard greeting among members of the Polish Falcons), "Bóg i ojczyzna" (God and Fatherland), and "Swój do swojego" (Support your own). Courtesy Alumni Memorial Library, St. Mary's College of Ave Maria University

to any Poland other than the one dreamed up to fill his own pocket and belly, has a counterpart in an earlier Łukaszkiewicz novel. *Dziwna dziewczyna* (The strange girl), set in the working-class Polonian enclave of Hamtramck, Michigan, criticizes the businessmen behind the joint venture schemes that sprang up in the wake of Poland's newly won independence. Appealing to patriotic loyalties, and playing on guilt over not reemigrating to help Poland directly, firms like Union Liberty and Polska Pożyczka Żywnościowa (Polish Food Loan) squandered the fortunes of thousands of immigrant families. In this novel Wojciech Gierdola, a wheeler-dealer real estate man with a criminal past, easily dupes honest families into investing their life savings in the "Union-Victory" company. The carefully described Union-Victory rally clearly delineates the emotional matrixes of Polishness during this period of transition, as immigrants were forced to decide between reemigrating to the homeland or admitting that America had become their new home, even if they did not yet think of themselves as Americans.

The crowded meeting hall is decked with American and Polish flags, and with banners reading "Polish money will build Poland," "Enriching ourselves, we will enrich Poland," and "Whoever believes in God is a member of Union-Victory!"[27] After a speech by a sham Polish war hero, Gierdola asserts that what the impoverished and war-ravaged homeland needs most is not the immigrants' blood, but the dollars they have earned in America. The most patriotic thing Polish immigrants can do, these scam artists argue, is to stay in America and invest their money in Poland. They should identify themselves as Poles and regard their earnings in American factories as Polish resources: Poland's fourth partition is to consider itself a colony of the reborn state. In this extended Poland, however, two groups are expressly excluded: the godless socialists and the Jews. "Who should rule Poland," demands Gierdola, "us or the Jews?" (189). With the cry, "To the gibbet with the Jews!" he hangs a Jew in effigy, shouting, "Union Victory only for Poles and Catholics!" (191). The leaders who would equate Polishness with Catholicism, Łukaszkiewicz suggests, are little more than petty thieves and self-serving hatemongers. Their vaunted patriotic idealism is no more than the script of a cynically brazen con game, exploiting old antagonisms not even out of a misguided sense of righteousness, but with purely mercenary calculation. And it is honest and diligent working-class Polonia and Poland itself, Łukaszkiewicz warns, that are fleeced.

But criticism of Polonia's secular powerbrokers did not begin with Łukaszkiewicz. More specifically, the scapegoating of Jews as enemies of Poland and Polonia that Łukaszkiewicz decries is explicit in a small number of early literary works. The most sinister of these is *Trzech pachciarzy* (Three Jewish tenants), written under the pseudonym Stary Związkowiec (The Old Alliancer).[28] One of the villains in this piece is the Jewish head of the "Pomniejszona,"[29] a Polonian fraternal agency clearly meant to represent the PNA. His assistant is a Christian lawyer who cheats grieving widows out of their death benefits and throws them down stairwells. (When he objects to being called a Jew like his colleagues, they taunt him, "Oj vay! Such a great purist and Polish patriot!"[30] Completing the trio is another Jew who "makes a living in America off Polish stupidity" (6). The language used by these three is the most vulgar and shocking to be found in all Polonian literature and, as much as their deeds, marks these characters as despicable. Besides cheating widows and orphans, they plot the downfall of their political opponent, the patriot-journalist Karyński. Karyński had been exiled to Siberia for his opposition to Russian rule and had escaped and made his way to America under an assumed name. At the same time they are accusing him within Polonia of spying for Russia, they denounce him to the U.S. government and to the Russian ambassador as a nihilist and a public enemy of the czar, who is a U.S. ally. They hope to use his escape from Siberia and his entrance into the United States under false pretenses as grounds for his deportation to certain death at the hands of the Russians. Although these plans fail, "the ringleaders of American Polonia, under the influence of Jewish villainy" succeed in blacklisting Karyński from their influential organization. Near the end the author drops the third person omniscient narrative and addresses readers in the first person: "No one here has yet spoken up for me; no one has revolted" (24) against the "Judas" (19) "who dresses his Jewishness in a Kościuszko uniform" (15).

A number of early works, like Stanisława Romanowska's *Nad Michiganem* (On Lake Michigan), concentrate in a less inflammatory tone on political maneuvering and power struggles that divide the immigrant community and defeat its efforts on behalf of Poland. The winning entry in a 1903 Polish National Alliance-sponsored literary contest, this novel features a circle of bankers, politicians, and vote-selling party hangers-on. Unity and patriotism, Romanowska charges, are only business tactics in Polonia. Under the partitions in Poland, the Polish language is honored as a means of maintaining Polishness, while in America, where one is free to be Polish, there is no effort to develop a literary tradition or respect for education. Only the dollar rules, and even good ideas are opposed because of petty jealousies and poorly understood notions of Polish patriotism: "Solidarity and unity within the Polish emigration in America are empty phrases."[31]

Much of *On Lake Michigan* centers around a Chicago aldermanic campaign in which Democrat and Republican interests converge with European Polish ones. In Romanowska's configuration, the Polonian Republicans, who openly oppose Russia, are the true patriots, while the conservative Democrats, like banker Nadętowicz, a "conciliator, Moscow-lover, [and] traitor," favor cooperation with Russia, oppose public protest against Poland's oppression, and manipulate the mass of immigrants against their own interests (28). As a result of their dividing the Polish vote, a German Democrat defeats the Polish Republican candidate.[32]

But Polonia's divisiveness is played out not only in the offices of its public institutions, but on the front stoops and in the backyards of its residential streets as well. Romanowska's heroine is a widow who has been cheated out of her husband's savings by a dishonest banker. When her only means of supporting her family, her sewing machine, is repossessed, gloating neighbors voice old-country class antagonisms: "Such a haughty noblewoman! She doesn't even chat with a person. She barely nods her head," says one. Another sniffs, "A great lady! Let her start taking in laundry. That will redden her hands a little!" (4).

These class tensions had wider implications for Polonia than merely determining whom one gossips with, or about, over the back fence. Helena Staś's *In the Human Market* takes aim at many of Polonia's usual targets: the sensual priest, the exploitative Church, the political maneuverers, the corrupt and arrogant fraternal leaders. But running through Staś's complex and sweeping exposé is the element of class tension between Polonia's leaders and their constituents, and, not unrelatedly, the divisive sexism of the Church and the fraternals, nowhere else treated so explicitly. These converge in Staś's discussion of the failures of Polish-American literature, which she blames on Polonia's intelligentsia, particularly its writers, editors, and publishers. The fictional experiences of Pani Łaź, "the first Polish-American woman author," have clear precedent in well-publicized real-life conflicts between Polonian women activists and Stanisław Dangel, manager of the PNA's *Dziennik związkowy* and *Zgoda*.[33]

Polish edition of *In the Human Market* by Helena Staś (1911). Courtesy Polish Museum of America, Chicago

Łaź, like Staś the struggling publisher of a woman's magazine, approaches the PNA newspapers for help and support. The vulgar manager, whose unsuspendered pants are in perpetual danger of falling down, dismisses her rudely: "Why the hell do you even come here, then go loiter around other offices and ogle all the editors, like that damn Jew over at the Resurrectionists?"[34]

"To me," she tries to speak up, "everyone is equal as a human being. And . . . the editor you maliciously call a Jew—which he may even be, I have to admit—he alone among all our editors in Chicago showed himself a true human being when times were hard for me."

"Then why don't you go flirt with him," spits the editor. "We get a good laugh at women with their heads screwed on wrong" (104–5). But Pani Łaź persists: "My literary skills aren't any worse than those of a lot of others you flatter. I know there are deficiencies in my work, but I beg you to give me the chance to make a living. I love this work. For me it represents everything; it takes the place of all life's pleasures" (106). But her writing "brings [her] into conflict with the Chicago intelligentsia" (155), not only with men unwilling to take her seriously, but with women whose agenda for Polonia ignores the needs of the working-class majority. Polonia's self-important leaders, Staś charges, drawn mainly from Poland's educated classes, are blinded by intellectual arrogance to the needs of their working-class constituents. As a result, they sabotage the development of genuinely Polonian artistic expression. Polonia's women activists, particularly "the literary women arriving here from the old country," Łaź charges, fail to understand the immigrant community they claim to serve. They belittle her attempts to create a distinctly Polish-American (working-class) literature: "As foreigners among our group and unaware of conditions, they saw in me a new direction and didn't spare me all kinds of infamy. . . . At every step they tried to poison my work. Their base attempts weren't even worthy of fishwives, let alone women of letters."[35]

Łaź describes an overheard conversation between an honest immigrant housewife and a society activist who is appalled to learn that the woman, who enjoys medieval romances like *Róża of Tanenberg*, does not know who Adam Mickiewicz is. The housewife tries to defend herself:

> "We don't have those books in the house because we don't understand them, but even though we don't know how to express ourselves very well, we still feel our Polishness inside. *By God, it is true!*[36] When we heard they were going to build monuments to Pułaski and Kościuszko my family and I cried

> with joy and we sent the president a handful of Polish earth that our mother left us on her deathbed. We gave the Poles the most precious gift we had."[37]
>
> The great-little literary woman snorted, "But what does that mean if you don't know who Mickiewicz, Słowacki, Krasiński, and so many other Polish writers are?"
>
> "Even though we don't know, we still feel our Polishness."
>
> "You don't know anything! . . . You are a lost nation for Poland; you bring shame to the name of Poland." (177)

But, Łaź wonders, "could all the works of Mickiewicz, Słowacki, and Krasiński have produced a greater love for the fatherland in that good soul?" (179). What Polonia's intelligentsia fails to understand, Staś charges, is that the Polishness they have worked to instill may reside in a different space for these former peasants, in land and family, rather than in an elite cultural tradition. And it may manifest itself in ways that specifically assert the legitimacy of being Polish in America. "The language is broken American," Łaź explains, "but the heart and soul are Polish" (179).

If Staś does not exactly propose that the immigrant housewife pick up

Helena Staś, frontispiece to American edition of *In the Human Market.* Courtesy Polish Museum of America, Chicago

the pen herself, she does call for a literature that addresses and legitimizes her experience:

> They don't understand Mickiewicz or Słowacki. . . . But they would understand a literature created for them, based on their lives. That's the only way the national spirit will survive in a foreign land. And so we should concentrate our strength on the creation of such a literature, and on awakening enthusiasm for it within the generations here. Taking up this idea, I have laid out my path and, disregarding the missiles of those who should be helping me, I go forward. (180)

Immigrant intellectuals who expected to assume unquestioned leadership positions found their power challenged by developing notions of social democracy, as well as by the open expression of old-world resentments as the various social classes were thrust into closer contact than they had ever been in Europe. Writing for the immigrant community alone, journalist-authors with varied visions for Polonia took on the individuals, institutions, and ideologies that were vital to its internal development and direction. Writers concerned themselves with matters of self-definition, demonstrating not the sense of powerless parochialism with which Slavic immigrants have been so often dismissed as silent and sullen drudges, but rather a conviction of dynamic self-determination, with international consequences as they pressured American politicians to support Polish independence. The concept of America became important mainly as it intersected with Polonia's and Poland's own concerns and issues.

Thus the fiction of social criticism takes on a very particular significance, as writers used novels, stories, and short tales to challenge (or uphold) delineations of power, to propose (or reject) specific cultural modes, and, not incidentally, to settle old scores with ideological opponents. These old-world social and political relationships are never absent from the debate over Polonian cultural, religious, and political goals, and are further complicated when the American immigrant experience is factored into the equation. If the arguments are sometimes vicious, modern readers need to understand the passionate convictions from which they grew and the seriousness of their implications for the future of Polonia and of Poland. Finally, the story of Polish-American writing is not one of unmitigated contentiousness and division. The next chapter discusses the most common recipe for (re)union.

6 ||| Love, Sex, and the State of Marriage

A Family Reunion

IF POLISH IMMIGRANT fiction was often the battleground on which writers enacted their own versions of the national struggle, it was also the field on which an honorable union could be proposed. Such models of reconciliation are most apparent in the "ethnic romance," in which questions of collective identity are explored and resolved through the drama (and more rarely the comedy) of sexual attraction and marital alliance. These romance stories articulate most explicitly the varied criteria by which Polishness could be measured and circumscribed.

It is no great surprise that writers should use the marriage plot to project their hopes for the nation. Marriages have often settled treaties, redrawn national boundaries, and united empires. Among peasants marriage was a common strategy by which holdings were joined and social and economic power consolidated. The choice of marriage partner has rarely been a simple matter of personal inclination, but it highlights the tensions in our overlapping identities, obligations, and loyalties, both individual and collective.

In addition, when public expressions of ethnic identity are discouraged or forbidden, as was the case to varying degrees in Polish territories under partition, ethnicity often retreats to the private, but not powerless, realm of home and family. This was a point exploited by Polish positivists like Maria Konopnicka who attempted to turn patriotic attention from armed revolt to social and cultural development. Her 1910 poem on the commemoration of an ancient victory over the Prussians admonishes readers, "Our every home will form a stockade."[1] Postinsurrection writers and activists refocused national aspirations, resituating Polishness in the mind and heart rather than

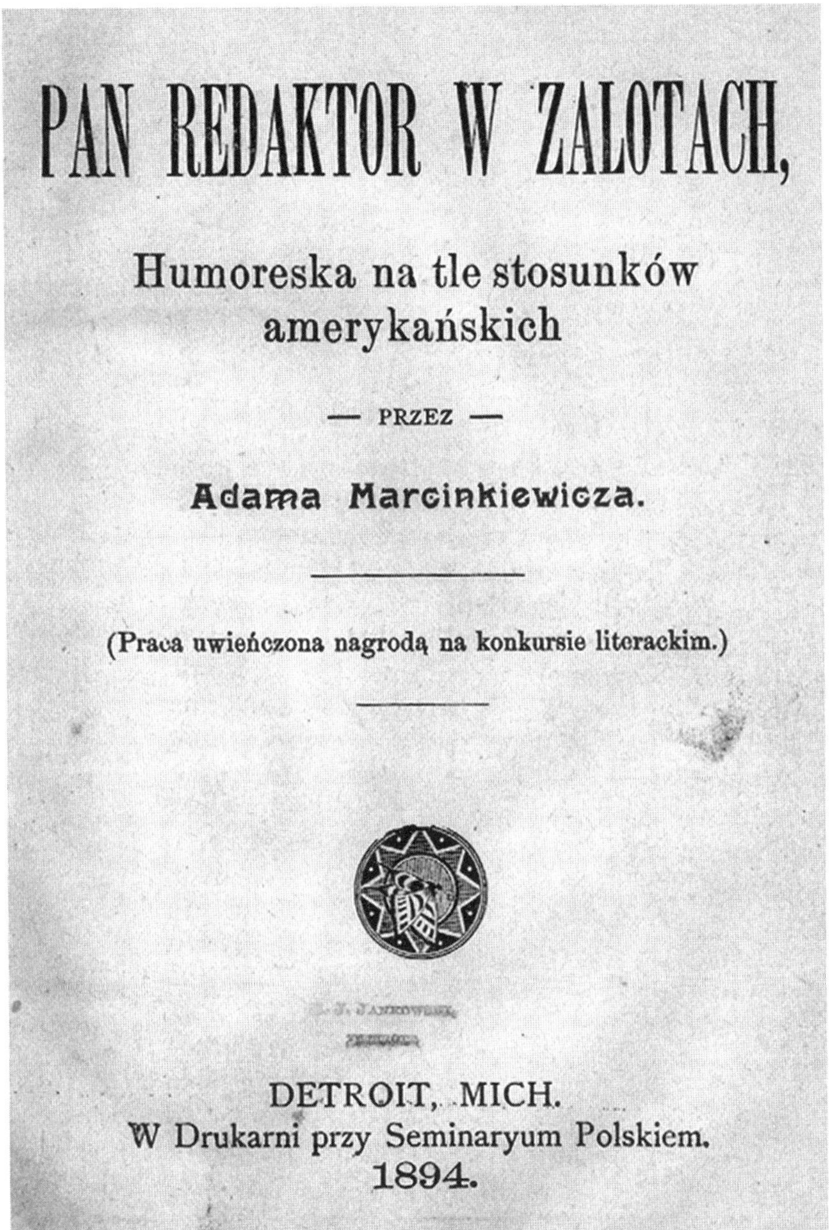

PAN REDAKTOR W ZALOTACH,

Humoreska na tle stosunków amerykańskich

— PRZEZ —

Adama Marcinkiewicza.

(Praca uwieńczona nagrodą na konkursie literackim.)

DETROIT, MICH.
W Drukarni przy Seminaryum Polskiem.
1894.

The Editor's Courtship, a political romance written by an immigrant priest, Adam Marcinkiewicz, and published by Detroit's Polish Seminary.

on the battlefield or halls of state. Created under these influences, immigrant romance narratives tend to conflate family and nation, modeling an ethnic identity rooted in familial intimacy, turning lovemaking into a matter of patriotic honor, and embodying Polish peoplehood, if not in an independent political state, then in the state of marriage. Although competing political factions and ideological visions were often contentiously and even maliciously acted out in Polonia's literature, nowhere did writers attempt to draw more compelling blueprints of an enduring Polishness than in their fictional treatment of love, sex, and marriage.

The terms of this interplay between national, ethnic, and family identities are not, of course, peculiar to the Polish case. America has its own ideology of peoplehood nuanced with the lexicon of kinship, in which, as Werner Sollors has noted, "family symbolism . . . [distinguishes] a 'wedded' national from an 'innate' ethnic identity." This tension between identities based on "consent" and "descent" is fundamental to America's own "typology of regeneration and rebirth."[2] Marriage has been formulated as the site on which fundamentally American conflicts between inherited and assumed identities are negotiated and reconciled.

Recognizing this significance, scholars of literary ethnicity have often explored themes of romance and marriage in English-language ethnic narratives. Because marriage is a way of essentializing alliances and creating new ties of blood, they have paid most attention to exogamous, or out-group, relationships as metaphors for the immigrant's increasingly intimate relationship with the new land and as signifiers of the new identities assumed in a country with its own mythology of expansive self-invention. In her study of ethnic women writers, Mary Dearborn has read in this trope of intermarriage their conflicted attraction to Americanization. However, like other models that use English-language works as their basis, Dearborn's focus on "one of America's most ideologically potent myths: that of the mixed marriage between a native-born white male and an eroticized and exoticized ethnic woman"[3] requires some reconfiguration as we look at marriage in immigrant texts written in Polish. Making no attempt to accommodate to or interpret for an audience of outsiders, and often drawing on historical experiences and relationships originating in Europe, these works present their own distinctive models of ethnic alliance and a radically different vision of the community's relationship to America.

Shared terminology and imagery may disguise divergent meanings. In his study of (English-language) Italian-American literature, Fred Gardaphé warns against "critical paradigms created by the dominant culture," which do not leave room for culturally specific meanings and categories of experience.[4] We have to see these Polish-American marriage tales through the lens of Polish history and culture, as well as that of the Polonian experience in America (perspectives that are not, after all, so easily separated). Otherwise, critical readings tend to support a fantasy of immigrant aspiration that says more about America's self-congratulatory myths than it does about the creation of an ethnic identity and culture.

Polonian writers used their own rhetoric of regeneration in order to make the American immigrant experience an agent of Polish national rebirth. The peasant immigrant, however, was to be recreated less as an American than as a Pole, with opportunities for individual development and progress in America turned to collective benefit. The very ideology of progress is weighted not so much with individual as with national aspiration. So while in both American and Polish minds marriage may have been granted the power to redraw lines of kinship, for Polish immigrant literary activists the roots of the family tree were set firmly in the Old World. Ethnic leaders saw in emigration an opportunity for the emergence and consolidation of a Polish identity, something hardly possible in the politically divided and socially stratified homeland. Polish immigrant writers construed marriage not as a shortcut to assimilation but as a means of forming and stabilizing a shared Polishness, of restoring the family lineage and inheritance threatened by internal disunity and coercion from without. America's freedom and opportunity was to lead to polonization rather than to Americanization. As fiction writers explored the meaning of Polishness along the ethnic fault lines of national and geographic origin, religion, language, political ideology, social class, and even personal choice and inclination, marriage served as a convenient metaphor for a national reunion contingent on alliances formed within and across these boundaries. Even after the restoration of the Polish state, novels of the interwar years, though describing different social and political realities, tended to resolve issues of ethnic identity in ways that underscored Polishness. For second-generation characters as for immigrant ones, marriage to a properly Polish mate was shown to bring not just domestic happiness but generational continuity, national and family honor, and a sustained relationship with the (Polish) homeland.

But who, precisely, was a properly Polish mate? While this question preoccupied writers, the answers they devised varied. It is precisely these variations that reveal the uneasy borders of Polishness, the contingencies of identity which Polonia's activists sought to define. By problematizing often interconnected cultural, religious, social, and political criteria of ethnicity, these works demonstrate the deep rifts left in the wake of the partitions, the preoccupation with issues raised by Poland's multicultural makeup, and the unclear relationship between American Polonia and the homeland. By turning now to some specific works of fiction, we can begin to uncover pressure points in Polonia's ethnogenesis and ways these early Polonian writers used the marriage plot to resolve complicated questions of identity and loyalty for their readers.

It comes as no surprise that immigrant writers consistently warned readers against intimacy with ethnic Russians and Germans, Poland's harshest oppressors, or that the personifications of these two enemies suggest the particularities of Poland's historical relationship with these powers. But it was not always so easy to determine who was a Pole, and who a German or Russian. In all three partition areas, ethnicity could be malleable and situational, with members of the same family sometimes choosing different ethnic identities. Norman Davies claims that "Poles kept to themselves" in the Russian partition, that "their children married amongst themselves, and looked with disfavor on any of their number who dared to break the unwritten rules of national solidarity."[5] That there was considerable anxiety over the issue, however, is evident in works like the 1904 religious tract *Wielka rana narodu polskiego, czyli małżeństwa mieszane* (The great national wound, or Mixed marriage), published in highly contested Silesia, which specifically warned against marriage between Pole and Russian. Marshal Śmigły-Rydz wrote, "Germany will destroy our body. Russia will destroy our soul."[6] The fictional treatment of Germans and Russians as suitors and spouses seems to reflect this perception of the two empires' differing relationships with subject Poland: Polonia's fictional Prussians are marauding and autocratic, while its Russians, as fellow Slavs, are treacherously seductive and duplicitous.

Poland's relationship with Russia was already weighted with the politics of sex, going back most memorably to the reign of the last king of Poland, Stanisław Poniatowski, whose lover, Catherine the Great, was one of the architects of Poland's dismemberment. But by the early twentieth century, imperial Russia was not the only perceived threat from the east. The rise of socialism and, to a lesser extent, Pan-Slavism, offered new configurations of Polish-Russian relations that were condemned and championed by competing national camps. Written in the wake of the failed 1905 revolution, Helena Staś's *Marzenie czy rzeczywistość* (Dream or reality) intertwines several strands of this interethnic and intergenerational conflict. When Staś's "emancipated" young heroine falls in love with a Russian ne'er-do-well, her father objects in traditional, politicized terms: "A Russian is an enemy of our country, an enemy of our language, an enemy of our creed!"[7] Wanda, in her dismissal of the Russian imperialist threat, demonstrates the emerging socialist one, also potentially compromising to Polish national aspirations: "I don't recognize national or religious feelings. Our motto should be, 'Not one nation and creed, but all humanity'—and we should strive for its union." Her father reduces her enthusiastic idealism to unnatural heartlessness: "To renounce national or religious feeling is to renounce family feeling."[8] And in truth, Wanda's rebellion and incipient internationalism, her insistence on sleeping with the enemy, lead to the emigration and dissolution of her family, to her two unhappy marriages, and to the suicide of her teenage son.

While the abandonment of national consciousness means the unraveling of family ties and the disruption of generational continuity, a return to the family fold signifies a renewal of patriotic passion. When the long-lost prodigal daughter at last steps down from the socialist soapbox, she takes up needle and thread for her living, and her domestic work both enshrines and eroticizes Poland's political struggle. Her masterpieces are two tapestries that hang in her bedroom. The one above her bed shows Poland divided between its three rapacious enemies. The other, facing her bed but hidden behind a curtain, portrays the nation's longed-for rescue by a Polish-American army. The narrator makes the connection explicit: "Because of her unhappy love for the Muscovite and for various perverse ideas, Poland, just like [Wanda], has gone through the vicissitudes of fate and, like Wanda, she will return."[9] Poland, seduced and betrayed through vanity, passion, and naiveté, is made responsible for its own political fall, a not uncommon charge among Poles and their enemies alike. But though Wanda's own family line is failed and her inheritance lost, there is hope for Poland in the untainted generations born in the American "partition."

If Russia seduces and betrays, Prussia dominates and subdues. In Henryk Nagiel's 1896 novel of international intrigue, *God's Punishment Crosses the Ocean,* for example (see chapter 3), Prussians are particularly singled out as calculating and passionless, even in love. When the marriage between a German baron and a countess from Poznań is poisoned by the "aversion of an ancient German aristocrat" to his Polish wife, the unhappy woman dies "of longing and regret, that she had married a German, and a man who'd never loved her."[10] The repercussions of this unhappy alliance are visited on their son, Konrad, who must choose between his dual loyalties.

In addition to the German specter, Nagiel's novel raises the troubling question of identity for those of mixed or uncertain bloodlines. Despite his integrity, his devout Catholicism, his self-identification as a Pole, and even his public revelation of his father's criminality, Nagiel's Konrad carries—nobly and tragically—the burden of his father's blood, and he loses the hand of the heroine.[11] But what is it that makes him a Pole like his mother, rather than a German like his father, or some combination of the two? Is it the influence of his patriotic, long-suffering mother? Or is it an innate goodness of character he has somehow inherited from her? These questions are never answered. The ambiguities of ethnicity are also suggested in Helena Staś's allegorical novella *Polski pień* (The Polish trunk), in which two suitors, both from the Prussian sector, vie for the same Polish(Irish)-American girl. Stanisław is a "purely Polish boy," while Fryc merely speaks Polish and "claims to be a Catholic."[12] Disowned by his family and rejected by Kasia, Fryc defaces, and eventually hangs himself from, a tree that Kasia and her immigrant grandfather have named for the Prussian-occupied city of Poznań.

What makes Fryc such an unconvincing Pole? Shared language and religion (and perhaps even blood, since the issue of his ethnicity is never resolved) are evidently not sufficient measures of Polishness: Fryc is still "a foreign power [that] had stolen into . . . 'Grandpa's Poland'" (21). And how is it that the influence of her immigrant grandfather turns little Kejty, alone of all her siblings, into Kasia, "a Polish jewel" (16)? That Nagiel, Staś, and other authors never satisfactorily define the basis of ethnicity, that they allow it to originate in the uncertain somewhere between predetermination and predilection, should not be too surprising—these are not either/or issues. However, most authors do grant Polishness, however defined and derived, the unquestioned ethical high ground, investing ethnic purity—whether a matter of blood or choice—with moral virtue, and the lack of it with, at best, imperfection, and at worst, defilement and degradation.

One might expect the issue of mixed parentage to take on added significance in America, where Poles were faced with new influences and possibilities. Only infrequently, however, are Polish immigrants shown in personal relationships with Americans. A rare example is Alfons Chrostowski's "Rok życia" (A year of life), serialized in 1889. "A Year of Life" quickly loses the Polish national themes with which it begins in order to concentrate on the scandals of the author's own personal life, since this odd and sordid novel appears to be a transparent fictionalization of Chrostowski's own failed marriage to an American woman, which ended in the author's attempted suicide and finally in divorce.[13] Whatever the novel's idiosyncrasies, the warning against an American spouse is explicit.

American interests and values are most often represented through other ethnic characters, however, particularly the Irish, with whom romantic liaisons are, at the very least, discouraged. Even a loving and dutiful Irish wife, in Staś's words, "could never be to [her husband] what a Polish woman could."[14] And more important, although an occasional Irish-Polish-American Katie may be successfully transformed into a Kasia, more often the children of such a union are neither Poles nor Polish-Americans, nor even Irish. Regrettably, they are Americans—not Crèvecoeur's celebrated new breed, but alien creatures speaking an unintelligible tongue.

This association of the Irish with Americanness is not random, since the Irish were the English speakers with whom Polish immigrants were most likely to have day-to-day contact. As factory foremen, as public officials, and as heads of the Roman Catholic hierarchy in this country, the Irish were the most obvious wielders of "American" power within the Polish immigrant's field of experience. And so some authors use the Irish spouse as a representative of the forces of economic exploitation and social oppression. In Stanisław Osada's *Z pennsylwańskiego piekła* (From a Pennsylvania hell), for example, Red Mary, an Irish barmaid married to a Pole, fails to seduce the novel's Mickiewicz-worshipping hero, so she stirs up discord within the small mining community, already crosscut with regional rivalries and prejudices. Her machinations finally lead to a fatal charge by the sheriff's militia against the hero and his followers, who are opposed to a company-maneuvered strike. The dying hero blames this treachery on "the cursed

Changing roles in the Polish-American family, as shown on the cover of a humor magazine published in Detroit (1933).

Stanisław Osada, journalist, novelist, and immigrant activist. Courtesy Polish National Alliance

little god of this land of business." But for Red Mary's husband, the American god acts through his Irish wife: "She possessed me. . . . Let that hour be damned in which fate joined me with that woman. . . . Everything bad had its beginning in her."[15]

If Osada's fiction contains a foreign whore, she is opposed by a Polish madonna, who at the death of her fiancé enters a Felician convent, joining "the powerful army of sister-teachers" dedicated to the education of Polish immigrant schoolchildren (100). The roles into which the conservative Osada inserts his women characters emphasize the purity and idealization of the Polishness his work proposes. The political intrigue and betrayal that fill Osada's novels are spurred by lustful, non-Polish, women who manipulate their Polish lovers and husbands into committing multiple treasons: against their immigrant countrymen, against their fellow laborers, against their own ethnic selves.

Nowhere is this pattern more insidious than in his fascinating and disturbing *W dniach nędzy i zbrodni* (In days of misery and crime). Once again, competing ideologies are represented by two women. One is Janka, an innocent orphan under the guardianship of the Polish immigrant who saved her from suicide. That immigrant is none other than Leon Czołgosz, who by the end of the novel will assassinate President McKinley. The lover who entraps Czołgosz in a violent web of physical and ideological passion is the revolutionary Róża, a character based primarily on Emma Goldman.[16] Róża is "not only a Jewess, but a Russian. . . . A Jew by birth," the novel's hero explains, and a Russian by culture. She speaks proper Polish, but not only was she raised in Russia, she also absorbed Russian social thought to such a degree that . . . what remained in her of Jewishness is only the strength of her hatred, the property of the inimitable race from which she came."[17] Osada's anti-Semitism, which not only this novel but his numerous other writings demonstrate, makes familiar, tangled associations between Jewishness, socialism, and Russianness, all of which Osada represents as dangerous to Polish interests. Familiar too is his characterization of the impassioned Róża: "dark and destructive sensuality is the dominant feature of Jewish heroines" in Polish literature from the beginning of the twentieth century to World War I.[18] Osada suggests that, in the end, only a pure Polish maiden could have saved Czołgosz from the bewitching Róża. But this maiden must eventually become a wife, and the mother of new generations of Poles on American soil.

Osada is not alone in warning against exogamy by spiritualizing and idealizing Polishness through the romantic relationships of which he approves, while sexualizing the relationships he condemns. Much of this literature depicts the Americanized Pole, of whatever generation, as seduced and demoralized by this country's materialism and lack of regulation. Particularly for female immigrants, Americanization becomes associated with emotional superficiality and promiscuity. In Czesław Łukaszkiewicz's *Guardian Angel and Guardian Devil,* for example (see chapter 4), a young immigrant's transformation from a Góral into a Pole is contrasted with the moral decline of his eager-to-Americanize village sweetheart, a Polish Sister Carrie who advances her position by trading up her lovers, finally becoming the mistress-housekeeper of a Polonian priest.

The seductiveness of America's economic opportunities and lack of social controls, particularly for women, is evident in many stories, among them Iza Pobóg's "Ich syn" (Their son), published in 1910, in which an immigrant engineer is forced into marriage with "an Americanized harlot unworthy of the name of Poland." Pobóg makes ethnicity a code for social class, as unassimilated immigrants like the bridegroom and his family are

Cover of *In Days of Misery and Crime* (1908) by Stanisław Osada, which includes an account of the 1901 assassination of President McKinley by Polish-American Leon Czołgosz. Courtesy Alumni Memorial Library, St. Mary's College of Ave Maria University

well educated, dignified, and honorable, while Americanized Poles are vulgar, morally degraded, and socially inferior.[19] An assimilated neighbor argues that the bride has bestowed an honor upon her reluctant husband: "So what if she's a laundress! She's a citizen of the United States." But the bride's poorly spoken Polish is further evidence of the disruption of "natural" social and family relations. The bride not only has violated class barriers, but unmans her husband linguistically: "I'm following my husband," she boasts in fractured Polish. Using a form of the masculine verb for getting married, *ożenić,* she says, "I married him today."[20] It is as though she had said, "I took him for my wife."

Like the Polish language, here Polishness itself is gendered, and the issue is not simply how to be a good Pole but how to be a proper Polish man or Polish woman. America, with its relative social freedom, was often represented as particularly compromising for immigrant women, who might confuse legality with morality: "Here there are no such things as harlots, just young girls free to do what they want because we don't need parental guardianship here—we have constitutional freedom." For a Pole, Pobóg implies, marriage with such a woman is not simply unfortunate, a matter of personal regret, but "unnatural," as the son explains to his parents: "The woman who forced herself on me with overpowering and devilish artifice . . . was not destined to be my life's companion." His parents disown him "because," they announce, "from the moment he lost his shame and sense of national dignity, he ceased to be our child."[21] Polishness, then, is not so much a matter of ancestry as it is a moral category. This union is untenable not just because it is loveless and personally unfulfilling but because it violates politicized sets of moral values and social hierarchies.

If Pobóg's little tale warns that Americanization leads to the abandonment of moral restraint and the transgression of class and gender barriers, it also walks a fine line between modeling an uncompromised Polishness to which working-class men and women might aspire and reminding those same readers of the centuries-old construct that Polishness is the exclusive domain of the nobility. Other works, such as Chrostowski's "The Polish Slave," would also reinforce the traditional social barriers that not only determined an acceptable pool of potential marriage partners but also restricted Polishness along lines of class. But writers like Łukaszkiewicz envisioned a more inclusive national identity, made possible by the opportunities for education and social contact that American Polonia offered immigrants. Thus the peasant protagonist of *Guardian Angel and Guardian Devil,* once so benighted that he mistook the Statue of Liberty for a saint, finds his proper mate in a young widowed noblewoman. Łukaszkiewicz argues for the oppressed peasant's potential as a full human being and as a Pole and, through this fictional marriage, for the reconciliation of traditionally antagonistic social forces.

Galician peasants, impoverished Warsaw gentry, Prussians, Russians, Irish, Jews, Americanized Poles—through the marriage plot, Polish-American fiction has brought them all into its discussion of proper Polishness. In different ways, all coexisted within or along Polish territorial or conceptual boundaries, in Europe or in America. Some are identified unequivocally as Poles, while others are sometimes explicitly differentiated from them. But even for these, their connection with Polishness is often intimate, highly charged, and sometimes fluid and overlapping. Thus immigrant writers used them to construct their varied versions of ethnic identity for their readers.

But Polonia's authors did not simply warn their readers about groups not to fraternize with. They also contrasted dangerous matches with desirable, approved ones, with marital unions that underscored these writers' ideologically implicated conceptions of Polish peoplehood. Spouses identified with Poland were ennobled and romanticized, and these marriages were represented as true, even inevitable, love matches. Werner Sollors reminds us of German critic Niklas Luhmann's observation that "falling in love" or "being made for each other" contains "a paradoxical tension between free choice and an ineluctably determined fate."[22] "Proper" unions tended to essentialize Polishness, situating it in indisputable impulses of the heart, in an instinctive gravitation of the soul. Certainly Polonian fiction invests this choice of a proper mate with a nearly deterministic attraction, even between Poles and non-Poles with whom Polish history prefigures such "natural" alliances. Thus, for instance, marriages between Poles and Lithuanians, such as that between two cousins in Nagiel's *God's Punishment,* who are at first cheated out of, but finally regain, their family inheritance, are completely unproblematized. Their marriage is emblematic of a hoped-for restoration of the Polish-Lithuanian Commonwealth. On the other hand, other Slavic ethnic groups closely linked with Poles geographically and linguistically, such as the Rusyns, are generally depicted as undesirable partners.[23]

In reality, despite differences of language and religion, a peasant Pole from Galicia would have had much more in common with a Rusyn spouse than with, say, a member of the petty gentry from Poznań. Intent on creating an overarching sense of Polishness, however, author-activists discouraged these differences, modeling successful marriages that crossed regional or class lines in ways that encouraged bonds based on a common commitment to a national cause. But evidence indicates that immigrants were keenly aware of these regional and class identities. Recent research into actual marriage patterns among immigrants to Chicago from one Galician village shows that, between 1893 and 1914, over 70 percent of their marriages contracted in Chicago involved partners from within ten kilometers of the home village. Though some spouses came from villages farther afield, only 2.3 percent of marriages involved a partner from outside Galicia.[24] Other accounts also stress the importance of local identities in matters of marriage: an immigrant widow from Poznań is reported to have lamented the marriage of her niece to a Polish peasant from Austria-Hungary: "I would have forgiven her for getting married without my permission, if she had just married a Pole. I don't want to see a Galician."[25] Despite the general perception among peasant immigrants that regional origin was an important consideration for successful marriage, authors intent on creating a unified national identity largely downplayed or ignored these differences, or attributed them to agitation by Poland's enemies.

With the proper influences and education, writers suggested, even Galicians could come to see themselves as (and maybe more important, be seen as) Poles. However, some authors raised the possibility of another more extraordinary transformation, one for which ethnic literary theory as it is commonly formulated does not prepare us. And that is that the process of polonization operates not just on those of "Polish" ancestry, but that Polishness is enticing enough to draw others to its fold and that these converts can become Poles. If immigrants from Poland and their children can be polonized, it is also occasionally possible to polonize the Other. And these Poles by choice may also be appropriate choices for mates. For certain authors, then, Polishness can be more than a matter of blood. It could also be an expression of politicized moral values and choices based on ideals such as freedom, nobility, and fearless self-sacrifice. Whatever one's claim to Polishness—blood or belief—it was finally against this moral component that proper Polishness could be judged, and treason measured.

The earliest example of the phenomenon of Polish conversion occurs in

Chrostowski's "The Polish Slave." When an immigrant is delayed in England on his way to the United States, he meets a beautiful, well-educated young woman of aristocratic family. She speaks flawless Polish, has a wide knowledge of Polish history and culture, and has a commitment to the Polish cause. But she is British. Inspired by the stories of her tutor, an emigré from the 1830 revolution, she has immersed herself in all things Polish. Her father jokingly charges the tutor with treason for making "a Pole out of his daughter."[26] In Chrostowski's story, it is not enough, or even essential, to be born in Poland, or to have Polish ancestors. Polishness can be a matter of personal inclination, though it seems to require categories of knowledge that are reserved for the educated and privileged.

Among the most remarkable of these conversion tales, however, is a novel produced nearly forty years later. "Adventures of a Polish Detective," previously discussed in chapter 3, was serialized in Buffalo's *Dziennik dla wszystkich* by an anonymous author in 1928 and 1929. After World War I, the finally realized dream of a resurrected Polish state, rather than mitigating questions of Polish identity, made them more pressing and immediate. With a restored homeland to return to, and increasing influences from outside the ethnic enclave, immigrants and their children were reconsidering their loyalties to Poland and to America. And within Poland itself, political, cultural, and religious forces were attempting to define and stabilize the multiethnic and diverse new nation. These forces resulted in generally more complex literary examinations of the meanings and obligations of Polishness as expressed through the marriage plot.

The detective story overlay, discussed in chapter 3, disguises a wide-ranging exploration of ethnic identities and intercultural relations. "Polish Detective" is the only Polonian novel to include, though somewhat tangentially and with idiosyncratic sidetracks, Mary Dearborn's element of immigrant and Native American intermarriage. Besides claiming a certain natural nobility of the oppressed Polish spirit, and the historical and spiritual legitimacy of the Polish presence in America, this connection is also a reminder that Poles came here because their native land had been overrun.

But if America is a Polish reservation or partition, then in the interwar years during which this novel appeared the homeland was again open to resettlement. The allure of a free Poland, and the author's vision for the resurrected state, is revealed through the novel's conversion subplot. "Adventures of a

Kidnapped on Her Wedding Night, reprinted in 1988 from a 1936 original. Courtesy Krystyna Osiecka

Polish Detective" culminates in a double wedding: Andrzej, a Polish-American Catholic, marries Rebekah, the daughter of a Jewish grocer; and Andrzej's social-climbing sister Marta marries Greenwood, an American factory owner. Polishness is not diluted through these "intermarriages," however. Rather, it is reconfirmed and redefined. First, marriage between Christian and Jew reunites strands of Polishness. Rebekah surprises her husband when she responds enthusiastically to his suggestion that they honeymoon in Poland:

"What a splendid idea. . . . One's native country is always the best."
"And here I thought . . . that you wouldn't agree to it."
"Why? Isn't it the country of my ancestors as well? We're all from Poland!"[27]

Given the novel's historical context, appearing as it did in the uneasy first decade of Poland's restored statehood, this proposal of an inclusive Polish state and the gentle suggestion that misunderstandings between Jews and Christians are the result of Christian myopia, might well be a prescription for redefining the nation. This novel suggests not simply that Jewishness is compatible with Polishness, but that Jews of Polish ancestry are simply and indisputably Poles. Polishness is as much a birthright for Rebekah as for her Catholic fiancé, and their marriage is a rejoining of Polish elements. While harder questions about the Christian-Jewish relations are avoided by Rebekah's eventual conversion to Catholicism, undertaken on her own initiative to seal the bond with her bridegroom, assimilation, with or without conversion, was certainly one of the conceptions of a unified Polish polity envisioned by progressives from at least the last quarter of the nineteenth century. And Rebekah's parents, who do not convert, are as pleased as she is to reclaim their rightful place in the new Poland.

Marta and Greenwood's relationship with Poland and Polishness, on the other hand, suggests that Polishness can also be chosen as an identity, regardless of ancestry. At the same time, it proposes a dormant blood connection just waiting to be awakened among second-generation, apparently assimilated, Polish-Americans. When Greenwood brings his bride to Poland on their honeymoon (actually, he tricks her into coming, since she had been interested only in visiting Western Europe), Marta falls in love with "the homeland she had never seen." Greenwood himself is so captivated that he determines to become a Catholic, sell his Buffalo factory, and reestablish his business in Poland: "I am starting to learn Polish and I want to become a Pole," he writes his in-laws. It is at his urging that "the whole Topieliński family was united on Polish soil: the parents; the Greenwoods, who were already called the Krasnodrzewskis; and young Andrzej and his wife with the rest of the relatives. Are they happy? Inquire of them at their Warsaw address and they'll tell you themselves."[28]

Catholics and Jews, former immigrants and their children, even Americans for whom Poland can be a kind of new frontier, are joined to reinvigorate

The Salesgirl from Broadway (1937), one of several novels by Melania Nesterowicz about the careers and romantic lives of second-generation Polish-American women.

and repopulate the newly independent nation. With this return to union, love for Poland becomes indistinguishable from love of spouse, love of family, love of an ideal that seems to guarantee prosperity and progeny.[29]

It was during the interwar period that Melania Nesterowicz, who had been writing fiction since the early years of the century, published several Polonian novels of manners centered around the romantic adventures of second-generation Polish-American "flaperki." These popular Polonian soap operas offer insight into the expanding range of ethnic possibilities opened by new social opportunities and a new Poland. The heroines of novels like *Sprzedawaczka z Broadwayu,* " Hot-Cha-Cha," and "Stella z Buffalo" are the first in their families to venture out of their neighborhoods into the commercial world, where they are seduced by materialism and embrace a new social independence. While their pursuit of an imagined America of wealth, glamour, and status at first compromises their connection to family and community, these secretaries, salesgirls, and nurses find a way back to an ethnic home of their own creation, ultimately rejecting relationships with old-blood Americans and finding fulfillment in marriage with a Polish or Polish-American man.

These novels fashion a dynamic model of American Polishness in which the threats of modernization and Americanization are rechanneled in order to empower the local community and reinforce, rather than undermine, ethnic loyalties. Nesterowicz's heroines use romantic relationships to refashion their identities, playing out alternative ethnic scenarios before "finding themselves" in their Polishness, before making a Polish home for themselves and their families. They follow a trajectory that seems to lead farther and farther away from home—from Buffalo's Polish East Side, from family and familiar ethnic touchstones. But the path is circular and these characters can find fulfillment only by reconstructing and reinhabiting their ethnic selves.

That path can take unexpected turns, however, and Polishness can stretch in unexpected new directions. In "Hot-Cha-Cha," the heroine's short-lived marriage to a wealthy American results in a dark-skinned child: the father's hidden ancestry includes a great-great-grandmother from a South Sea island. Recognizing that in racially stratified America her son will face daunting obstacles, his mother and a group of Polish-Americans settle on this island, establishing a New Poland. Here is a retelling of the immigrant epic in which the founding myth is rewritten in recognition of America's troubled pluralism.

Without ceasing to love America or the American Polonia of her parents, a second-generation woman envisions an alternative world of tolerance in which one's roots in varied soils can be honored and nurtured. When he gets old enough, she decides, her son will learn the Polish language and travel with her to Poland, where his dark skin will presumably be no obstacle. Likewise, new emigrants will not only find a home on this Polish colony but the aboriginal inhabitants will welcome them as linked to themselves by new ties of blood. This New Poland will be a multiracial, multicultural paradise.

The fantasy of escape is also what propels these young women into the arms of American men, whom they imagine carry the key to the American ancestral mansion. These relationships, holding the promise of a life outside Polonia, of the Americanization through marriage so prominent and so positive in the general discussion of ethnic literature, are not only doomed to failure, but even in their best moments threaten the second-generation's relationship to family, to community, and to a finer self. American wealth is linked consistently not with the mythical drive, determination, and creative vision of the legendary self-made man, but with inherited privilege perpetuated through bigotry and resulting in arrogance, corruption, and dishonor.

The second generation is shown to be painfully aware of the low regard in which Poles are held within America at large, of "the poisonous propaganda of the one hundred percenters against the 'undesirable' immigrants from Eastern and Southern Europe [that] revealed itself at every step."[30] Not even American birth is a passport to nativeness. "I was born in America," Stella keeps reminding people, who despite surprise at her perfect English never manage to see her as anything but a foreigner.[31]

What initially attracts these women to American society is not only a Hollywood-inspired dream of the high life and the hope of material gain, or the desire to be accepted as an American. Collectively, Nesterowicz suggests, immigrant Polonia has been judged inadequate by its second generation —intellectually, culturally, and materially—and has failed to provide an attractive alternative for its educated and worldly children, particularly its young women. It is their experiences in the white-collar workforce that open their eyes to these alternatives. After beginning to earn her own living as a stenographer in a downtown office, Stella announces, "I'm a free woman, independent of my father and mother."[32] Not only does she rebel against her parents' "old-fashioned" ways, refusing to carry a bag lunch to the office or to bring her American beaus into the house, she also rejects the "life in Poland" she sees ahead of her on the East Side: "a life like the one her girlfriends led. Children, a squalid apartment, furniture bought on installment, with no possibility of rising to the sphere of millionaires, where sensation and amusement make life pleasant, where you don't have to worry about trifles, where even though women don't have a slew of children they still manage to be happy."[33]

Nesterowicz clearly understands the dreams and ambitions that entice the wayward daughters of working-class Polonia away from this life. At the same time, she exhibits sympathy toward the struggles of working-class first-generation immigrants like salesgirl Irena's mother, who "cleaned offices downtown" when she arrived from the old country, and like Stella's, who "for thirty-odd years . . . had not stirred beyond Buffalo."[34] The moral voice in Nesterowicz's novels belongs to these immigrants and is echoed by the young women who do choose to marry neighborhood boys and whose struggles with poverty are sweetened by their love for their husbands and for their children. Like Stella herself, her American lover fails to recognize the virtues and attractions of such a life: "What to do?" wonders Stef Mitchell. "Move in with the Kowalskis. Marry Stella and every morning eat the breakfast her mother makes, put my 'luncz' in my pocket and go to work with my wife. And at night head to the saloon for a beer with her father and listen to him tell stories about Piłsudski in broken English."[35]

Stella's father, broken English and all, is shown to be a man of honor. And eventually, whatever its faults and failings, however annoying its gossip and scrutiny, this Polish neighborhood pulls Nesterowicz's heroines back to the fold. It finally proves all the more attractive in contrast to the strange places through which these young women have wandered, even as Polish-American husbands become all the dearer in contrast to the American admirers who fail the tests of mature and responsible love. The new commitment to their Polish-American lovers and husbands translates into a parallel commitment to American Polonia, including the old ethnic neighborhood, which is refigured through these unions into the hope of Poland and America. Stella Kowalski's father describes a future in which Polish-Americans are Buffalo's "dominant element":

"There will be as many of us in Buffalo as grains of sand on the banks of Lake Erie, and we will become a cohesive group that will not break its ties with Poland but will cooperate closely with the former homeland in cultural and artistic matters. Our Polish genius will emerge in all the fields of science, art, industry, and business. . . . In the future our Stella and Stan will take the position they deserve in the American homeland."[36]

For the children of Polish immigrants, America is now the homeland. But what has brought Stella's father to this conviction, and brought Stella and Stan together, is their renewed love for Poland. The second generation is bound not just to an American ethnic neighborhood but finally, it must realize, to Poland itself. Stan's enlistment in Poland's struggle for independence turns him from a street corner "sheik" into a "serious, soulful soldier, with exquisite manners." Looking about her on a trip to the still embattled Warsaw, Stella sees both a nation and a family: "These people were not foreigners—they were her people, close to her. They were the brothers she hadn't seen for so long, and had now rediscovered." Polonia must love Poland, Nesterowicz tells her readers, in order to love and reproduce itself. "All my hopes are fulfilled, and my sorrows have flown," rejoices Stella, the new bride. "It's Poland that did that," Stan answers. "You're right," says Stella. "It's Poland."[37]

Through the metaphor of marital alliance and misalliance that the ethnic romances articulated, Polonian authors encouraged the immigrant community to read itself as part of a Polish family, exploring ways of constructing communal identity and of reproducing a Polish sensibility and historical consciousness. Whatever the statistics on increasing out-marriage or on weakened ties to Poland among succeeding generations, the guidelines laid out by Polonia's immigrant authors have remained part of an idealized ethnic consciousness. Despite Polonia's increasing diversity, despite diverse ways of being Polish-American, and despite the necessarily contingent borders along which a common peoplehood can be proposed, the ideal remains that Polishness entails the perception of a people bound to each other along the clearly contestable lines of ancestry, but, perhaps more critically, as eternally connected to a land across the ocean. The message of Nesterowicz and her fellow immigrant writers is that, no matter how distant, no matter how complicated by other loyalties and affections, Poland and Polishness are always waiting to be reembraced.

EPILOGUE |||

Continuities

Polish Immigrant Literature Then and Now

THE LITERATURE OF turn-of-the-century immigrants is all but forgotten today, and the names of its writers have faded even from Polonian history. Perhaps these works became irrelevant as the issues they engaged so passionately became less pressing, as the incidents and personages they described passed from community consciousness. Perhaps, in fact, the issues that mattered so much to well-educated immigrant writers failed to find lasting meaning in the lives of working-class immigrant readers. Perhaps American prejudices and the push for assimilation made Polish books, and immigrant memory, a matter of shame. Later generations, often with little or no knowledge of the Polish language, would certainly find these books inaccessible, if they found them at all. Cheap production values and the appearance of ephemerality must have doomed many old copies to the fireplace, the junk pile, or the paper drive. American archives and libraries would have been largely unaware of their existence. And Polish-American repositories have long suffered from uneven collecting and preservation practices.

Scholars who did happen upon some of these old books or newspaper stories may have been uncertain about what to do with them, how to fit them into the inadequate disciplinary framework: Was this Polish literature? American literature? Should these works be studied as artifacts? As examples of popular culture? As sociological records? Only with the rise in interdisciplinary studies, and with the recognition of a multilingual American culture, has a space begun to emerge for the serious study of works like these, from all of these perspectives.

Like the later generations of other ethnic groups, the children, grandchildren, and great-grandchildren of Polish immigrants have made their own literary contributions, for the most part in English, and through nonethnic publishing companies. Postwar emigré authors writing in Polish form a distinguished company—Czesław Miłosz, Jan Lechoń, Stanisław Barańczak—but their work bears little in common with their turn-of-the-century counterparts, and for the most part they did not support existing Polonian publishing enterprises, nor form their own in this country. Even popular postwar novelists like sociologist Danuta Mostwin, whose fiction often deals with issues of immigrant adjustment, tend to utilize European publishers like Veritas in London and Instytut Literacki in Paris.

But beginning with the loosening of diplomatic obstacles in the 1970s, and augmented by the declaration of martial law in 1981 and the political and economic uncertainties of the eighties and nineties, American Polonia has experienced a renewed influx of immigrants. While the body of Polish-language writing emerging from modern immigrant Polonia is more varied and sophisticated than that produced a century ago, it is this latest wave of immigrants whose overall patterns of literary production are most similar to those of the stara emigracja. Like their turn-of-the-century counterparts, newcomers are establishing their own popular journals and publishing companies. They are serializing contemporary Polish-language crime novels set in American cities[1] and producing new exposés of corruption and exploitation within immigrant institutions. They are using popular fiction to explore their changing relationship to the homeland and to families left behind. And like their fellow writers a century ago, they are accused of sensationalism, slander, and political collusion.

There are a number of perhaps not immediately apparent similarities between turn-of-the-century and modern immigrants that might help account for some of these commonalities. Although the postwar emigration and the Solidarity-era group are generally thought of as linked by their shared political struggle against communism and as distinct from the turn-of-the-century migration "for bread," both the turn-of-the-century and the current migration might better be called, in the words of contemporary author Zofia Mierzyńska, "political-economic" movements, in which both motivations coexist.[2]

Indeed, the very difficulty of naming and defining what is often, rather inaccurately, called the post-Solidarity migration, points to the difficulty of separating political from economic motivations. This group includes legal immigrants, such as family members of citizens and permanent residents. It includes political activists, many of them well educated, who were granted asylum after martial law or found some other means to legalize their residency. Like the early immigrants faced with the prospect of returning to a restored Poland after World War I, these emigrés were often torn when the free elections of 1989 offered the possibility of repatriation.

But the largest segment of this group is made up of *wakacjusze* ("vacationers")—that is, of Poles from various social strata who come to this country as visitors, usually with the intention of working illegally, and who overstay their visas, sometimes by many years.[3] The U.S. Immigration and Naturalization Service puts their number at seventy thousand as of 1996.[4] The intention of these illegal vacationers may or may not be to remain in the United States, and it often changes according to personal circumstance. As in the old emigration, the imperative to earn hard currency abroad can sweep entire villages and regions, as chain migration facilitates the immigrant's entry into community employment and housing networks. Together these groups, legal and illegal, form a fluid community focused, like turn-of-the-century immigrants, on circumstances in Poland and, also like them, holding an often uncertain commitment to a future in the United States. It is this ambiguous relationship to America and to Poland that haunts the literature they produce.

The appearance in the last twenty years of new Polish-language publications in the United States and Canada, as well as the nature of these books, newspapers, and magazines, reflects some of the issues that connect this latest wave of newcomers with a long history of immigrant cultural production. The strong ties to journalism of turn-of-the-century immigrant literature and publishing are continued into the present, as modern authors use their acquaintance with contemporary issues and events to create fiction drawn from the daily experiences of their readers and serialize their works in newspapers, print them in low-circulation journals and through small-scale immigrant presses, and self-publish them, just as their early counterparts did.[5] As in an earlier era, journalists often double as authors of fiction. But even more important, this connection with journalism has again encouraged a popular literature aimed at a general audience, though a better educated and more sophisticated one.

Contemporary authors have continued to draw inspiration from the immigrant community's day-to-day activities and problems. Melania Nesterowicz acknowledged this connection in the 1930s: "Generally, after returning from the editorial office if I didn't have a meeting or some pressing work, I wrote the chapter of a novel treating what I had seen or heard in the course of the day."[6] Modern immigrant literature's affiliation with journalism continues to blur the distinction between fiction and nonfiction and to address immediate immigrant issues. One of the most popular of the immigrant journalist authors of the latest migration was Zofia Mierzyńska. Through the window of her work the elements that unite immigrant literature of divergent eras and circumstances come into clear focus.

Before returning to Poland in the mid-1990s, Mierzyńska wrote for several Polonian papers (including *Gwiazda polarna,* established in 1908 and once affiliated with the Worzałła Brothers publishing company). She produced a Polish-language radio soap opera, *Jackowo story,* set in one of Chicago's old Polish neighborhoods, now dominated by wakacjusze, and her several novels about new Polish immigrants provoked indignant protest. One reader called her most popular novel, *Wakacjuszka* (The vacationer), "Trash with neither literary nor ideological value. It's only about sex, chasing after the dollar, and cheating each other. . . . I think it's the work of communists."[7]

Accusations like these echo criticisms launched against turn-of-the-century immigrant writers, whose works often revealed uncomfortable family and community issues, exposed institutional corruption, and took potshots at political adversaries. Under different historical circumstances, these earlier writers were labeled socialists, or Russian-lovers, or Prussian sympathizers, or sometimes, regrettably, Jews. But this name-calling underscores the issues of ethnic loyalty based on conditions in Poland that have always been sources of contention within Polonia, and that continue to frame the tensions between and within Polonia's several immigrant waves. Mierzyńska's fiction concentrates on the social worlds of contemporary immigrants as they negotiate the gap between their inflated expectations and the disillusioning realities of life in America and as the lives they left in Poland become more and more irretrievable. "My books are based on authentic experiences and incidents," Mierzyńska explains. "I use fiction only in terms of the names and occupations."[8] Hanna Świderska, writing in *Kultura,* praises *The Vacationer* as a long-overdue "sociological record."[9]

In 1910 Helena Staś called for an immigrant literature "created for [immigrants], based on their lives."[10] The need for such a literature is no less real at the turn of the next century, as continuing waves of newcomers confront existing ethnic communities, grappling with their own particular issues of adjustment, forging their own social and cultural networks, and creating their own Polonias. Despite enormous historical changes, despite the particularities of each cohort's experience in the United States and in Poland, the function and focus of immigrant literature remains largely the same, expressing their day-to-day struggles and concerns, interpreting their daily experiences and social worlds in a transnational synthesis of old- and new-world issues and cultural patterns.

Mierzyńska's own argument for a popular literature that accurately addresses the immigrant experience might well have come from Staś's pen ninety-some years ago: "People like to read about themselves, about matters that relate to them, issues that make them both happy and sad. Often I hear complaints from writers, particularly here in emigration, that these people don't read, that they don't appreciate [literature]. [But] if writers write only for themselves, not taking their readers into consideration, then they shouldn't really complain that people don't read their work."[11]

The concerns of these modern immigrant readers are very similar to those that earlier immigrants expressed in their own literature: economic survival; family relations; cultural issues like language maintenance, community resources, and networks of power; conditions in the country of origin; and shifting relationships to the new country and to the old. Mierzyńska writes with a consciousness of these similarities:

> The facts and events that I described in *The Vacationer* aren't a new phenomenon that we haven't encountered before. The problem of the so-called Chicago marriage, of renouncing our own children, of mutual antagonisms, and so on, exist today as they did one hundred years ago. In their work *The Polish Peasant in Europe and America*, William Thomas and Florian Znaniecki, relying on documents, letters, excerpts from court proceedings, etc., present the history of Polish emigrants along with their problems and complaints, which are not so different from those today.[12]

In fact, the letter that Mierzyńska's "vacationer" writes home to her husband could have come right out of Thomas and Znaniecki, or out of the turn-of-the-century epistolaries, even to its characteristic opening: "My dear husband, in the first words of my letter, Let Jesus Christ be Praised."[13]

But despite the immigrant's intentions to return to Poland, these old-world ties can become more and more tenuous. "Someone once said," Mierzyńska writes, "that anyone who sees America once, will never again know peace. If he returns, he'll think about what's here. If he finds himself here, he'll long for what he left behind. . . . We're like birds who've lost their nests and, tossed in the wind, struggling in the downpour, we're trying to find them again" (3:61).

In *The Vacationer*, Mierzyńska draws out these shifting loyalties through her main character, Aniela, a woman in her forties who leaves her husband and children in Poland and comes to Chicago, meaning to stay just long enough to earn money for a tractor. She earns the price of the tractor, and a cultivator, and still she stays: "Franuś was writing me that it was enough already. . . . But I had the fever, maybe I'd caught that American sickness. Nothing mattered but the almighty dollar" (2:57). Within a few years, Aniela has decided to use her American dollars not to continue improving her home in Poland but to buy a brownstone in the heart of Chicago Polonia, where she becomes a landlady to new vacationers.

The uncertainty of the immigrant's position, particularly for women, becomes additionally clear in Mierzyńska's *Zawód: Hałskiper* (Occupation: Housekeeper), which consists of vignettes from the lives of a group of women working illegally in the Chicago suburbs, sleeping in shifts in squalid basement rooms, cleaning houses by day and offices by night, with every second Sunday free. Some continue to daydream about their return to families and homes in Poland, about expensive presents for their husbands, education for their children, about opening a little clothes shop in Białystok, about a comfortable life in Poland without struggle.

But for most of these women there is finally no going back. Some have gotten married and are raising children who are already Americanized. Others are no longer the people they were, and the personal and social worlds they left in Poland no longer exist for them. The most drastic tolls are taken on family ties: this one's husband is living with another woman, "in front of the whole village."[14] This one's took the twenty thousand dollars his wife had sent during three years in America and asked for political asylum in West Germany—with their neighbor's wife. But it's not only the husbands left behind who have found comfort in others. "Chicago marriages" help the women overcome the cheerlessness of their working lives. And besides, by sharing living expenses with a "bojfrend," they can send more money home.

This money is also a source of family disintegration. The vacationers are reminded of "the children left behind, far away, who don't even remember anymore what their father or mother looks like.[15] Of the husband or wife now dressed head to toe in American Spandex, driving the Polonez bought with American dollars, drinking American coffee with American 'krim' for breakfast—and not at all looking forward to your return!"[16] When Aniela realizes that her family wants her back only for the money and gifts she will bring, she imagines telling them, "Everything that I brought I give to you, everything will be yours. The dollars. And the miniskirt. And the motorcycle. But I have to go back [to America], because I see that there is no place for me with you" (2:82).

Perhaps the biggest impediment to return is the gradually widening gulf that results from long separation, from the accumulation of new, unshared experiences. Living apart from their families, the vacationers have made their own lives for themselves, and though those lives may be difficult, they are independent: "After a couple of years they've gotten used to freedom, to fun, and now they should go back to their husbands, their wives, their children? It'd be hard to get used to that all over again" (3:26). Their expectations of family life, and of relationships between men and women, have been changed by a combination of American cultural influences, economic power, and personal independence.

Among the issues these immigrants share with their earlier counterparts is a preoccupation with internal exploitation and betrayal. In America, Mierzyńska suggests, family and national bonds do not translate into common interests or mutual understanding. Quite the opposite. "What hurts worst," Aniela says, "is that a Pole acts like a wolf with other Poles; one would drown another in a spoonful of water" (1:61). It is not American capitalists who exploit the illegal workers but the other immigrants who run the employment agencies, who rent the unheated porches, who cheat their customers and take payoffs from their employees: "Poles are the worst; greedy, jealous, looking to take advantage of each other" (1:37). A Polish shipping agency accepts payment for automobiles, then closes its office and disappears. Aniela must split her housekeeping earnings fifty-fifty with a Polish employment agency. She buys her overnight office-cleaning job with her engagement ring and two bottles of whiskey. And she still has to sleep with her boss.

Just as many turn-of-the-century immigrants developed a national consciousness, a sense of themselves as Poles, through their exposure to new ideas in the immigrant community—through literature, through the immigrant press, through cultural and political institutions and the proximity of immigrants from various regions and social strata—the uneducated vacationer Aniela begins to think of her experience in national terms only in the United States. At first, when a radio interviewer berates her for planning to return to Poland, to the "regime," she says, "I don't want to go back to any Reżim, but to Franek. Maybe you've mistaken me for someone else. My Frania's name is Socha, not Reżim" (2:48).

But as she advances in Jackowo society, as she acquires money and prestige, Aniela's identity begins to organize itself in ways that engage a wider web of interconnections and relationships with a national ideal: "The homeland is not the structure," she realizes after attending a Polonian ball, "not a better or worse government, which is fleeting, which changes. Our homeland is the land where the plain stretches out before you. It's the mountains, the summits raised like beaks toward heaven. It's the sea, with its sandy dunes. It's the grave of a mother and father somewhere in a village cemetery" (2:16). Aniela's internalized Polishness recalls nineteenth-century attempts to formulate a "nation [that is] not a collection of people living on territory defined by certain borders, but rather the collection of their own ideas, feelings, and thoughts."[17]

Like Polish immigrants generations earlier, Aniela helps establish a village emigrant organization, the "Society of Friends of Our Rector," which sends money back to the home parish for a weekly mass and "deliberate[s] together how to fight communism." However, the current immigrants show the same propensity for the infighting that defeated so many efforts among the earlier immigration, and their first project is to "uncover all the spies sent here. . . . Each one pretends that he came for the dollar, but really the communists sent him here to watch and listen." The connection between an American experience and a developing political understanding of old country conditions is articulated by the society's president: "Many of us were not concerned with politics until now, but . . . now things will be otherwise. . . . We live in a country where everything is permitted, and we are free to fight the red plague" (3:14). This same widening of horizons coupled with freedom from political oppression led Michał Kruszka to claim in 1885 that "in the New World we have the best opportunity to exist as Poles."[18]

Polish immigrant writers before World War II, influenced largely by the Polish social and literary movements of positivism and organic work, felt compelled to direct their creative energy toward social and political goals. The most fundamental of these were the restoration of Poland's statehood and, relatedly, the development of a Polish national consciousness among immigrant readers, most of whom were former peasants without a well-established sense of themselves as Poles. Modern-day immigrants may not need an American experience to awaken an awareness of themselves as Poles, but they continue to write about the transformations of identity that living in emigration imposes. Disagreements over just who could properly be called a Pole, over the obligations Polishness demanded, and over the direction social and political action on Poland's behalf should take preoccupied early Polonia's writers both before and after national independence. But if in more recent years the deliverance of the nation from communism is no longer the issue it once was, community concerns have reemerged over Polonia's relationship to the "new" Poland. Literature reveals immigration, past and present, as a personal and social process of negotiation and accommodation. While the road back to the homeland may be much more tentative and problematic for modern-day immigrant writers than for those of the stara emigracja, the shifting relationship to families, to Polonia, and to Poland continue to be fundamental issues.

Although most studies stress the differences between the several waves of Polish immigration, and the consequent stresses to Polonian community, cultural, and institutional life, the literature created by immigrants at the turn of the twentieth and twenty-first centuries also suggests unexpected commonalities. Today's readers are better educated than those of the stara emigracja, but the necessity of a popular literature based on immigrant experiences and concerns is no less real. While these issues are shaped by each immigrant cohort's very specific historical circumstance, they may also reflect concerns inherent to immigration itself.

The study of current immigrant works in Polish reminds us of historical continuities that connect Polish America's various immigrant waves, particularly and perhaps unexpectedly the turn-of-the-century and current waves, and enriches our understanding of what is still a dynamic and evolving Polonia. Their common patterns of production, form, and theme, as well as the very particular issues and concerns they reveal, also have significance for the more general study of ethnic literature and of the continuing creation of ethnic identity and culture in the United States and underscore the importance of issuing English translations of these works in order to facilitate comparative study. What we learn from Polish-language writers and their works in this country contributes to our knowledge of Polish cultural and political history, to a more complete reading of American ethnic literature, and to a fuller understanding of America's vital and evolving multiculturalism, to which the various Polonias continue to add their voices.

PROFILES |||

Selected Polish Immigrant Authors and Publishers

Bałdyga, Kazimierz (1893 or 1895–after 1929). Born in Warsaw, Russian Poland. Served in Haller's Army. Radio personality and contributor to several newspapers, including *Kuryer narodowy* and *Nowy świat* (New York), *Rekord codzienny* (Detroit), *Weteran* (Cleveland), *Gwiazda polarna* (Stevens Point, Wis.).

Barć, Franciszek (1883–1958). Born in Czudec, Austrian Poland. Educated in Rzeszów. Emigrated 1903. Attended University of Detroit. Worked on several newspapers, including *Polak w Ameryce* (Buffalo), *Dziennik zjednoczenia, Naród polski,* and *Przyszłość* (Chicago), *Tygodnik obywatelski* (Hamtramck, Mich.), *Dziennik polski,* and *Ognisko domowe* (Detroit).

Bartosz, Adam (1894–1980). Born in Góra Ropczyska, Austrian Poland. Emigrated 1913. Illness kept him from education in Poland; in U.S. he attended night school, interrupting studies to earn money and marry. Eventually finished high school at night, while working as newspaper editor. Law degree from University of Baltimore. Editor, *Jedność Polonia* (Baltimore), *Rolnik* and *Gwiazda polarna* (Stevens Point, Wis.). Wrote plays and poetry. Active in PNA. Papers at Milwaukee Urban Archives, University of Wisconsin, Milwaukee.

Bójnowski, Łucjan (1868–1960). Born in Swierzbutowo, Russian Poland. Emigrated 1888. Ordained 1895. Rector, Sacred Heart Roman Catholic Church, New Britain, Conn. Under his leadership a church, two grade schools, a high school, a home for the aged, and an orphan asylum were built in New Britain. Founded Daughters of Mary of Immaculate Conception order of Catholic nuns. Established newspaper *Przewodnik katolicki.* Supporter of Dmowski's right-wing Endeks. Died in New Britain. Papers at Connecticut Polish American Archives at Central Connecticut State University.

Borzęcki, Władysław (1899–1976?). Born in Lwów, Austrian Poland. Studied law at University of Kraków. Served in Polish army, 1918–22. Emigrated 1923. Worked as bank clerk (Związek Spółek Zarobkowych Bank, New York), private music teacher, soloist. Involved in Polish arts clubs (New York). Journalist on several newspapers, including *Kuryer narodowy* and *Nowy świat* (New York); American correspondent for *Ilustrowany kuryer codzienny* (Kraków).

Burke, Karol (1892–after 1926). Born in Widowicz, Austrian Poland. Emigrated 1917. Served in Haller's Army, WWI. Published memoirs of the war years in *Sokół* (Pittsburgh), which he edited.

Chełchowski, Telesfor (1884–1917). Occasionally, Szczepan Chełchowski. Emigrated 1907. Poet, playwright, satirist. Editor of socialist paper *Bicz Boży* (Chicago). Died of tuberculosis in Texas sanatorium.

Chrostowski, Alfons Mieczysław (ca. 1860–after 1920). Occasionally, Count de Chrostowski. Father spent six years in Siberian exile for part in 1863 insurrection. Educated in Moscow, where involvement in revolutionary circles resulted in expulsion under police guard to home town. Emigrated before 1887. Play *Nihiliści* (The nihilists) performed by workers' theater groups in U.S.; finally banned in New York at insistence of Russian consul. Other revolutionary works published anonymously in European periodicals. Editor, *Postęp* and *Świat* (New York), *Reforma* (Chicago), *Ojczyzna* and *Jutrzeńka* (Cleveland). Member of New York Ognisko group of leftist journalists and social activists; supporter of early independent church movements. All traces of him seem to disappear within Polonia by early 1900s, but he is listed in 1920 census as 48-year-old playwright.

Czupka, Julian (1854–1924). Born in Czortków, Austrian Poland. Educated in Tarnopol, Austrian Poland. Received Ph.D. 1879. Emigrated 1882. Graduate of New York University Law School. Editor, *Osa* (New York), *Polonia* (Baltimore). Contributor of humorous poetry and prose to these papers and to *Kukuryku* (Buffalo). Member of New York Ognisko group. Left journalism to practice law in Philadelphia and Wilkes-Barre, Pa. Died in Wilkes-Barre.

Czuwara, Stanisław (1882–1955?). Served in Haller's Army.

Dangel, Stanisław (1873–1938). Also Dangiel, Dangel-Langowski. Supporter of PNCC. Editor, *Straż* (Scranton, Pa.), *Narodowiec* and *Wiadomości codziennie* (Cleveland); *Hasło polskie* (Pittsburgh). Stint as manager of PNA newspapers *Dziennik związkowy* and *Zgoda* (Chicago) marked by controversy, accusations of harassment and unprofessionalism. Activist, KON. Returned to Poland sometime between 1919 and 1921 to take over family estate in Kutno, where he died. Biography in *Polski słownik biograficzny.*

Drzazga, Renat (?–?). Affiliated with PNCC.

Dyniewicz, Władysław (1843–1928). Born Władysław Dywicz in Chwałków, Prussian Poland. Emigrated 1866. Blacksmith in Poland; worked for railroad before buying small Polish bookstore and expanding into one of Polonia's most influential newspapers, *Gazeta polska narodowa/Gazeta polska w Chicago,* and first major publishing enterprise, Polish American Publishing Company. Died in Chicago. Biography in *Polski słownik biograficzny.*

Haiman, Mieczysław (1888–1949). Born in Złoczów, Austrian Poland. Emigrated 1913. Worked as laborer, then as journalist, 1917–35. Became director of newly created Polish Museum of America, 1935; wrote many historical studies of Polonia. Awarded Polonia Restituta and Silver Laurel of Polish Academy of Literature, many other honors. Biography in *Polski słownik biograficzny.* Papers at Polish Museum of America, Chicago.

Hodur, Franciszek (1866–1953). Born in Żarki, Austrian Poland. Emigrated 1893. Ordained 1893, Scranton, Pa. Pastor, Nanticoke, Scranton (1895–97).

Founded PNCC, 1904. Consecrated as bishop of PNCC, Utrecht, 1907. Wrote extensively, fiction and nonfiction. Papers at Central Diocesan Library and Archives of PNCC, Scranton. Biography in *Polski słownik biograficzny.*

IWANOWSKI, FRANCISZEK (1889–1933?). Emigrated 1911?

JABŁOŃSKI, FRANCISZEK HIERONIM (1863–1908). Born in Inowrocław, Prussian Poland. Studied philosophy at Louvain before emigrating 1883, where he continued theological studies before involvement in PNA. Editor of various newspapers, including *Dziennik polski, Krytyka, Opiekun, Orzeł polski* (Milwaukee), *Dziennik narodowy, Kuryer chicagoski, Dziennik związkowy* and *Zgoda* (Chicago). Died in Chicago. Some information at <www.pna-znp.org/jablonski.htm>.

JAX, ANTONI (1850–1926). Occasionally, Jaks. Born in Gniezno, Prussian Poland to middle-class family. Emigrated ca. 1889. Involved in writing and performing for theater since youth; became one of principle writers for Polish stage in America.

JESIEŃ, WACŁAW S. (1886–after 1911). Born in Częstochowa Piotrowska. Served in Haller's Army. Lived in Pittsburgh.

KARAŚ, JÓZEF (ca. 1891–?). Born in Lubla, Austrian Poland. Served in Haller's Army. Wrote for *Nowiny polskie* (Milwaukee). Some information at Józef Piłsudski Institute.

KARASIEWICZ, JÓZEF (1881–1969). Editor, *Dziennik polski* (Detroit).

KARŁOWSKI, WIKTOR (1848–?). Participant in 1863 uprising. Fought in French Foreign Legion in Mexico and Algeria, 1870–71. Emigrated ca. 1871. Editor, *Gazeta polska narodowa/Gazeta polska w Chicago. Polski słownik biograficzny* reports he died in railroad accident, 1896, but contemporary accounts indicate this widely circulated story was mistaken.

KMIECIAK, MICHAŁ (?–after 1910). A director of PNA.

KRUSZKA, WACŁAW (1868–1937). Born in Sławomierz, Prussian Poland. Graduated from Gregorianum, Rome, and Jagiellonian University, Kraków, 1893. Emigrated 1893. Ordained, St. Francis Seminary, St. Francis, Wis., 1895. Served various parishes in Wisconsin before settling as pastor of St. Adalbert's (Milwaukee). Brother of Michał Kruszka, politician and publisher of *Kuryer polski* (Milwaukee). Lobbied extensively in U.S. and Rome for America's first Polish-American bishop, resulting in the investiture of Paweł Rhode in Chicago. Wrote prolifically on Polish and Polonian history and social and religious issues. Memoir, *Siedm siedmioleci* (Seven septenniums), is rich source of contemporary detail about Polonia. *History of the Poles in America* (1905) has been published in translation. Died in Milwaukee. Biography in *Polski słownik biograficzny.*

LAUDYN, STEFANIA (1872–1942). Also Laudyn-Chrzanowska, Laudynowa. Born Stefania Borowska in Rochaczów, Mohyłew, Russian Poland (now Belarus). Educated at Moscow University. First husband, Kazimierz Laudyn (d. 1908), was 1863 insurrectionist. Before emigrating, she wrote several plays and political works. Active throughout life in European Pan-Slavic women's organizations. Emigrated 1909. Married Adam Chrzanowski 1910. Editor, *Głos Polek* (official organ of Polish Women's Alliance, Chicago). Social activist in various Polish and Polonian causes, including Polish Society of Writers and Journalists in North America. On some issues, such as women's rights, was quite progressive. Only work translated into English is *A World Problem: Jews—Poland—Humanity* (banned in some libraries for anti-Semitism). Returned permanently to Poland in mid-1920s, but continued to contribute to New York's *Kuryer narodowy.* With Adam Chrzanowski owned Bristol Hotel, Zakopane, Poland, where she died. Biography in Schultz and Hast, *Women Building Chicago.*

ŁEMPICKI, STANISŁAW (1880–1935). Born in Zamki. Emigrated 1901. Wrote drama, poetry, nonfiction. Worked on *Gazeta polska* (Chicago), *Kuryer polski* (Milwaukee). Died in Milwaukee (not Stevens Point, as sometimes reported). Biography in *Polski słownik biograficzny.*

ŁUKASZKIEWICZ, CZESŁAW (1882–1946). Born in Kraków, Austrian Poland. Father was 1863 insurrectionist. Emigrated 1914, to organize for (Piłsudskiite)

KON. Imprisoned by U.S. government for six months in 1917 as German sympathizer. Author of string of anticlerical novels and political satires, many historical analyses and works of political theory. Regular contributor to *Ameryka-Echo* (Toledo, Ohio). Editor, *Chicagoski kuryer niedzielny* and *Kuryer narodowy* (Chicago), *Postęp* (Baltimore), *Kuryer nowoyorski* and *Wici* (New York). Received Polish Legionnaire's Cross, Independence Cross, and Polonia Restituta, other honors. Did diplomatic work and lectured in Poland, 1930–34. Died in Chicago. Biography in *Polski słownik biograficzny.*

MARCINKIEWICZ, ADAM (1867–1939). Born in Przecław, Austrian Poland. Received law degree in Kraków. Ordained in Detroit, 1896. Pastor in Buffalo and New York, 1896–1918. Pastor of St. Albertus, Detroit, 1918 until death. See <www.pgnys.org/polpriests/marcinkiewicz.html>.

MORAWSKI, WOJCIECH (1873–1954). Born in Sukowy, Prussian Poland. Studied law in Kraków, Berlin, Freiburg, Paris. Received Ph.D. in Vienna. In 1905 left Poland under taint of unknown scandal. Editor, *Kuryer narodowy* and *Wolna Polska* (New York). Lecturer in Polish, Columbia University, 1919. Conducted diplomatic work for Poland, early 1920s. Received Polonia Restituta and Legion of Honor awards. Assisted Nobel prize winner Władysław Reymont with English edition of his novel *The Peasants.* Died in New York. Biography in *Polski słownik biograficzny.*

MORSKA, CELINA (?–after 1927).

NAGIEL, HENRYK (1859–1899). Born in Warsaw, Russian Poland. Attended Warsaw University Law School. Before emigrating, wrote a couple of novels. Emigrated to Paris, 1888. Arrived in U.S. ca. 1889. Worked on many early newspapers, including *Kukuryku* and *Krytyka* (Buffalo), *Kuryer nowoyorski i brooklyński* (New York), *Dziennik chicagoski, Nowe życie, Reforma,* and *Telegraf* (Chicago). Member of New York Ognisko group. In addition to fiction, wrote overview of Polonian press (1895). Returned to Poland 1896, where he contributed to Lwów's *Słowo polskie.* Died in Lwów. Biography in *Polski słownik biograficzny.*

NASTAŁ, STANISŁAW (1899–1947). Born in Stara Wieś, Austrian Poland. Studied journalism in Poland; graduated from military academy. Emigrated 1907(?). Cavalry capt., Haller's Army, WWI. Director of Polish radio show in Milwaukee, where he died.

Nesterowicz, Melania (1876–1951). Born Melania Habdank-Białobrzeska in Warsaw, Russian Poland. Intended to study medicine in Switzerland, but in 1894 married Stefan Nesterowicz (*which see*). As a result of her husband's business failures, emigrated first to Brazil, then to U.S., ca. 1902. A progressive unaffiliated with any political camp, began work as journalist ca. 1907 with *Ameryka-Echo* (Toledo). Editor, *Dziennik dla wszystkich* (Buffalo). Wrote many works of fiction; wrote regularly on political and social issues, sometimes anonymously or under pseudonym Jan Kłos. Received Polish Legionnaire's Cross, Polonia Restituta, Silver Laurel of Literature, many other honors. Died in Wilkes-Barre, Pennsylvania.

Nesterowicz, Stefan (1851–1931). Born in Russian Poland. Before marriage to Melania Habdank-Białobrzeska (*see* Nesterowicz, Melania) in 1894, was world traveler. Business failures forced him to emigrate to Brazil, then to U.S., where he and his family arrived ca. 1902. Pharmacist by profession. Various business and scientific projects fell through; earned living as newspaper agent and journalist, initially with *Ameryka-Echo* (Toledo), for which he wrote satirical pieces and travelogues. Later established comedy magazine *Motyl* (New York). Returned to Poland 1922. Died in Lwów. Biography in *Polski słownik biograficzny.*

Neuman, Kazimierz (1843–1907). Occasionally Nauman. Born in Poznań, Prussian Poland. Injured in the insurrection of 1863. Emigrated 1889. Firmly in religionist camp; wrote many short, satiric pieces. Editor of several papers, including *Opiekun, Orzeł biały,* and *Słowo* (Milwaukee), *Przyjaciel młodzieży* and *Dziennik chicagoski* (Chicago). Died in Chicago. Biography in *Polski słownik biograficzny.*

Niedźwiedzki, H[enryk?] (?–after 1910?). Lived in Toledo, possibly also Cleveland.

Niemir, Jan (?–after 1880).

NOWINA, B. (?–after 1929).

ORŁOWSKI, JÓZEF (1862–1943). Born in Lwów, Austrian Poland. Received law degree in Poland. In 1905 debarred for misuse of funds; sentenced in Vienna to four years in prison. Sentence commuted 1907; Orłowski emigrated. Friend and colleague of Paderewski, whose National Department he supported. Wrote several works of fiction and nonfiction, all from anti-German perspective. Died in Chicago. Biography in *Polski słownik biograficzny.*

OSADA, STANISŁAW (1869–1934). Born in Pruchnik, Austrian Poland. Served in Austrian army; as result of participation in underground student movement, fled to Switzerland, where he was involved with the Rapperswill group of emigré political theorists. Emigrated to U.S., 1893. Social activist and publicist on many fronts; began work with socialists, ended with conservatives. Deeply involved in Falcon military-gymnastic movement. Helped found Polish Society of Writers and Journalists in North America. Worked for many papers, including *Dziennik milwaucki* (Milwaukee), *Reforma* and *Głos ludu* (Buffalo), *Kuryer ilustrowany* (New York), *Nowe życie, Sztandar, Dziennik polski, Gazeta handlowa,* and *Sokół* (Chicago). Correspondent for several European papers. In addition to two novels, wrote prolifically on Polish and Polonian cultural and political issues. Supported conservative National League. Died while visiting Poland. Biography in *Polski słownik biograficzny.*

OSTROWSKI, JANUSZ (1886–1960). Born in Poznań, Prussian Poland. Graduated from Jagiellonian University. Journalist for *Dziennik polski* and *Rekord codzienny* (Detroit). Instructor, Alliance College (Cambridge Springs, Pa.), 1912–14. Also a poet. Received Silver Laurel award from Polish Academy of Literature.

PARYSKI, ANTONI ALFRED (1865–1935). Born Antoni Panek in Bocheń, near Łowicz, Russian Poland, to illiterate parents. Worked as postal clerk in Łowicz before emigrating in 1883. Worked at various jobs, including typesetter and journalist for *Gazeta narodowa* (Detroit), *Gazeta polska* (Chicago), *Krytyka* (Milwaukee), *Wiarus* (Winona, Minn.). Wrote short fiction and nonfiction under many pseudonyms, including Parysso, M. Brass, Opinia, Łowiczanin, Brat M., Parisot. Independent thinker and astute businessman, often reviled by religionists. Established Polonia's most successful newspaper and publishing company, *Ameryka-Echo* (Toledo, Ohio). Died in Toledo. Company records held by Immigration History Research Center. Biography in *Polski słownik biograficzny.*

Piotrowska, Helena (1873–1928). Born Helena Sawicka near Kowno, Russian Poland. Attended one year at a women's college in Kraków before emigrating with family, 1889. Married Stanisław Piotrowski in Chicago, 1894. Member of Socialist Labor Party and frequent contributor of patriotic articles and occasional fiction to Polonian and American press. Editor, *Siła* (Buffalo). After teaching in Buffalo public schools and Eastern Kentucky State Normal School, received a master's degree from Columbia University. Bolek's *Who's Who in Polish America* reports she died in 1901, but Piotrowska was active in World War I and in Polish White Cross. Died in Buffalo.

Pobóg, Iza (?–after mid-1920s). For a short time, editor of beleaguered women's edition of PNA weekly *Zgoda* (Chicago). Correspondent for *Kuryer ilustrowany* (Milwaukee). Contributed fiction, poetry, articles on social and political issues to various Polonian newspapers; published one novel, *Cudowny kamień* (The miraculous stone), set in Poland. Also published a novel and a collection of poetry in Poland. Lived for at least a time in New York. Returned to Lublin in 1922, but reportedly came back to U.S. a few years later.

Popławski, Piotr (?–after 1937).

Przyprawa, Jan J. (1884–1944). Born in Przeciszów, Austrian Poland. Emigrated 1910. Recruiter for Haller's Army, in which he served. Editor, *Zgoda* and *Dziennik związkowy* (Chicago), *Polonia* and *Monitor* (Cleveland).

Pszczoła, Janusz (?–after 1918).

Rekwart, Halina Urszula Drelenkiewicz (1894–1958). Died in Los Angeles.

Romanowska, Felicja (1875–1944). Occasionally Romanowska-Kończalska. Emigrated 1907 from Lwów. Singer with La Scala Opera, Milan; also performed around U.S. and taught music in Los Angeles, where she settled. Her name was used as a pseudonym by a group of Polish writers headed by Józef Mackiewicz.

Romanowska, Stanisława (ca. 1867–after 1909). Music teacher in Chicago. Novel on political maneuvering in Chicago won first prize in 1903 PNA-sponsored literary contest.

Sichrawa, Mieczysław (?–after 1945). Volunteer in Haller's Army. Wounded in action, WWI and II; interned by Nazis. Editor, *Weteran* (Chicago).

Skarga, Paweł J. (?–after 1926). Probably lived in Wisconsin.

Ślisz, Stanisław (1856–1908). Born in Kołaczyce, Galicia. Received law degree from Jagiellonian University. Emigrated 1885. His brother Józef established first Polish bookstore in Buffalo, 1896. Writer firmly in Roman Catholic camp, translator, editor of several newspapers, including *Krytyka* (Milwaukee), *Czas, Wiara i ojczyzna,* and *Kropidło* (Chicago), *Ojczyzna, Dziennik dla wszystkich, Polak w Ameryce,* and *Polak amerykański* (Buffalo). Confined to wheelchair. Died in Buffalo.

Słupski, Zygmunt (ca. 1860–ca. 1925). Editor, *Bocian* and *Telegram* (Buffalo), *Patrjota* (Philadelphia). Owned steamship ticket agency in Philadelphia. Returned to Poland ca. 1891; continued as journalist in Poznań.

Stachowicz, Stanisław Z. (ca. 1890–1964). Born in Jacmierz, Austrian Poland. Recruiter for Haller's Army in Chicago. Editor, *Polonia* and *Weteran* (Cleveland).

Staniewski, Alfons J. (1879–1941). Born in Święciechów, Russian Poland. Beginning in 1894, was active in Polish Socialist Party in Warsaw; fled country under the name Janicki, 1898. After stays in Switzerland, Holland, and Scotland, he settled in England, where he worked for labor movement and became British citizen. Arrived in Canada in 1910; eventually settled in Toronto. Wrote under various pseudonyms, including Ajotes. Editor, *Związkowiec* (Toronto).

Staś, Helena (1868–1930). Also Helena Męczyńska Staś. Born in Piotrkowo, Russian Poland. Emigrated ca. 1887. Contributed fiction, poetry, articles on patriotic and social issues to various Polonian newspapers, including *Ameryka-Echo* and *Dziennik polski* (Detroit). An independent voice, unaffiliated with any political or religious camp, though active in Polish Women's Alliance and Falcons. Had no higher education, but called for distinctive Polish-American literature that would address needs and experience of working-class immigrants. In addition to sporadic writing, taught school and ran candy store for a time in Milwaukee. Established *Ogniwo*, women's and children's monthly magazine (Chicago). Established theosophical discussion groups and *Nowa era*, theosophical monthly (Milwaukee). Editor, women's and children's section, *Kuryer polski* (Milwaukee). Returned to Poland as correspondent in 1927, permanently in 1928. Joined Baptist Church. Died in Kalisz, Poland.

Stefański, Leonard (ca. 1896–?). Emigrated 1913. Served in Haller's Army.

Szczutowski, Henryk (?–after 1909). No information on this author, despite frequent contribution of humorous sketches to leftist newspapers.

Szpaczek, Jan (?–after 1917).

Szwajkart, Stanisław (1857–1918). Born in Tarnopol, Austrian Poland. Studied at University of Lwów. Emigrated 1881. Held many jobs, including music teacher, musician, clerk. Journalist, *Wiara i ojczyzna*, *Dziennik chicagoski.* Also wrote for German-language immigrant papers. Died in Chicago.

Tarczyński, Rudolf (1875 or 1876–?). Born in Piotrków area, Russian Poland. Began work as journalist in 1901 in Rome, where he graduated from the Gregorian University. Returned to Poland as professor of Polish language and literature. Ca. 1909, left Poland for political reasons; newspaper correspondent and Falcon activist in France before coming to U.S., 1926. First lt. in Haller's Polish Army. Editor, *Ognisko domowe* (Detroit). Professor of Polish Literature at Polish Seminary, Orchard Lake, Mich., and University of Detroit. Contributor to newspapers in Poland. Returned to Poland in 1937 and to France during WWII.

TRUSZKIEWICZ, FRANCISZEK (ca. 1895–?). Emigrated 1915; settled in Cleveland. First lt. in Haller's Army.

WACHTL, KAROL H. (1879–1946). Originally Wachtel. Born in Jarosław, Austrian Poland. Studied law and medicine at University of Lwów. Emigrated 1903. Received Ph.D., De Paul University, 1920. Active in PRCU and in Polonian theater as actor and playwright. Also poet, educator, historian. Edited several newspapers, including *Promień* (La Salle, Ill.), *Dziennik chicagoski* and *Naród polski* (Chicago), *Kuryer narodowy* (New York). Supporter of Dmowski. Returned to Poland 1923; disillusioned with conditions there, came back to U.S. 1926. Buried in Queens, N.Y.

WALDO, ARTUR L. (1896–1985). Born in Radom, Russian Poland. Emigrated 1913. Contributed to various newspapers, including *Zorza* (Pittston, Pa.), *Dziennik zjednoczenia* (Chicago), *Trybuna codzienna* and *Weteran* (Detroit). Fought in Haller's Army. Returned to U.S. 1921. As advisor in Warsaw on American Polonia, was working in Poland at outbreak of WWII; fought with Polish Army until 1940, when he returned to U.S. During war, worked for U.S. as coordinator of information for Polish affairs. Very active in Polonian theater as playwright and actor. Published many works on Polonian history in Polish and English. Died in Arizona. Papers at Central Archives of Polonia, Orchard Lake, and Polish Museum of America.

WALUS, FRANK J. (ca. 1897–?). Emigrated 1913 from Drohobycko, Austrian Poland. Settled in Lowell, Mass. Volunteer, Haller's Army, WWI. Published memoirs and sketches about war in *Weteran* (Cleveland) and *Kurjer codzienny* (Boston). Employed as printer.

WATRA, JÓZEF (1887–1963). Also Przewłocki-Watra. Born in Tuchów, Austrian Poland; emigrated ca. 1905. Wandered extensively (American southwest, Mexico, Honduras, Alaska, Canada); lived among several Native American tribes and learned their languages. Worked as sailor, teacher, miner, blacksmith, cowboy, bricklayer, factory worker; fictionalized experiences in several novels published in Poland. Finally settled in Milwaukee, where he became political activist and editor of *Nowiny polskie* .

Wedda, Józef (?–1947). Born in Wisconsin. Journalist and businessman in Detroit. Member of Detroit's Civil Service Commission, 1932–45. With brother, Jan, operated Wedda Brothers Publishing Co. Editor, *Praca* and *Rekord niedzielny.* Author of English-language novel about Polonia, *Jasna Polana.*

Woicki, Józef (?–after 1907). Lived in Waterbury, Conn.

Wójcik, J. (?–after 1910).

Wrotnowski, Bronisław (ca. 1878–1946). Began newspaper work in Poland 1898. Journalist, *Gwiazda polarna* (Stevens Point, Wis.); editor, *Jaskółka.* Wrote under pseudonym Marian Bronisławski. Died in Detroit.

Yolles, Piotr P. (1893–1958). Born in Zabłotów, Austrian Poland. Jewish. Graduated from University of Cerniowce (now in Romania). During WWI, served in Austrian Army; wounded. Emigrated 1920. Master's degree in social work, Columbia University, 1925. Studied journalism, New York University. Editor, *Dziennik nowoyorski* and *Nowy świat* (New York). Founded and directed Brooklyn's Polish Day Nursery. Published *Ciernie* (Thorns), novel set in Poland. Received many honors, including Cross of the Legion of Honor. Sometimes wrote under pseudonym Włóczęga (The wanderer).

Zaborska, Tekla (?–after 1895).

Zagroda, Jerzy (?–after 1895).

Zahajkiewicz, Szczęsny (1861–1917). Born in Stanisławów, Austrian Poland. Teacher in Lwów, where he published poems and edited a paper. Emigrated 1889 at request of Resurrectionist Fathers, to teach in Chicago Polonia. Active in Falcons. Editor, *Anioł* and *Naród polski* (Chicago). Wrote many plays, poems, humorous pieces. Died in Chicago.

Zasławska, Alina (Anna) (1882–1911). Emigrated 1905 from Odessa. Primarily a poet. Died in Hartford, Conn.

Zawadzki, Marian (1885–?). Born in Kraków. Volunteer in Haller's Army. Lived in Detroit.

Żuławski, Czesław (1880–after 1937). Emigrated 1905 from Sambor, Austrian Poland. First lt. in Haller's Army. Contributed stories about World War I experiences to *Weteran* and *Dziennik związkowy.* Edited *Hallerczyk.* Lived in Baltimore.

Notes

Introduction

1. Chametzky, "Styron's *Sophie's Choice,* Jews and Other Marginals, and the Mainstream," 435–36.

2. The theater has probably received the most attention to date of any aspect of Polonian cultural life. In English, for instance, see Waldo's chapter in *Ethnic Theatre in the United States,* ed. Maxine Seller; Cygan, "'New Art' for Polonia"; and Cuba, "Polish Amateur Theatricals." In Polish, there is Orzechowski's full-length study, *Teatr polonijny w Stanach Zjednoczonych.* Many histories of Polish America also include some discussion of the local theater movement, and substantial collections of plays are held by several of the major repositories for Polonica, including the Alumni Memorial Library at St. Mary's College and the Connecticut Polish Archive at Central Connecticut State University. The Burton Historical Collection at the Detroit Public Library also contains the papers of immigrant actors and playwrights.

3. In 1893 the Manistee library numbered thirty-seven paid members and contained over a thousand volumes. The previous year, 750 books had been borrowed, at the rate of two to five cents per item, or for free with the payment of a five-dollar membership fee (*Kuryer polski,* 20 February 1895). See also Dunikowski, *Wśród Polonii w Ameryce,* 46. Cleveland established its reading room in 1891, with fifty members and one thousand volumes (*Kuryer polski,* 19 October 1891). Polonian reading habits will be discussed in more detail in chapter 2.

4. Waldo, *Zarys historii literatury polskiej,* 6.

5. While the term is sometimes used to designate an organized community of ethnic institutions, *Polonia* here refers simply to the Polish diaspora—that is, to Poles and their descendants living outside Poland.

6. Blejwas, "Voiceless Immigrants," 5; Wachtl, *Polonia w Ameryce,* 233.

7. Several of my own translations of short immigrant texts have been published and are listed along with the originals in the bibliography of primary sources.

8. Although Sienkiewicz was in the United States from 1876 to 1878 and published a number of works based on his observations here, he was always a visitor, never an immigrant, even of the sojourning variety. First published in 1897, *Za chlebem,* a tearjerker about an old immigrant and his daughter, was often serialized in the Polish-American press. Sienkiewicz's works were probably the most popular, and certainly the most prevalent, of all the literature printed in Polonia.

9. Maciuszko, "Polish-American Literature," 163–82. One area of Maciuszko's expertise is Polish literature in English translation.

10. Zaborowska's *How We Found America* concentrates on writers already fairly well represented in literary and historical scholarship: Mary Antin, Elizabeth Stern, Anzia Yezierska, Maria Kuncewicz, Eva Hoffman, and even Vladimir Nabokov. The unfortunate impression left by this selection is that no immigrant women were writing in Polish before the arrival of the World War II intellectuals.

11. Jan Niemir's *Jak się zemścił borowy Zielonka nad Wojtkiem Bruchyłą* (1881, 1890). Apparently only the second printing of this work is still extant.

12. Peterson, *Popular Narratives and Ethnic Identity,* 96.

13. Gladsky, *Princes, Peasants, and Other Polish Selves,* 1–2.

14. Some immigrant authors of works about American Polonia set other novels and stories in Poland or in other countries or time periods. Helena Staś, for example, used biblical settings for some of her later stories. See *Kobieta wobec Chrystusa* and "Marya i Marta." Iza Pobóg's full-length novel *Cudowny kamień* is set in Poland, as is Józef Orłowski's *O chłopską skórę.*

15. See, for instance, Barszczewski, *Polacy w Ameryce, Obrazki amerykańskie,* and *Czerwony mesyasz;* and Przewłocki-Watra, *John Big Foot* and *Prawdziwy mężczyzna.* These authors are among those discussed in Klimaszewski, "Sami o sobie?" and *Pod znakiem potu, łez, i dolara.* Another work by an immigrant author but published only in Poland is Iza Pobóg's *Cawboy.*

16. Among those who went back to Poland but later returned to the United States are Czesław Łukaszkiewicz, Iza Pobóg, and Karol Wachtl. Stanisław Dangel, Stefania Laudyn, Henryk Nagiel, Stefan Nesterowicz, Zygmunt Słupski, Helena Staś, and Rudolf Tarczyński returned to and remained in Poland. Works published in both the United States and Poland are Wacław Kruszka's *Siedm siedmioleci,* Stanisława Romanowska's *Nad Michiganem,* Zygmunt Słupski's *Politykier,* and Helena Staś's *Na ludzkim targu.*

17. Symonolewicz-Symmons, *Ze studiów nad Polonią amerykańską,* 99–100.

18. Dearborn, *Pocahantas's Daughters,* 71.

19. Pochmann, "Mingling of Tongues," 676.

20. Newman, "Ethnic Literary Scholar," 3.

21. Gardaphé, *Italian Signs, American Streets,* 9.

22. Fine, *The City, the Immigrant, and American Fiction.*

23. The essentially oral, declamatory character of the immigrant letter was brought home to me in a video tape made by a friend on a recent trip to Poland. When a distant relation, a sixty-five-year-old peasant woman, was asked to say a few words on tape to an American relative who had not been able to make the trip, she drew herself up and recited in highly ritualized style a speech several minutes long that contained all the elements of the turn-of-the-century immigrant letter described

by Thomas and Znaniecki, beginning with "Niech będzie pochwalony Jezus Chrystus" (Let Jesus Christ be praised).

24. Gieysztor et al., *History of Poland,* 486.

25. Spiller, "The Cycle and the Roots," 3–18.

26. Staś, *Na ludzkim targu* (1910), 179.

27. Brożek, *Polish Americans,* 163–64. Where this claim comes from is a mystery, since it's doubtful that Brożek himself had read any of these works.

28. *Dziennik związkowy,* 15 January 1918; Federal Works Agency, *Chicago Foreign Language Press Survey Records.*

29. Osada's two novels, *W dniach nędzy i zbrodni* and *Z pennsylwańskiego piekła,* will be discussed in detail in later chapters. Wachtl's literary efforts include a collection of short stories, *Podarek nowy,* and anthologies of poems *Ciche pieśni* and *Pieśni orężne* as well as several plays, written between about 1910 and the mid-1920s. Waldo's novel *Czar miasta Kościuszko* will also be discussed later, as will Kruszka's sketch "Na progu dwudziestego wieku."

30. Kruszka, *A History of the Poles in America,* 1:301.

31. Wachtl, *Polonia,* 234. Wachtl may even have been gentle with Chełchowski, since much of his work consists of vulgar (if entertaining) attacks on the clergy.

32. Waldo, *Zarys historii,* 47–48.

Chapter 1

1. Davies, *Heart of Europe,* 175. Having noted these shifting political borders and national designations, I will continue to use the term *Polish* to designate all Polish-speaking immigrants, and *Poland* to refer to the land from which they came, regardless of the temporal status of Poland's statehood.

2. Among conservatives, however, *popierać swoje, swój na swoje,* and similar slogans came to carry an embedded anti-Semitism. They were especially employed in economic wars against Jewish business owners. However, in patronizing Jewish businesses, many Christian Poles felt they were continuing a familiar and comfortable relationship along patterns well established in the old country.

3. The principal architect of the messianic ideology is Poland's "national poet," Adam Mickiewicz (1798–1855). However, in Polish culture the image continues to be perhaps as pervasive, and as controversial, as America's own conception of itself as a promised land. It can be modified, refuted, and railed against, but not ignored.

4. Davies, *Heart of Europe,* 268. For a useful contemporary account of educational strategies, see Bobrowski, *Praca oświatowa, jej zadania, metody, organizacja.*

5. Jacobson, *Special Sorrows,* 40.

6. For a discussion of shifting definitions of this literature see Pigoń, "Główne problemy literatury ludowej." See also Stauter-Halsted, *The Nation in the Village,* 113–14.

7. Gieysztor et al., *History of Poland,* 486.

8. Quoted in Greene, *American Immigrant Leaders,* 117, 119. The right to pray in Polish reflects efforts in Prussian and Russian Poland to restrict Polish-language worship; these efforts were replayed in the United States, where conflicts with Roman Catholic leadership arose over the hiring of Polish-speaking priests in neighborhood parishes.

9. See Haiman, *Polacy w walce o niepodległości Ameryki.*

10. The first book was Marcin Rosienkiewicz's *Dialogues to Facilitate the Acquisition of the English Language by the Polish Emigrants/Rozmowy, do ulatwienia nauki jenzyka angielskiego, dla emigrantow polskich* (Philadelphia, 1834). The lack of Polish orthographic characters necessitated taking some liberties with standard Polish spelling. The first periodical was the monthly *Poland : Historical, Literary, Monumental, and Picturesque,* established in 1842 and probably lasting only about four issues. Wepsiec, *Polish American Serial Publications,* 109 .

11. Panna Maria means "Virgin Mary."

12. Both Parisville, Michigan, and Polonia, Wisconsin, have made claims for dates earlier than these, which would change the order of settlement.

13. In Poland, the emigration to Western Europe that followed the November Uprising is called the Great Emigration (*wielka emigracja*). This should not be confused with America's Great Migration, the Great Wave of immigration, mostly from Eastern and Southern Europe, to the United States between approximately 1870 and 1924.

14. See Michalski, "The Prussian Crucible."

15. Dziembowska, *Pamiętniki emigrantów,* "Pamiętnik nr. 32," 2:155. Conflicts between Poles from different partition areas was especially a factor in the numerous "church wars" that arose in late-nineteenth-century Polonia. See, for instance, Orton, *Polish Detroit and the Kolasinski Affair.*

16. See Erdmans, *Opposite Poles,* 19–23; Pula, *Polish Americans,* 14–20; Bukowczyk, *And My Children Did Not Know Me,* 6–15.

17. Polonian writers continued to employ this image long after Poland had achieved independence. See, for instance, Edward Alan Symanski's collection of poetry *From the Fourth Province,* published in 1952.

18. See Thomas and Znaniecki's classic *The Polish Peasant in Europe and America.* The tendency to identify oneself and one's neighborhood by parish affiliation persists, and is common among other Catholic ethnic groups as well. See also Dolan, *The American Catholic Experience,* 204–8.

19. Editorial, *Kuryer polski* (Milwaukee), 21 May 1892.

20. Davies, *God's Playground,* 2:62. The Polish *szlachta* is a rather exceptional case among European nobility, making up between 8 and 12 percent of the Polish population. See Davies, *Heart of Europe,* 297–99, 331–36. A competing conceptualization of Polishness argued that it resided in the *lud,* the "people." See Porter, *When*

Nationalism Began to Hate, 30. Russian Pan-Slavists, hardly disinterested theorists, claimed that the only true Poles were the peasants, because Polish high culture had been contaminated by Western European and Latin (that is, Roman Catholic) influences. Milosz, *The History of Polish Literature,* 282.

21. In fact, these tensions continue to exist, accounting in part for misunderstanding between the descendants of the *stara emigracja* and the postwar and post-Solidarity immigrant cohorts. See Blejwas, "Old and New Polonias"; Erdmans, *Opposite Poles.* Issues of social class inform internal arguments over the content, legitimacy, and very existence of Polish-American culture, even among third-, fourth-, and fifth-generation Polish-Americans. As recently as 1997 the letters to the editor column of *Gwiazda polarna*'s English-language monthly supplement, *GP Light,* was the site of a contemporary restatement of arguments that could have been written in 1897. One defender of the nobility accused Polonia's leaders of airing "Jewish, peasant, clerical and otherwise superficial points of view" while "deprecating Poland's true noble traditions." *GP Light,* November 1996. Another countered with accusations of the nobility's traitorous collusion: "I, for one, can sleep easy at night knowing that it was not my [peasant] ancestors who sold Poland's glory to her enemies for thirty pieces of silver" (*GP Light,* September 1997). And on a bathroom wall of my 1920s-era house in an old Polish neighborhood I found the penciled notation, *Szlachta = warchoły, szarlatany* (The nobility are troublemakers and charlatans).

22. Franciszek Bujak, *Żmiąca: Wieś powiatu Limanowskiego: Stosunki gospodarcze i społeczne* (Kraków: Gebethner i Spółka, 1903), 100; quoted in Stauter-Halsted, *Nation in the Village,* 59. Except for the war years themselves, there had always been a steady return migration. According to American sources, between 1908 and 1914 an average of thirty thousand immigrants returned to Polish lands annually. This includes my own great-grandmother and (American-born) grandmother, who were among the 35,028 who returned in 1914. See tables in Brożek, *Polish Americans,* 234. Between 1908 and 1923 this made for a return rate of 40 percent. Wyman, *Round Trip to America,* 11.

23. Jabłoński, "Dzieci wisielca." See also Stauter-Halsted, *Nation in the Village,* 1–2.

24. Segel, *Stranger in Our Midst,* 4.

25. Wojciech Morawski, Henryk Nagiel, Józef Orłowski, and Stanisław Ślisz were trained as lawyers. Morawski, Orłowski, and Julian Czupka held Ph.D.s from European universities, and Karol Wachtl received his doctorate in the United States. Czesław Łukaszkiewicz, Stefania Laudyn, Stefan Nesterowicz, Janusz Ostrowski, Stanisław Szwajkart, and Antoni Paryski all had some postsecondary education. Adam Marcinkiewicz completed his law degree in Poland and became a priest in the United States. Piotr Yolles studied law in Europe and did his graduate work at Columbia in social work. Helena Piotrowska earned a master's degree at Columbia.

26. Quoted in Kruszka, *History of the Poles,* 1:301. The writer was referring to

the authors of religious, historical, and political nonfiction, as no fiction writer had emerged by this date.

27. For an account of the identity-building efforts of another of these groups, see Magocsi, *Rusyn-American Ethnic Literature*.

28. Institutional histories, varying in objectivity, exist for the major organizations. For the PNA, there is Osada and Olszewski's six-volume *Historia Związku Narodowego Polskiego,* published between 1957 and 1967. The first volume had been written by Stanisław Osada many decades before. It is supplemented by Donald Pienkos's *PNA: A Centennial History of the Polish National Alliance of the United States of North America.* Pienkos is also the author of the Falcons' centennial history, *One Hundred Years Young.* An earlier four-volume history of the Falcons by Artur Waldo is especially rich in photographs, incidental details, and personal anecdotes. The PRCU was covered by Karol Wachtl in 1913, but Mieczysław Haiman's 1948 update, *Zjednoczenie Polskie Rzymsko-Katolickie w Ameryce,* is notable for its extensive use of fully documented newspaper and other primary sources. A centennial history by John Radzilowski is in progress. Finally, the Polish Women's Alliance is the subject of a three-volume history begun by Jadwiga Karłowiczowa in the 1930s and updated to 1981, *Historia Związku Polek w Ameryce.* Donald Pienkos is completing a centennial history. For the history of Polonian socialism, see Cygan, "Political and Cultural Leadership in an Immigrant Community."

29. See, once again, Orton's *Polish Detroit.* The Polish National Catholic Church grew out of several decades of immigrant dissatisfaction with the American Roman Catholic hierarchy, particularly over local control of parishes and their finances. Several independent Catholic churches were finally united under Rev. Franciszek Hodur of Scranton, Pennsylvania, in 1904. By the mid-1990s, Roman Catholicism and National Catholicism had reconciled, though they remain separate institutions with a number of important doctrinal differences (perhaps most notably, the fact that National priests are allowed to marry). Studies of the PNCC include Kubiak, *The Polish National Catholic Church in the United States of America from 1897 to 1980;* Andrews, *The Polish National Catholic Church in America and Poland;* Fox, *The Polish National Catholic Church;* and Wlodarski, *The Origin and Growth of the Polish National Catholic Church.*

30. Quoted in Dunikowski, *Wśród Polonii,* 139.

Chapter 2

1. Waldo, *Rok książki polskiej w Ameryce,* 8. Another firm, the New York–based Polish Book Importing Company, was a major supplier of Polish-language books printed in Europe.

2. Sollors, "Immigrants and Other Americans," 570. See also Di Pietro and Ifkovic, *Ethnic Perspectives in American Literature,* particularly the sections on Hungarian, Portuguese, Croatian, Slovenian, and Serbian immigrant literatures.

3. For Polish-American journalism see Kowalik, *The Polish Press in America* and Wepsiec, *Polish American Serial Publications.* For a contemporary account, we have Kruszka's *History of the Poles in America to 1908.* Kruszka's annotation of almost every Polonian serial up to 1905, no matter how short-lived, imparts a sense of just how active (if not lucrative) the early press was.

4. The Polish Army in France, popularly called Haller's Army, included over twenty thousand Polish-American immigrant volunteers, many of whom remained in Europe after the Armistice and fought in the Polish-Russian War of 1920–21. Most eventually returned to the United States. See Hapak, "Recruiting a Polish Army in the United States."

5. Although these two papers were published by the Polish People's Publishing Co., books were issued with the imprint of the newspapers, rather than that of the parent company. In the case of *Bicz Boży,* I am aware only of works that specify that they were self-published ("Nakł. Autora"), or which give no publisher, but name *Bicz Boży* as printer. This is the case for several other "publishers" as well. Since the difference between publisher and printer is not always definable, and since the choice of printer carries ideological significance, I have noted the printer for those items that carry such a reference. These are identifiable in the citations and bibliography by the notation "Druk" (printed by).

6. Known mainly as a music publisher and record producer, Sajewski also published many Polish-American plays. For the company's history, see Spottswood, "The Sajewski Story."

7. Establishing numbers is a problem of definition. Some affiliated organizations (for instance, the Polish National Alliance and its newspapers, *Dziennik związkowy* and *Zgoda,* as well as PNA branches in different cities) produced books under separate imprint. Other organizations whose essential purpose was social, political, or religious occasionally published books related to their activities, history, or ideology. Some quite active book producers were actually only printeries. Incomplete records complicate the problem.

8. *Dziennik chicagoski,* 27 March 1893, 3 June 1893, 15 March 1894; Federal Works Agency, *Survey Records.* The prizes were apparently awarded despite the uproar, since records indicate that Słupski's novel *Politykier* was published in Chicago in 1894, as the contest's first-prize winner. A second novel, *Z życia Polaków w Ameryce* appeared under pseudonym in 1897 as the second-place winner. Peterson also reports disappointing results for German-American literary contests. Peterson, *Popular Narratives and Ethnic Identity,* 95.

9. Waldo, *Sokolstwo,* 1:399.

10. A strange footnote to this mystery relates to Felicja Romanowska, a professional singer and music teacher who also occasionally published fiction, including a story in the same 1910 PNA almanac. In 1933 a crime novel parody written under the pseudonym Felicja Romanowska, *Wileńska: Powieść kryminalna,* was serialized in a Polish newspaper. The actual authors were Józef Mackiewicz, Jerzy Wyszomirski, Stanisław Mackiewicz, and Walerian Charkiewicz. Editor Wacław Lewandowski devotes an entire introductory chapter in a 1995 reprint of the novel to the question of authorship and the source of this pseudonym. The authors themselves refused to disclose the secret but insisted that there never was a Felicja Romanowska. There is no mention of immigrant author Felicja Romanowska, though she was alive and active as a singer at the time the novel was written, nor of Stanisława Romanowska, whose identity as an author actually could be in question. And though both Romanowskas were professional musicians, there seems to be no relationship between them.

11. The Dyniewicz and Paryski firms went through several name changes, and discrepancies occur in the scholarship. Paryski's company was known at different times as Ameryka, as Paryski, and as Ameryka-Echo. For the sake of clarity, I will refer to it in the text and in bibliographical notations as Paryski, unless the imprint on an extant work designates otherwise. However, much of Paryski's output did not list a publisher at all. The situation is slightly different for Dyniewicz's firm, which merged with the Smulski company to become the Polish American Publishing Company. Samsel puts the merger at 1911 ("Polish Catholic Book Publishing in the United States," 49). Kłossowski says it probably did not occur before 1920 and credits Józef Chrzanowski of the Polish National Publishing Company with forming the Polish American Publishing Company after Smulski's death in 1928 ("Śmiałym los sprzyja," 202). In any case, the Polish American Publishing Company's connection to Dyniewicz should not be overlooked. Brożek's claim of a connection to the Resurrectionist's Polish Publishing Company is mistaken (*Polish Americans,* 161–62).

12. Kłossowski, "Śmiałym los sprzyja," 204.

13. Ibid., 207.

14. The Dyniewicz firm also published the first book Paryski authored, *Nieposłuszna* (The disobedient girl), released under the pseudonym Antoni Parysso in 1886.

15. Paryski was not the only publisher singled out. Michał Kruszka fought the clerical injunction against his Milwaukee paper, *Kuryer polski,* in court. He lost. For a 1903 account by Jesuit Karol Janowski on accusations of the anticlericalism of the Polonian press, see Grzebień, *Burzliwe lata Polonii amerykańskiej,* 235–41.

16. Another version has him fleeing service in the czar's army. See "Paryski, Antoni," *Polski słownik biograficzny.* Wojciech Chojnacki suggests that the real reason was some sort of romantic entanglement ("Antoni A. Paryski," 2).

17. Łukaszkiewicz, *Nauczyciel wychodźtwa,* 17–18.

18. Ibid.

19. Dziembowska, *Pamiętniki emigrantów,* "Pamiętnik nr. 4," 1:205.

20. [Stefan Nesterowicz], "Listy Hyacynta Poczciwiny," 101. Nesterowicz also proved himself a keen social observer in his travelogue *Notatki z podróży po Ameryce Północnej,* which contains detailed accounts of even the smallest Polonian colonies in the American South. It was translated by Marian Moore Coleman and published as *Travel Notes* (1970).

21. Staniewski, *Sen na jawie,* 7.

22. This echoes Paryski's charge against Powderly, of course. Similar claims were made by conservative Stanisław Osada in his 1909 novel *Z pennsylwańskiego piekła.*

23. Staniewski, *Sen na jawie,* 25.

24. Dziembowska, *Pamiętniki emigrantów,* "Pamiętnik nr. 20," 1:489. See also "Pamiętnik nr. 2," 1:165–185; 2:479.

25. Ibid., "Pamiętnik nr. 5," 1:218–19.

26. In cases in which I am aware of a serialization in addition to a separately printed edition, I have so noted in the bibliography. While copies of all these works are difficult to locate, because of the availability of microfilmed Polish-American newspapers, limited as it is, a serialized version is in all cases the most accessible. Finally, there were items I was not able to locate at all, in any format. When these appear to be within the scope of this study, they are included in the bibliography and noted as "not extant."

27. Wojciech Chojnacki, "Czytelnictwo, piśmiennictwo i działalność wydawnicza polskiej grupy etnicznej w USA," 116.

28. Studnicki, "Nadzwyczajne polskie przedsiębiorstwo w Ameryce."

29. Chełminski, "From *Gwiazda* to the *Ameryka-Echo,*" 4. Wojciech Chojnacki puts the numbers at fifteen hundred and seven million, respectively ("Czytelnictwo," 122), while Wachtl claims two thousand and five million (*Polonia w Ameryce,* 227). And according to Łukaszkiewicz, the company printed two million books in 1913 alone (*Nauczyciel wychodźtwa,* 34).

30. Regina Koscielski, in her often reprinted "Illiterate Peasants I Have Known," recalls that "'Ameryka-Echo,' known as an anti-clerical weekly, offered religious books to new subscribers and succeeded in putting large volumes of bonus 'Lives of Saints' in numerous homes! Bibles were owned by Polish Protestants."

31. Another account recalls, on another occasion, finding Czupka sleeping on a billiard table in a neighborhood bar. Bautro, "Wspomnienia z lat 1891 do 1926." See also Waldo, *Sokolstwo,* 1:142–43.

32. Czupka, *Obrazki z Ameryki* [70, 72]. (The last four pages of this sketch, after page 68, are unnumbered, probably the result of a printing error. Pagination resumes on page 70, but there are five intervening pages. The numbers in brackets refer to unnumbered pages, as they should logically be numbered.) Czupka is writing about New York's *Ognisko,* to which he and Henryk Nagiel contributed. See also Nagiel, *Dziennikarstwo polskie w Ameryce;* Cygan, "Political and Cultural Leadership."

33. The Paryski Company papers are held by the Immigration History Research Center at the University of Minnesota. The majority of the surviving material, however, dates from after 1939. Scattered records of Milwaukee's *Kuryer polski* are in the Urban History Archives at the University of Wisconsin, Milwaukee.

34. Osada, *Prasa i publicystyka polska w Ameryce,* 10; quoted in Olszyk, *The Polish Press in America,* 37. Throughout most of the 1930s, Paryski paid author Czesław Łukaszkiewicz a moderate monthly stipend, with occasional lump sum payments. But it is unclear whether these were payments for the Łukaszkiewicz novels Paryski published from 1923 to 1935, or for the author's other occasional writings and services.

35. These appear with the notation "Nakł. autora" (published at the author's expense).

36. Staś, "Dla dobra literatury poslko-amerykańskiej [*sic*]," *Dziennik polski,* 21 August 1907.

37. Wojciech Chojnacki, "Czytelnictwo," 119.

38. Studnicki, "Nadzwyczajne polskie przedsiębiorstwo"; Tadeusz Korzon's *Historya nowożytna* (Modern history), *Historya starożytna* (Ancient history), and *Historya wieków średnich* (History of the Middle Ages); and Kazimierz Gorzycki's *Historya polski* (History of Poland) were all listed in Paryski's catalogue by 1913.

39. Bukowski, *Działalność literacka i społeczna Hieronima Derdowskiego w Ameryce,* 35–36.

40. Hering, "Dzieje 'Gwiazdy Polarnej,'" 23.

41. [Rosiński], *Antoni A. Paryski,* 46.

42. Studnicki, "Nadzwyczajne polskie przedsiębiorstwo."

43. *Ameryka-Echo,* 26 November 1910.

44. Wójcik, "Przygody agenta."

45. Krzyżanowski, *A History of Polish Literature,* 444.

46. Staś, "Wspomnienia."

47. Although she appears to have been in Toledo at approximately the time this article was printed, Staś was probably not an *Ameryka-Echo* agent. Only two identifiably female names appeared in Paryski's published list of agents: S. Buczyńska of Toledo, in 1910, and Amelia Kolińska, who collected in Philadelphia, Camden, and Wilmington along with two male agents, in 1906.

48. K[arasiewicz], "Los pracownicy pióra."

49. Ibid.

50. All statistics are from American government sources. Polish sources, available from 1920 on, give comparable numbers. Brożek, *Polish Americans,* 234.

51. Printed on glossy paper, with a color cover and quality graphics, the monthly *Jaskółka* was the latest and most professionally produced of a string of Polonian literary magazines, as well as one of the longest running (1927–35). In addition to literature,

it featured a humor section and articles on current events, high and popular culture, geography, and history.

52. As late as 1943 one thousand copies of Łukaszkiewicz's *Przygody Głupkowiaka z Mędrkowiakiem* and *Listy księdza Świeczki,* first published more than a decade earlier, were being reprinted. This is all the more remarkable because these novels concern the contested 1928 PNA convention, in which rival factions fought for control of the organization until the matter was settled in court. It was hardly topical fifteen years later.

53. See Kister, "*Pegazy na kredytowej,*" 105. This is a history of the company by the wife of its original owner, Marian Kister.

54. Gąsiorowski, *Ach, te chamy w Ameryce,* 96–98.

Chapter 3

1. Denning, *Mechanic Accents,* 24. These two series fall into the loose category of crime, rather than detective, fiction relying on fantastic plots rather than on characterization, and depending not so much on deductive reasoning and superior powers of observation to solve the crime as on the detective's ability to corner the criminal, whose guilt is already obvious.

2. Paryski's 1913 catalogue indicates that these two are Jastrzębska adventures.

3. Wojciech Chojnacki, *Bibliografia wydawnictw zwartych Polonii amerykańskiej,* 31–32.

4. Denning, *Mechanic Accents,* 35–37.

5. Brooks, *When Russia Learned to Read,* 142.

6. Only four volumes of *Bibliografia polska, 1901–1939,* edited by Janina Wilgat, had been published as of 2002.

7. Wojciech Chojnacki, "Czytelnictwo," 119.

8. *Ofiara hypnotyzmu,* 7.

9. Davies, *Heart of Europe,* 330.

10. Panek, *Probable Cause,* 16.

11. See, for example, the Wróblewski, Gościak, and Kozłowski family correspondence.

12. Popiel's seduction by all things German (and, indeed, foreign) is especially emphasized in F. C. Anstruther's retelling of the story in *Old Polish Legends,* first published during World War II. The political uses to which these tales could be fashioned is obvious.

13. Klein, *The Woman Detective,* 225.

14. The casting of a Pinkerton as a mad scientist may have been particularly satisfying to immigrant readers. The adventures of the fictional detective Nat Pinkerton,

as already indicated, were often reprinted by Polonian publishers. William Pinkerton, on the other hand, was the very real brother and business partner of Allen Pinkerton, organizer of the Pinkerton detective agency, so often deployed against immigrant strikers. These agents, fictionalized as the Winkertons, are depicted with bitterness in Nagiel's *God's Punishment.*

15. Czarnik, "Wybory beletrystyczne 'Dziennika chicagoskiego,'" 175; Kruszka, *History of the Poles,* 1:306.

16. In 1889 or 1890 (Nagiel came to the United States in 1889), a Warsaw publishing house released his "crime novel" *Sęp,* which reportedly became popular in the United States. Unfortunately, I have not been able to locate a copy of this novel to determine whether it was the source of the pulp detective of the same name or whether Nagiel might have authored the later Sęp series. The latter possibility seems unlikely, however. Not only had Nagiel died in 1899, while the pulps did not appear until a decade later, but stylistic differences distinguish the anonymous tales from Nagiel's 1896 novel. Still, the connection may be more than coincidental. Another Nagiel crime novel, *Tajemnice Nalewek* (Secrets of Nalewki), was published in Poland after Nagiel's death. See *Polski słownik biograficzny,* s.v. "Nagiel, Henryk"; Kruszka, *History of the Poles,* 1:358, n. 9.

17. Nagiel, *Kara Boża,* 297.

18. The "artist-painter" may be the same lost soul of Czupka's "Dwaj malarze" (Two painters) in *Obrazki z Ameryki,* 69–77. Gryziński, the "doctor of law from Galicia," who becomes one of the novel's major characters, may be Czupka himself, who earned his law degree in Europe and later graduated from New York University's school of law. Nagiel worked with him on the short-lived Buffalo humor weekly *Kukuryku* and on New York's *Ognisko.* For a discussion of the Ognisko group, see Cygan, "Political and Cultural Leadership." The café to which Nagiel refers is Klementyna "Mama" Budzyńska's on East Second Street, which he also described in *Dziennikarstwo polskie w Ameryce.* See also Waldo, *Sokolstwo,* 1:128–29.

19. One story has it that Russian schoolteachers, well aware of its implications, refused to call their pupils by this name. One of those children whose parents chose this name for its patriotic meaning was Józef Teodor Konrad Korzeniowski, called Konrad as a boy (and later known as Joseph Conrad). As a child, Conrad spent several years in Siberian and Russian exile with his family because of his father's revolutionary activities.

20. Davies, *Heart of Europe,* 218. The morality of this "functional treason" was a matter of hot debate. See Eile, *Literature and Nationalism in Partitioned Poland,* 38–40.

21. One novel that turns on these debates is Orłowski's *W żelaznych kleszczach,* which will be discussed in chapter 5. It opens with a woman's murder.

22. Nagiel, *Kara Boża,* 272–73. Other works that portray the Russian as sexual seducer include Osada's *W dniach nędzy i zbrodni* and Staś's *Marzenie czy rzeczy-*

wistość. In *Polski pień,* another work by Staś, however, a Prussian suitor is never even considered by the Polish-American object of his affections.

23. Authorship was never revealed, but several candidates emerge. One possible author is Melania Nesterowicz, the editor of *Dziennik dla wszystkich* at the time and the (often anonymous) author of other novels about Buffalo Polonia that the paper serialized. Although rather more carefully plotted than other Nesterowicz works, the novel is full of details of Buffalo life that indicate a close acquaintance with the city. Another possibility is Bronisław Wrotnowski, the author of several serialized crime novels, who advertised *Jaskółka,* the monthly magazine he edited, in the Buffalo newspaper around this time. Finally, another candidate is Stanisław Gąsiorowski, a Polish journalist who spent time in the United States, occasionally wrote fiction about American Polonia, and was *Dziennik dla wszystkich*'s regular correspondent from Warsaw in the 1920s.

24. *Szumowiny* was also sold in book form in 1933. It's unclear whether *God's Punishment* was reprinted in 1930, when it was once again advertised for sale, or whether an existing stockpile of old editions was then being uncovered and sold. At any rate, the release came in the wake of a renewed interest in crime fiction.

25. "Przygody polskiego detektywa," *Dziennik dla wszystkich,* 6 November 1928.

26. Ibid., 19 November 1928.

27. Ibid., 29 December 1928.

Chapter 4

1. Chrostowski, "Niewolnik polski," *Jutrzenka,* 10 January 1894. Chrostowski, part of the Ognisko group of immigrant socialists, was a controversial figure. Wacław Kruszka called him "completely gone astray, but talented" (*Historya polska w Ameryce,* 5:99.) I offer this translation of the original Polish "zupełnie wykolejony, ale zdolny," as an alternative to that in the recently published English-language version of Kruszka's work, *A History of the Poles in America to 1908,* "totally deranged but nevertheless talented" (1:309). Jankowski's translation continues: "Today [in 1905] no one is interested in him, but Henryk Nagiel has already noted that 'if not for his moral shortcomings he could occupy a certain position in literature not only in America but also in Europe.' . . . Unfortunately, his was a totally wasted talent" (1:309–10).

2. See Barth, introduction to *Ethnic Groups and Boundaries.* For a discussion of this internalized Polishness as a strategy of national preservation, see Porter, *When Nationalism Began to Hate,* 17–21.

3. Gladsky makes a similar argument for Polish American literature written in English. Gladsky, *Princes, Peasants,* 5–6.

4. For example, L., "Testament Wuja Jacentego"; "Trzy nikle"; Helena P[iotrowska],

"Z nędzy"; Melania Nesterowicz, "Historya białego domku" and "Siódme przykazanie"; "Samouczek M. Rosenbauma."

5. T. K., *Przygody Lejbusia* , 49–51.

6. Milosz, *History of Polish Literature,* 255. Paryski, for instance, published a series of gawęda collections, containing stories like "The Child Who Was Sold to the Devil," "The Barkeep and the Four Thieves" (in *Gawędziarz polski no. 1,* ca. 1912), and "Was She a Faithful Wife" (*Gawędziarz polski no. 5,* ca. 1912).

7. See, for instance, Staniewski, *Ciekawe gawędy Macieja Grzędy* (1911).

8. [Neuman], "Gawęda tygodniowa," *Dziennik chicagoski,* 16 September 1899.

9. See *Kuryer polski* (Milwaukee), 18 September 1893. When Neuman left the *Kuryer* to set up the rival paper *Słowo,* the following editorial appeared: "No one here in America is ashamed of his background; no honest person needs to be ashamed. So why is the editor of *Słowo* ashamed? Anyway, everyone here already knows that Neuman is of Jewish extraction, born in misery at Kleparz [Market] in Kraków; it's also known that he later lived in Poznań, where he passed as a Pole." Neuman's own writings were staunchly Catholic. One decidedly anti-Semitic novel, *Trzech pachciarzy,* has also been attributed to him, probably mistakenly. See chapter 5, n. 28 .

10. Karol Wachtl was also the object of persistent rumors that he was Jewish. See, for instance, "Mnich i żyd" *Dziennik związkowy/Zgoda,* 5–6 February 1908. Anna Cienciala suggests that this false claim, rather than a break in relations with his brother Stanisław, a prominent actor in the immigrant theater, may have been behind his decision to change his name from Wachtel. Cienciala, "Foundations of Polish-American Scholarship," 51–52. He changed the spelling of his name after his return from Poland in the mid-1920s, a period of growing anti-Semitism.

11. Julian Czupka, "Irlandczyk z Smorgonii" (The Irishman from Smorgonia), *Obrazki z Ameryki,* 28. The character of Mac Adlo may be based partly on Pike Landusky, a miner and saloon owner in Maiden, Montana. See Kowalczyk, "'Pike' Landusky, Montana Frontiersman."

12. "Listy Wojtka do starego kraju," *Dziennik chicagoski,* 10 March 1898.

13. Czupka, "Tyrolczyk" (The Tyrolean), *Obrazki z Ameryki,* 1–14. My translation of this story appears in the *Multilingual Anthology of American Literature,* edited by Marc Shell and Werner Sollors.

14. "Bankier" [The Banker], *Obrazki,* 3. This is the second story in the collection, but it is numbered as beginning with page one. The stories that follow are numbered normally. Antoni Wiśniewski's Manhattan tavern was located at 212 Broome Street.

15. Czupka, *Obrazki,* [3].

16. Czupka himself never returned, however.

17. "Tera pozdrawiam i kłaniam si tobi sto tysiensuf razy i odpisz mi, a ja ci stond napisze jeszcze wiele ciokawych rzeczuf. Kłaniaj si także kumom, i kumam, a somsiadowi Karasiowi powiedz, niech jeszcze zaczeka z kupnem łonki, aż poszlę

papiry. Twuj na wieki kochajoncy monsz Bazyli." *Ameryka-Echo,* 7 September 1907. In addition to being published in book form, these letters were serialized and under slightly varied titles continued to appear in slightly different forms. See Thomas and Znaniecki's introduction to "The Peasant Letter" section of *The Polish Peasant in Europe and America* for a discussion of the conventions of letter writing, including the importance of "bows," ritualized greetings in highly stylized language which reconfirmed family and social relationships.

18. It is very likely that this series, which appeared in 1898, was also authored by Neuman, who had begun editing the paper two years before.

19. In response to the 1893 depression, Jacob S. Coxey led a march of several hundred unemployed laborers and their supporters from Massillon, Ohio, to Washington, D.C. Local activists also orgainzed their own marches on the capital. One of these organizers was Jan (sometimes Józef) Rybakowski, an engineer from Galicia and editor of a socialist weekly in Chicago. In early June, 1894, Rybakowski and about three hundred marchers, made up predominantly of Polish, German, Bohemian, and Russian immigrants, set off from Chicago. They passed through immigrant settlements in Michigan, Ohio, and Pennsylvania with the intention of gathering support. On August 24, 1894, the march was routed by sheriff's deputies outside Buffalo, New York.

20. The principle of "Za waszą wolność i naszą" (For your freedom and ours) encouraged Poles in Europe and America to gain battle experience and advance freedom's cause by coming to the military aid of other countries. For a discussion of Polish-American literary constructions of the Spanish-American war, see Matthew Frye Jacobson, "Martial Art: Literature and Romantic Militarism in Turn-of-the-Century Polonia."

21. "Listy Wojtka do starego kraju," *Dziennik chicagoski,* 16 February 1898.

22. Szydłowska-Cegłowa, "Funkcje stylistyczne i artystyczne gwary polsko-amerykańskiej," 202.

23. Morawski, *Na dwóch półkulach,* 69.

24. Staś, *Na ludzkim targu* (1910), 179.

25. Chełchowski, "Legjonista 'Dzioł,'" 30.

26. Stanisławowo refers to the neighborhood surrounding Chicago's first Polish church, St. Stanislaus Kostka. In 1895 the Rev. Antoni Kozłowski led parishioners in a secession from neighboring St. Hedwig's, over issues of the American Catholic Church's financial and administrative control of ethnic parishes.

27. [Neuman], "Moi trzej przyjaciele," *Dziennik chicagoski,* 4 December 1902.

28. Ibid., 2 December 1902.

29. Ibid.

30. A promised second novel following Władek to America never materialized.

31. Chrostowski, "The Polish Slave," *Jutrzenka,* 6 March 1894. In early installments, the hero is named Filip. No explanation is offered for his change in name.

32. Chrostowski, "The Polish Slave," *Jutrzenka,* 6 March 1894.
33. Ibid.
34. Morawski, *Na dwóch półkulach,* 65–66.
35. "Listy Wojtka do starego kraju," *Dziennik chicagoski,* 19 March 1898.
36. Łukaszkiewicz, *Anioł stróż i djabeł stróż,* 85.
37. Jacobson, *Special Sorrows,* 21.

Chapter 5

1. See Blejwas, "Stanisław Osada: Immigrant Nationalist," 25.
2. Iwanowski, "'Od nagłej, a niespodziewanej,'" 80–82.
3. L., "Tchórz," *Dziennik chicagoski,* 30 May 1900.
4. "Maszyna piekielna," *Dziennik chicagoski,* 31 March 1900.
5. Rev. Vincent Barzyński, quoted in Parot, *Polish Catholics in Chicago,* 52–53.
6. Hodur, "Faryzeusze i Saduceusze," *Straż,* 17 April 1897.
7. Serialized in *Rola Boża* under the pseudonym Chrystomir Cień. The name *Chrystomir,* of course, has *Christ* as its root, with the ancient Slavic *-mir* signifying honor. *Cień* means shade.
8. Brożek suggests that up to three-quarters of Polish-American children attended parochial schools in the peak years before World War I. These numbers declined considerably after the war (148). Despite school closings and demographic changes in the remaining student body, the parish school remains a fundamental component of Polonia's self-conception.
9. Józef, *Dzielny Michałek sierotka,* 47–48. The publisher is the "Society of Friends of the Polish National School." The author may be Józef Zawistowski.
10. "Chrystus przed sędzią pokoju," *Straż,* 20 January 1900.
11. Neuman [Dada, pseud.], "Niezależne piekło."
12. Interestingly, however, the well-publicized and often violent "church wars" that occurred in so many parishes, which focused on issues of local control over parish finances and the appointment of parish priests, found little overt expression beyond scattered barbs. For one example, see "Listy Wojtka do starego kraju," *Dziennik chicagoski,* 2 February 1898.
13. Józef Piłsudski became Chief of State when Poland regained its independence in 1919. A socialist and longtime political activist, he had commanded the Polish Legions during the First World War. Although he left the government in 1922, Piłsudski returned to power in a 1926 coup. His authoritarian regime continued until his death in 1935.
14. Wachtl, *Polonia w Ameryce,* 230; Osada, *Prasa,* 74.
15. As a journalist, Łukaszkiewicz sometimes took his inspiration from Polonia's

own scandals. *The Nun's Veil,* for instance, contains an episode transparently based on the 1919 trial of Stanisława Lipczyńska, housekeeper to Fr. Andrew Bieniawski of Isidore, Michigan. Lipczyńska was sentenced to life in prison for the murder of a young nun. Łukaszkiewicz's novel treats the murder of a nun of the same name by a priest's jealous housekeeper-mistress. The story was widely reported in the press and was even the inspiration for a play and movie, *The Runner Stumbles.* For a wildly idiosyncratic account of this incident, see Natsolim [Harry Milostan], *The Errant Nun.*

16. Łukaszkiewicz, *Księży chleb* (1930), 36.

17. Łukaszkiewicz, *Zakonny welon* (1935), 61.

18. Łukaszkiewicz, *Ucieczka grzesznych,* 25. These Polish-American nuns are members of the Sisters of St. Felix, commonly known as Felicians. The order was founded in Poland. Felician nuns first arrived in America in 1874, with the principal mission of teaching immigrant children.

19. Staś's own relationship to the Church is ambiguous. Her fiction is highly spiritual and sometimes portrays priests sympathetically, but Staś herself strayed in and out of connection to conventional religious institutions, for which she was at times maliciously ridiculed in the Polonian press. For many years an active theosophist, she founded a theosophist study group and weekly newspaper in Milwaukee, and died a Baptist. *In the Human Market*'s two long chapters in which an eccentric old woman describes a universe formed of "father-spirit" and "mother-matter" can probably be taken as a statement of Staś's own cosmology.

20. These charges were fueled by the fact that Laudyn had lived and studied in Moscow before emigrating, and by her vocal Pan-Slavism, a cause that Poles generally considered a front for Russian hegemony. Two years later she rejoined *Głos Polek,* apparently with no ill feelings on either side.

21. Laudyn, "Doktorka," 38. This image is reminiscent of an often quoted song usually attributed to Julian Czupka, "Ameryka, to śliczny, wolny kraj" (America, that beautiful free country): "There's money to be made / And lots of work to do / You'll look for it till you're blue / Running night and day, / And if you have degrees / From two faculties / You'll get a job, and how / Milking cows!" Wachtl, *Polonia w Ameryce,* 241.

22. Łukaszkiewicz, *Ucieczka grzesznych,* 213.

23. Shortly after Łukaszkiewicz's arrival in the United States, he published *Moskalofile.* For more about KON's role in World War I era Polonia, see Francič, *Komitet Obrony Narodowej w Ameryce;* Hapak, "Recruiting a Polish Army"; and Pienkos, *For Your Freedom through Ours.*

24. Orłowski, *W żelaznych kleszczach,* 204. This novel was based on the story of Prof. Holt of St. Louis, who was implicated in a plot to sabotage the American war effort and murder J. Pierpont Morgan.

25. Chełchowski, *Baczność! Jenerał Tabaka ma głos!* (Chicago: Nakł. autora, 1913), 12.

26. This dissatisfaction, of course, was repeated after World War II, and more recently after the fall of communism.

27. Łukaszkiewicz, *Dziwna dziewczyna,* 185.

28. This work has been attributed to Kazimierz Neuman by even as reputable a source as the *Polski słownik biograficzny.* This is a curious claim, however, if only because *Three Jewish Tenants* was published in 1913, six years after Neuman's death. But there are other reasons to doubt any connection. Neuman was hardly an "Old Alliancer" (a Polish National Alliance activist)—even a disillusioned one, having been firmly in the Catholic camp, as editor of the *Dziennik chicagoski.* And there is the irony of attributing this highly anti-Semitic work to Neuman, whose enemies accused him of being Jewish and whose earlier works problematized Jewish and Polish mutual exclusiveness. Nowhere is Neuman as simplistic, or as unambiguously anti-Semitic, as is the author of *Three Jewish Tenants.* The confusion over his attributed authorship was probably caused by the similarity in title of a genuine Neuman work, *My Three Friends,* and by a misprint in Alphonse Wolanin's *Polonica Americana.*

29. While *Pomniejszona* can refer to a miniature Poland, it also carries the meaning of diminished.

30. Stary Związkowiec, *Trzech pachciarzy,* 10.

31. Stanisława Romanowska, *Nad Michiganem* (Chicago, 1903), 39–40. See also chapter 2.

32. In 1931 there was indeed a heated aldermanic election that pitted Pole against German. See Kantowicz, *Polish-American Politics in Chicago,* 67, 70. However, there does not appear to be a clear correspondence between the events in Romanowska's novel and the actual election.

33. Staś, *Na ludzkim targu* (1910), 173. See *Kuryer polski* and *Dziennik związkowy,* February–June 1909.

34. Staś, *Na ludzkim targu* (1910), 104. Staś began *Ogniwo,* a woman's and children's monthly magazine, in 1909. Printed on glossy paper, with high-quality graphics and photographs, it lasted just two years. The PNA manager is probably referring to Karol Wachtl (Wachtel), editor of the Resurrectionist Order's *Dziennik chicagoski.* See chapter 4, n. 10.

35. Staś, *Na ludzkim targu* (1910), 173. An episode in which Pani Łaź asks Polonia's doctors to advertise in her paper and is turned down because she wrote a piece critical of Darwinism, has precedent in an unsuccessful appeal Staś made to the Association of Polish Physicians. See *Dziennik związkowy,* 8 March 1909. Staś's "great little literary woman" is perhaps Stefania Laudyn, who had arrived in 1909 with an already established reputation as a playwright, political writer, and feminist organizer, and who within a year took over the editorship of *Głos Polek.* She may also have been taking a potshot at Iza Pobóg. It is not known when Pobóg arrived in this country or what her professional background was, but the two sparred with each other in the

pages of *Dziennik związkowy* and *Kuryer polski* (Milwaukee) in the fall of 1908 and spring of 1909. Staś's "Rezon Kaśki" is a thinly disguised attack on Pobóg.

36. This phrase is rendered in English.

37. After many years of lobbying and fundraising within Polonia, statues of Revolutionary War heroes Kazimierz Pułaski and Tadeusz Kościuszko were erected in Washington, D.C., in 1910, to great publicity and fanfare. For a discussion of these monuments as proof of Polish-American legitimacy, see Øverland, *Immigrant Minds, American Identities,* 94–96.

Chapter 6

1. Quoted in Davies, *God's Playground,* 2:136.

2. Sollors, *Beyond Ethnicity,* 152, 153.

3. Dearborn, *Pocahantas's Daughters,* 10.

4. Gardaphé, *Italian Signs, American Streets,* 9.

5. Davies, *God's Playground,* 2:108–9.

6. Quoted in Davies, 2:109. Edward Śmigły-Rydz was a follower of Piłsudski and headed the Polish government from 1936 to 1939.

7. These charges refer to concrete Russian policies against the Polish language and Roman Catholicism. See Davies, *God's Playground,* 2:81–111. Staś herself emigrated from the Russian partition in the mid-1880s, a period of particularly stringent regulation of Polish culture, and must have brought with her firsthand knowledge of these measures.

8. Staś, "Marzenie czy rzeczywistość," *Gazeta polska w Chicago,* 29 August 1907. For an examination of the conflict between internationalism and the national struggle, see Cygan, "Political and Cultural Leadership."

9. Staś, "Marzenie czy rzeczywistość," *Gazeta polska w Chicago,* 12 September 1907. Polish is a gendered language, in which the word for Poland, *Polska,* is feminine.

10. Nagiel, *Kara Boża,* 16.

11. See chapter 3 for a discussion of the significance of these characters' names.

12. Staś, *Polski pień,* 18, 19.

13. The novel was accompanied by a series of articles on U.S. marriage and divorce law. When the Buffalo paper *Gwiazda* printed a feature on Chrostowski's difficulties, he protested that "one hundred ordinary people can get married or shoot themselves" without raising the public's eyebrow. In the midst of the serialization of his novel, an anonymous poem appeared in *Ognisko* advising the author not to continue this public airing of dirty laundry.

14. Staś, *Polski pień,* 6–7.

15. Osada, *Z Pennsylwańskiego piekła,* 97–98.

16. Osada has played wildly with historical fact but maintains enough of a

connection to make his novel all the more intriguing. The actual link between Goldman and Czołgosz has been proven tenuous, despite her arrest soon after the McKinley shooting. And there is no evidence that either Czołgosz or Goldman was on the Coxey-inspired 1893 march of Rybakowski's army of the immigrant unemployed, with which the first section of the book is concerned. Osada himself, however, was along for at least part of this march, which originated in Chicago and was routed by sheriff's forces in Buffalo. The character of Róża is probably also based in part on Róża Rybakowska, who accompanied her husband on his march as a spokesperson and liaison, and perhaps even on Rosa Luxemburg. Janka appears to be at least partly inspired by another marcher, Helena Siemianowska of Cleveland, called in contemporary newspaper accounts the army's Joan of Arc.

17. Osada, *W dniach nędzy i zbrodni* (Milwaukee, 1908), 60. What the accusation of being "raised in Russia" may mean here is unclear, since the same could be said of many Polish Christians whose loyalties are not questioned on this basis. Osada himself came from Austro-Hungarian territory.

18. Opalski and Bartal, *Poles and Jew,* 110.

19. Among the other Polish immigrant works that express this equation of Polishness with natural dignity and honor, and Americanization with vulgarity and materialism, is Melania Nesterowicz's *Z życia analfabety.* However, the leftist Nesterowicz made the tragic hero of her story a poor peasant immigrant striving for an education who is rejected by his frivolous Americanized fiancée.

20. "Ja idę za mój husband. Ja sze dziś z niego ożeniła."

21. The rather odd fact that this Americanized Polish wife is described as a redhead carries further implications of foreignness and sensuality. (See, for instance, the earlier-mentioned F. C. Anstruther retelling of the Polish legend of corrupt King Popiel and his "licentious" wife, who was "wicked, red-haired and German" [22]). Because red hair, quite rare among Poles (and among Germans, for that matter!) is so often a metonym for Irishness (and the bride is accused of running around with Irishmen), Pobóg's story suggests the already alluded-to identification of Americanness—with all its attendant immorality and family upheaval—with the Irish.

22. Sollors, *Beyond Ethnicity,* 168.

23. See again, for instance, Łukaszkiewicz, *Anioł stróż i djabeł stróż* for the depiction of a flagrantly unfaithful Rusyn wife.

24. Knothe, "Recent Arrivals," 301–38.

25. Dziembowska, *Pamiętniki emigrantów,* "Pamiętnik nr. 29," 2:126.

26. Chrostowski, "Niewolnik polski," *Jutrzeńka,* 15 August 1894. The implication is that this pair will marry. However, the novel appears never to have been completed.

27. "Przygody polskiego detektywa," *Dziennik dla wszystkich,* 27 May 1929.

28. Ibid. Krasnodrzewski would translate literally to something like Beautifulwood or even Redwood.

29. "Adventures of a Polish Detective" is only one of a handful of novels in which falling in love with a man or woman is linked to falling in love with Poland, or in which a honeymoon trip stirs deep, unexpected love for the "homeland," particularly in second-generation Polonians. See also Waldo, *Czar miasta Kościuszko,* and [Nesterowicz], "Stella z Buffalo."

30. [Nesterowicz], "Stella z Buffalo," *Dziennik dla wszystkich,* 12 April 1927.

31. Ibid., 18 December 1926.

32. Ibid., 15 December 1926.

33. Ibid., 22 December 1926.

34. [Nesterowicz], "Sprzedawaczka z Broadwayu," *Dziennik dla wszystkich,* 14 November 1932; "Stella z Buffalo," *Dziennik dla wszystkich,* 7 February 1927.

35. [Nesterowicz], "Stella z Buffalo," *Dziennik dla wszystkich,* 28 February 1927.

36. Ibid., 21 May 1927.

37. Ibid., 10 May 1927.

Epilogue

1. See Roy, "Marylin Monroe z Greenpointu," serialized in the weekly *Panorama* (Chicago), 1994.

2. Mierzyńska, "Rozmowa z Zofią Mierzyńską."

3. See Erdmans, *Opposite Poles,* 57–83.

4. United States Immigration and Naturalization Service, <www.ins.usdoj.gov/text/aboutins/statistics/illegals.htm>. Poland, ranking tenth among nations contributing illegal immigrants to the United States, was the only European country among the top fifteen. The INS does, however, note that the numbers of Poles dropped over 25 percent since 1988, probably because of the changing political and economic conditions in Poland.

5. See also Erdmans, *Opposite Poles,* 83. Among other contemporary immigrant authors whose works reflect the modern Polish community is playwright Janusz Głowacki, now based in New York, whose work has appeared in both Polish and English. As with the earlier emigration, Poles who returned to Poland after spending time in the United States have also turned their experiences into fiction. See, for instance, works of Edward Redliński, including *Dolorado* (Chicago 1984; reprint, Poland 1994) and *Szczuropolacy* (Rat-Poles).

6. Quoted in Waldo, *Zarys historii,* 33.

7. Letter to the editor, *Dziennik polski* (Detroit), 2 August 1985. The novel was reprinted in Poland in 1992, where its print run of fifty thousand was sold out in two months. Mierzyńska, interview with the author, December 1997.

8. Mierzyńska, interview with the author, December 1997.

9. Świderska, "Eldorado—dolorado," 118.

10. Staś, *Na ludzkim targu* (1910), 179.

11. Quoted in Mierzyńska, "Rozmowa."

12. Ibid.

13. "Kochany mój mężu, Franiu! W pierwszych słowach mojego listu Niech Będzie Pochwalony Jezus Chrystus." Mierzyńska, *Wakacjuszka,* 2:72.

14. Mierzyńska, *Zawód: Hałskiper,* 57.

15. This is reminiscent of the turn-of-the-century immigrant song "Jak jechałem z Ameryki" (When I journeyed from America): "And my children did not know me, / For they fled from me, a stranger. / 'My dear children, I'm your papa; / Three long years I have not seen you.'" Pawlowska, *Merrily We Sing,* 154–55.

16. Mierzyńska, *Wakacjuszka,* 3:60.

17. Maurycy Mochnacki, quoted in Porter, *When Nationalism Began to Hate,* 20. But for contemporary Poles seeking their place in a wider cultural landscape, this inner Poland can also be a haunting shadow. The protagonist of Edward Redliński's *Dolorado,* who visits the United States for the chance "to think about something more important than Poland," is told that he will find this impossible: "You'll carry Poland with you, like a humpback, like brain cancer" (53). The impulse is reminiscent of the famous lines of Jan Lechoń, published long before he emigrated: "And in the spring let me see spring, not Poland." Quoted in Miłosz, *History of Polish Literature,* 385.

18. Quoted in Greene, *American Immigrant Leaders,* 117.

Bibliographic Essay

Strategies in Recovering Polish Immigrant Writings

From the very beginning of this project, which has now extended over ten years, it was clear that there would be two basic, ongoing challenges. The first challenge was identifying and locating primary materials, that is, novels and other forms of fiction written in the Polish language by immigrant authors and published in the United States before the outbreak of World War II. The second challenge was uncovering biographical background on the authors of these works. Those tasks have become easier over the years with the availability of Internet resources, an increased interest in genealogy, and the developing field of American literature studies in languages other than English. The following discussion is intended not only to facilitate further research into Polish immigrant writing, but to point out the nagging blank spots that remain.

Constructing a bibliography of Polish immigrant Polish-language writing began with two fundamental but flawed sources, Artur Waldo's *Zarys historii literatury polskiej w Ameryce* and Stanisław Osada's *Prasa i publicystyka polska w Ameryce,* both of which are maddeningly incomplete and sometimes misleading. Much of Karol Wachtl's study, for instance, consists of year-by-year listings of works written in Polish or English by Polish immigrants, Polish-Americans, or by Americans about matters Polish or Polonian. The criteria for inclusion are not specified, and the works are for the most part undifferentiated by type or genre, so that papers submitted by seminary students are included along with military manuals, collections of sermons, Polish grammars, and translations of Polish classics. Waldo generally provides no information beyond date, name, and title, so it is not even certain how many of these works were actually published. Still, his bibliography, compromised as it is, contains the only reference in print to certain works. Alphonse Wolanin's guide to the holdings of the Polish Museum of America, *Polonica americana,* fills in some of the blanks, but was never meant to be a comprehensive listing of Polonian imprints and contains some troublesome misprints. It was necessary to treat these sources as leads to follow, rather than incorporating them without question.

Of invaluable help was the work of two Polish bibliographers, Wojciech and Władysław Chojnacki. Wojciech Chojnacki's *Bibliografia wydawnictw zwartych Polonii amerykańskiej, 1867–1900,* is a reliable listing of all Polish-American imprints before 1900 and offers a comprehensive view of nineteenth-century Polonian publishing. For Polish-American publications, it is more reliable than the standard bibliographies of

Polish nineteenth-century imprints compiled overseas by the Karol Estreichers, father and grandson. (A bibliography of twentieth-century Polish imprints, comparable to Estreicher, under the editorship of Janina Wilgat, is in progress, but has not yet reached the letter D.) What is more, it lists repositories and some private collections in which these nineteenth-century works can be found, or in whose catalog they are included but are missing. It also identifies authors who wrote under pseudonym or whose works were printed anonymously but whose authorship is known. But the cutoff date of 1900 falls before the real explosion of Polonian publishing. And as complete as Chojnacki's bibliography is for Polonia's earliest works, it doesn't help at all in identifying the large body of literature published in periodicals. It is also not annotated, so it can be difficult to discern whether an item was written in the United States or simply reprinted here, whether it is a work of fiction or nonfiction, and whether it concerns immigrant life.

A source that fills in some of these gaps is Władysław and Wojciech Chojnacki's listing of Polonian almanacs, *Bibliografia kalendarzy polonijnych.* Although the tables of contents are not listed, contents relevant to Polonia—including short stories—are sometimes noted. This bibliography offers a good place to start in locating works that were not published under separate imprint and also lists repositories, including many small ethnic libraries, that own each title. In the end, however, it is still necessary to examine each almanac, page by page. Many were printed with incomplete, or wholly without, tables of contents. And in the end the only way to determine the relevance of some stories was to skim through them.

This points to another major obstacle in identifying this literature: much of it appears only in newspapers and other periodicals that are not indexed. Only *Rola Boża* has a published index; the Polish Museum of America also holds a typescript index to *Jaskółka.* So it is necessary to physically scan through issues of Polish-American periodicals. This is made infinitely easier—even possible—largely as a result of a 1970s microfilming project funded by the National Endowment for the Humanities, so that films of the most common newspapers are now held by some of the major immigrant repositories and available on loan through the Center for Research Libraries. (For this reason, my bibliography of primary sources lists repositories for those periodicals available only in hard copy, but not for those that have been microfilmed.) As a result, the newspaper fiction is often easier to access than titles that appeared only in book or pamphlet form.

But complete runs do not exist for all the filmed titles, and some titles were never filmed at all. It is possible to examine hard copies for some of these (once again, the Polish Museum is the richest repository), but for many of the earlier or more obscure titles listed by Jan Wepsiec, it appears that only scattered issues, or even none, are extant. This accounts for some missing dates in the bibliography. What is more, the eye is fallible and there is doubtless much material that I overlooked.

Identifying the works themselves was just part of the challenge, however. Trying to fit them into the context of the authors' lives could be fascinating and maddening. While some of the authors' careers are well documented, for many others even the most basic information was lacking. Once again, the Polish-language sources mentioned above, particularly Wachtl and Osada, as well as Waldo's four-volume history of the Falcons (*Sokolstwo*), are sometimes helpful but often partisan and occasionally misinformed. Though consulted as a standard reference for Polonian history, Francis Bolek's *Who's Who in Polish America* contains too many glaring mistakes to be considered at all reliable, while it overlooks some of Polonia's most important writers, journalists, and social activists. The *Polski słownik biograficzny,* the definitive Polish source for biographical information, lists relatively few Polish immigrants and is an ongoing project that has so far reached only the letter *R.* Still, the information it contains can be considered reliable (though apparent mistakes occasionally surfaced, such as the death date for Wiktor Karłowski).

In many cases, biographical information had to be inferred from references and notes in other sources, such as Wepsiec's bibliography of Polish-American serials, which chronicles periodical editors and publishers in painstaking detail. And valuable information—not only about authors but also about publishing activities, library development, and organizational life—was often buried in the newspapers themselves, in articles, advertisements, editorial notes, and of course in obituaries. For most of this, once again, there is no index, but Polish-American genealogical societies have published indexes to birth, death, and marriage notices for *Dziennik chicagoski* and *Jedność-Polonia.* These are useful only in locating people who lived in Chicago or Baltimore and whose survivors paid for the printing of an obituary. Since *Dziennik chicagoski* was a Roman Catholic newspaper run by the Resurrectionists and one of several Polish dailies in Chicago, it is also far from a complete representation of Polish deaths in that city.

One very important English-language source must be mentioned here: the *Chicago Foreign Language Press Survey Records,* compiled between 1936 and 1941 by the Works Progress Administration (renamed the Work Projects Administration in 1939). It consists of translations into English of selected newspaper articles from the foreign press beginning in the nineteenth century, with a substantial Polish section. Although none of the newspaper fiction is included and it is not helpful for biographical detail about individual authors, its articles documenting literary contests, publishing efforts, and journalistic squabbles would be very difficult to locate otherwise.

In order to construct any kind of picture of early Polonian authors, however, it is still often necessary to do the most basic kind of genealogical research, using ship manifests, naturalization records, census indices, vital statistics, city directories, and social security records. This has become easier over the years as more and more of this material became available on the Internet. But this also necessitates repeating old searches again and again using new tactics and resources. The commercial website <www.ancestry.com> allows users to search a large number of databases at once, and even turned up some obscure printed resources, but other services like Rootsweb <www.rootsweb.com>, the Gencom project <www.gencom.com>, and the Ellis Island research site <www.ellisislandrecords.org> are also useful. The Polish Genealogical Society of America <www.pgsa.org> offers several important searchable online databases, including the *Dziennik chicagoski* death notices, Haller's Army volunteer lists, Polish Roman Catholic Union of America death benefit listings, and records of marriages in Chicago Polish parishes through 1915. Other local Polish genealogical society sites, including those from Buffalo and Detroit, are helpful as well. Still, on some authors these efforts have so far turned up little or no information or have led to more questions than answers. I pursued this search most rigorously for the more prolific and important writers, which sometimes led to strange detours and further mystery, so that even for some of the writers about whom the most complete record exists, vital pieces that would help us understand their work are still missing.

For scholars wishing to examine the novels and short stories firsthand, this bibliography includes a list of the major repositories where they can be found, compiled from various sources. Understandably, although these items occasionally turn up in collections in Poland, they are much more common in the United States. American college and university libraries are the richest resource. A large number of titles are held at the Immigration History Research Center at the University of Minnesota, which also has an excellent collection of Polish immigrant newspapers on microfilm, as well as the Paryski Company records.

The University of Pittsburgh's holdings are also notable, as they include the library of the Polish National Alliance's now closed Alliance College. Processing and preserving this enormous amount of material is a monumental, ongoing project that the university is fulfilling most professionally. Another growing collection, under excellent administration and supplemented by microfilmed newspapers, is housed at Central Connecticut State University. The State University of New York, Buffalo, holds microfilm copies of many publications. And several other universities, including Southern Illinois University, Edwardsville, and the University of Wisconsin, Milwaukee, have smaller collections of Polish-American imprints, in the case of the latter fleshed out by important archival collections on the local Polonia. An independent and very rich source of Polonian imprints is the Balch Institute in Philadelphia, whose holdings include a good selection of almanacs.

One of the most important resources is the Alumni Memorial Library at St. Mary's College of Ave Maria University, in Orchard Lake, Michigan. This is a collection with which I am intimately familiar, because I have been its curator for the last several years. Since the Orchard Lake Schools, of which St. Mary's College is a component, has been serving Polonia in one form or another since the 1880s, it contains not only the Polish-American imprints themselves, but many other works, often quite obscure, that were published in Europe around the same time as the Polonian materials and that help round out the historical picture. Catalogs of all the above repositories are accessible online, and some items are available through interlibrary loan.

Local public libraries appear to be only minor sources of this material, with the exception of the New York Public Library, which does not share its materials through interlibrary loan. And it seems that only a very limited number of items were ever deposited with the Library of Congress. But the libraries and archives of ethnic organizations may hold more that is as yet undocumented. (And the holdings of some ethnic organizations, like the Polish Institute of Arts and Sciences in America, while under excellent administration and well cataloged, are largely outside the subject area and time period of this study.) Any of these repositories may still yield information about local authors and publishing companies. In addition, random copies of publications continue to turn up at bookstores in older Polish neighborhoods, as well as at rummage and estate sales and through online auctions.

Finally we come to two of the major archives organized and administrated by Polonia itself. Affiliated with the Orchard Lake Schools but not part of St. Mary's College is the Central Archives of Polonia. Its collections are partially documented in several published catalogs, but its unpublished holdings are actually much more extensive and include books (Polish-American imprints among them), newspapers, and the papers, photographs, and artifacts of miscellaneous Polish-American individuals and organizations, including Bolek and Waldo. The collection is not accessible online and researchers may find it difficult to access items not yet noted in the printed catalogs—which do not list books. For this reason, its holdings are not indicated in this study's bibliography of primary sources. However, it can be a source of biographical and historical detail, and as more of the enormous amount of material at Orchard Lake is documented it will undoubtedly prove more useful to scholars of Polish immigrant writing and publishing.

Also suffering from a lack of technology and funds is the invaluable collection of the Polish Museum of America in Chicago, organized and administered by the Polish Roman Catholic Union of America. In addition to large display spaces, the museum includes a library and archive, which together form a treasure trove of material relevant to this study. Of the many items that have survived in single copies, most of them are held by this repository. (For the sake of ease, I've listed those held by the library and those by the archives under the single rubric of Polish Museum of America.) Besides Polish-American imprints, the museum also owns microfilmed and original newspapers, many of them, again, available nowhere else in the United States. In addition, there are individual and institutional papers, photographs, and biographical materials from all geographic areas of American Polonia.

Clearly, then, the bibliography of primary sources and the accompanying author biographies can only be considered works in progress. But we now have some idea of what to look for and where to find it. It is hoped that further research will not only turn up more titles and a fuller picture of the writers who created them but also locate copies of some of the known works that seem to have disappeared.

Bibliography

Primary Sources

Abbreviations

ACPL	Allen County (Indiana) Public Library
BAL	Balch Institute (Philadelphia)
BGU	Biblioteka Główna Uniwersytetu A. Mickiewicza (Poznań)
BJ	Biblioteka Jagiellońska (Kraków)
BN	Biblioteka Narodowa (Warsaw)
BPP	Biblioteka Polska (Paris)
BUL	Biblioteka Uniwersytetu Łodzkiego (Łódź)
BUW	Biblioteka Uniwersytetu Warszawskiego
CCSU	Central Connecticut State University (New Britain)
CLP	Carnegie Library of Pittsburgh
CPL	Cleveland Public Library
EPFL	Enoch Pratt Free Library (Baltimore)
FP	Franciscan Library (Pulaski, Wis.)
HFC	Holy Family College (Philadelphia)
HIS	Hoover Institute, Stanford University
HU	Harvard University
IBL	Biblioteka Instytutu Badań Literackich Polskiej Akademii Nauk (Warsaw)
IBP	Instytut Polonijny, Uniwersytet Jagielloński (Kraków)
KSU	Kent State University
LC	Library of Congress
LO	Loyola University
MCM	McMaster University (Hamilton, Ont.)
ML	Biblioteka Muzeum Literatury im. Adama Mickiewicza (Warsaw)
MLN	Michigan Library Network
MLS	Milwaukee County Federated Library System
MU	Madonna University (Livonia, Mich.)
NYPL	New York Public Library
OSS	Ossolineum Library (Wrocław)
OSU	Ohio State University
OX	Oxford University

PCI	Polish Cultural Institute (Winona, Minn.)
PLH	Polish Library Home (Cleveland)
PMA	Polish Museum of America (Chicago)
PWA	Polish Women's Alliance (Chicago)
SIUE	Southern Illinois University-Edwardsville
SMOL	St. Mary's College of Ave Maria University (Orchard Lake, Mich.)
STU	Stanford University
SUNYBN	State University of New York, Binghamton
SUNYBU	State University of New York, Buffalo
UC	University of Chicago
UKS	University of Kansas
UMN	University of Minnesota, Minneapolis
UND	University of Notre Dame
UPITT	University of Pittsburgh
UWM	University of Wisconsin, Milwaukee
UWMD	University of Wisconsin, Madison
WHS	State Historical Society of Wisconsin (Madison)
WPL	Westerville (Ohio) Public Library
WSU	Wayne State University
YU	Yale University

Included here are works of fiction written by immigrants in the Polish language, and published by immigrant companies in the United States before World War II.

Many works were published anonymously or under pseudonym. Works that were published anonymously, but for which it is possible to attribute authorship, are listed with the author's name in brackets. Works that were published under pseudonym, but for which we know the author, are listed under the author's name, with the pseudonym in brackets and cross-referenced. If authorship cannot be established, the work is listed under the pseudonym, if there is one, or under the title.

Ajotes. *See* Staniewski, Alfons J.

Aka [pseudo.]. "Sympatyczny środek" (A nice way). *Rózga,* 15 January 1910. PMA.

"Amerykański raj" (American paradise). *Dziennik związkowy/Zgoda,* 2 October 1908.

"Awantura z moją żoną (humoreska)" (A quarrel with my wife: A humorous story). In *Wielki kalendarz uniwersalny, czyli Powszechny dla wszystkich stanów polskiego narodu na rok 1921,* 1:141–43. [Stevens Point, Wis.: Bracia Worzałłowie] Nakł. i Druk. Polskiego Wyd. Kalendarzy Europejskich, [1920]. PMA.

Bałdyga, Kazimierz. *Opowiadania żołnierskie* (Soldier stories). 1928. Not extant?

———. "Taki zwykły wytarty kwoder" (Just a common old quarter). In *Wielki kalendarz uniwersalny, czyli Powszechny dla wszystkich stanów polskiego narodu na rok 1927,* 2:207–17. [Stevens Point, Wis.: Bracia Worzałłowie] Nakł. i Druk. Polskiego Wyd. Kalendarzy Europejskich, [1926]. PMA.

Barć, Franciszek S. "A Miesiączek się uśmiechał" (And Miesiączek kept smiling). In Waldo, *Czyn zbrojny,* 168–72.

[Bartosz, Adam]. "Hello, Wirusy! Ciekawe przygody Wojciecha Ogurka, piklem przezwanego, ku zbudowaniu i pocieszeniu rodoków, jego ciężkom łapom nagryzmane!" (Hello, old campaigners! The interesting adventures of Wojciech Ogórek, nicknamed Pickle, for the edification and amusement of his countrymen, scribbled with his own heavy paw). *Jednośc-Polonia,* [before January 1926]–25 December 1926.

———. "Z naszych kunerów" (From our corners). *Jednośc-Polonia,* 7 January 1928–8 April 1938.

Bazyli [pseud.]. "Historya moich sztucznych zębów i żeniaczki: Humoreska" (The story of my false teeth and marriage: A humorous story). In *Wielki wybór humoru: Najwiekszy wybór najdrowszego humoru, artów, dowcipów, fraszek, anegdot, opowiadań, i wierszyków,* 157–58. Toledo: Paryski, n.d. SMOL.

———. "Historya moich sztucznych zębów i żeniaczki: Humoreska," *Rózga,* 5 March 1910. PMA.

Bicz, Jan [pseud.]. "Rady mojego przyjaciela" (My friend's advice). *Dziennik polski,* 6 January 1923.

———. "Z tematów detroickich i hamtramickich" (About Detroit and Hamtramck matters). *Dziennik polski* 22 (November 1922–6 June 1923).

"Biedny milioner (Historya o biednym bogaczu i bogatym nędzarzu amerykańskim)" (The poor millionaire: The story of a poor rich man and a rich beggar in America). In *Kalendarz maryański dla polaków w Ameryce na rok 1918,* 214–36. [Stevens Point, Wis.]: Nakł. i Druk. Polskiego Wyd. Kalendarzy Europejskich, [1917]. PMA.

"Bóg z tobą!" (God be with you!). In *Wielki kalendarz uniwersalny, czyli Powszechny dla wszystkich stanów polskiego narodu na rok 1920,* 2:65–73. [Stevens Point, Wis.: Bracia Worzałłowie] Nakł. i Druk. Polskiego Wyd. Kalendarzy Europejskich, [1919]. PMA.

Borzęcki, Władysław. "Bohater Lwowa" (The hero of Lwów]. In Waldo, *Czyn zbrojny,* 262–65.

Bronisławski, Marian. *See* Wrotnowski, Bronisław.

Burke, Karol. "Uśpieni rycerze" (Latent knights). In Waldo, *Czyn zbrojny,* 302–6.

Chełchowski, Telesfor [Szczypawka, pseud.]. *Baczność! Jenerał Tabaka ma głos! Zbiór wesołych gawęd głównego dowódcy wojsk polskich w St. Zj* (Attention!

General Tobacco has the floor! A collection of merry tales of the commander-in-chief of the Polish armies in the United States). Chicago: Nakł. autora, 1913. CCSU, PMA.

———. "Baczność! Jenerał Tabaka ma głos! Zbiór wesołych gawęd głównego dowódcy wojsk polskich w St. Zj." *Bicz Boży,* 20 August 1911–6 September 1914. PMA.

———. *Baczność! Jenerał Tabaka ma głos! Zbiór wesołych gawęd głównego dowódcy wojsk polskich w St. Zj.* [Chicago]: n.p., 1915. YU.

———. *Baczność! Jenerał Tabaka ma głos! Zbiór wesołych gawęd głównego dowódcy wojsk polskich w St. Zj.* Steven's Point, Wis.: Worzalla's Sons, 1915. CCSU, PMA, SMOL.

———. *Co Jenerał Tabaka mówi o wojnie?* (What does General Tobacco say about the war?). Not extant?

———. "Gospodyni Jędza: Wesoła bajeczka duchowna" (Housekeeper Hag: A merry clerical tale). In *Kalendarz humorystyczny "Bicza Bożego" na rok 1914,* 33–47. Chicago: *Bicz Boży,* [1913]. BAL, PMA.

———. *Humorystyczne listy z terenu wojny* (Humorous letters from the war front). Chicago: Nakł. autora; Druk. Bicza Bożego, 1915. BN, PMA (missing).

———. "Humorystyczne listy z terenu wojny." *Bicz Boży,* 6 December 1914–3 January 1915. PMA.

———. "Jak Bartłomiej Potulny dostał się do nieba za protekcją swojego bortnika-socjalisty" (How Bartholomew Milquetoast got into heaven through the protection of his socialist boarder). *Bicz Boży,* 1 January 1912. PMA.

———. "Jak robotnik dwuch księży wyżywił" (How the laborer supported two priests). In *Kalendarz Bicza Bożego 1913,* 66–76. Chicago: Bicz Boży, 1912. BAL, PMA.

———. "Korespondencja księdza proboszcza" (The rector's correspondence). In *Kalendarz Bicza Bożego 1916,* 23–66. Chicago: Bicz Boży, [1915]. BAL, PMA.

———. "Legjonista 'Dzioł'" (Legionnaire Joe). In *Humorystyczny kalendarz "Bicza Bożego" 1917,* 30–35. Chicago: Bicz Boży, 1916. BAL, PMA.

———. "Listy głodnej żony i sytego męża" (Letters of a hungry wife and a sated husband). *Bicz Boży,* 20 August–3 September 1916. PMA.

———. "Przygoda 'Wielebnego Ojca' Byczka" (The adventures of "Reverend Father" Bullock). In *Kalendarz Bicza Bożego 1913,* 27–29. Chicago: Bicz Boży, 1912. BAL, PMA.

———. "Znalazł środek (opowiadanie z życia Polaków w USA)" (He found a way: A story from the life of Poles in the U.S.A.). In *Kalendarz humorystyczny "Bicza Bożego" na rok 1914,* 135–36. Chicago: Bicz Boży, [1913]. BAL, BUL, PMA.

Chrostowski, M. Alfons. "Niewolnik polski: Na tle stosunków polsko-amerykańskich"

(The Polish slave: Based on Polish-American conditions). *Jutrzenka,* December 1893–November 1894+.

———. "Rok życia" (A year of life). *Ognisko,* December 1888–22 June 1889.

———. *Uwiedziona* (The seduced girl). Toledo: Paryski, 1891. PMA (missing).

"Chrystus przed sędzią pokoju: Legenda spisana podług opowiadania polskiego ludu Nanticoke" (Christ before the justice of the peace: A legend based on a story of the Polish people in Nanticoke). *Straż,* 12–20 January 1900.

Ciekawy górnik (The curious miner). Scranton: Straż, n.d. UMN.

Cień, Chrystomir. *See* Hodur, Franciszek.

"Ciężka, twarda dola polskiego kandydata" (The cruel, hard fate of a Polish candidate). In *Książka roczna (kalendarz) "Ameryki-Echa" na rok 1934,* 285–86. Toledo: Paryski, [1933]. PMA.

"Cud" (The miracle). In *Kalendarz humorystyczny Bicza Bożego na rok 1915,* 33–39. Chicago: Bicz Boży, [1914]. BAL, PMA.

"Cudowne drogi opatrzności: Obrazek z życia polskich emigrantów" (The miraculous way of providence: A picture from Polish emigrant life). In *Kalendarz św. Michała na rok Pański 1913,* 35–47. Techny, Ill.: Society of the Divine Word, [1912]. PMA.

Człowiek w żelaznej klatce (The man in the iron cage). [Toledo: Paryski], 1911. PMA.

Czupka, Julian. *Obrazki z Ameryki* (Pictures from America). Wilkes-Barre: Górnik, 1897. PMA.

———. "Obrazki z Ameryki." *Jedność-Polonia,* 25 December 1926.

———. "Tyrolczyk" (The Tyrolean). Trans. Karen Majewski. In *The Multilingual Anthology of American Literature: A Reader of Original Texts with English Translations,* ed. Marc Shell and Werner Sollors, 348–57. New York: New York University Press, 2000.

Czuwara, Stanisław. "Wędrowiec" (The wanderer). In Waldo, *Czyn zbrojny,* 307–12.

Dada. *See* Neuman, Kazimierz.

[Dangel], Stanisław. *Rezolutna Marysia: "Narodówka"* (Resolute Mary, nationalist). Scranton: Towarzystwa Przyjaciół Polskiej Narodowej Szkoły, n.d. PMA, UMN.

Dangel-Langowski, [Stanisław]. "Na zawsze" (Forever). *Ameryka,* 15 June 1895.

———. "Sprzedana dusza: Szkic" (The sold soul: A sketch). *Ameryka-Echo,* 27 April 1895.

———. "Sprzedana dusza: Szkic." *Straż,* 22 December 1897.

de Pillar, S. *See* Słupski, Zygmunt.

"Dobra nauka: Nowelka" (A good lesson: A short story). *Strumień* (Westfield, Mass.), July 1909, 91–93. PMA.

Drelenkiewicz-Rekwart, Halina U. "Niedoszła gwiazda" (The would-be movie star). In *Kalendarz związkowy na rok 1936,* 179–83. Chicago: Dziennik Związkowy, [1935]. CCSU, PMA, UPITT.

———. "Trzech 'daddies' za wielu . . . : Nowelka" (Three daddies too many: A short story). In *Kalendarz związkowy na rok 1936,* 99–101. Chicago: Dziennik Związkowy, [1935]. CCSU, PMA, UPITT.

"Druh Fajka ma głos!" (Brother Pipe has the floor!). *Bicz Boży,* 21 November 1915–3 September 1916. PMA.

Drzazga, Renat. *Dzika kaczka: Obrazek z życia polskiego dziewczęcia w Ameryce* (The wild duck: A portrait from the life of a Polish girl in America). Scranton: Nakł. Komisji Oświaty przy P.N. Spójni, n.d. SUNYBU, UMN.

Espejotes [pseud.]. "Smok cytrynowy" (The lemon dragon). *Dziennik chicagoski,* 30 January–2 February 1899.

"Gawędy Bazylego Szturkajły" (The tales of Basil Poker). In *Wielki wybór humoru,* 129+.

———. *Rózga,* December 1909–September 1910. PMA, UPITT.

"Gawędy Pafnucego Zioberki" (The tales of Pafnucy Ribs). *Ameryka-Echo,* 28 March–30 May 1908.

"Gawędy Williama Szturkajły" (The tales of William Poker). In *Wielki wybór humoru,* 237+.

———. *Rózga,* October–December 1910. PMA, UPITT.

"Gdzie się podział przejechany?" (Where is the one who got run over?) *Rózga,* 8 January 1910. PMA.

"Gomuła ma głos" (Gomuła has the floor). *Djabełek,* May–June, August–September, November 1933.

Gruba Hanka Piróg i jej siedmiu bortników (Fat Hanka Dumpling and her seven boarders). Detroit: Rekord Codzienny, n.d. PMA.

Gwiazda, Maciej [pseud.]. "Murzyn o Polsce" (The Negro's opinion of Poland). *Ameryka-Echo,* 5 December 1920–9 January 1921.

"Gwiazdka w obozie: Z życia polsko-amerykańskiego" (Christmas Eve in camp: From Polish-American life). In *Kalendarz misyjny na rok 1919,* 42–45. Erie, Pa.: Nakł. Księży Misyonarzy Św. Wincentego á Paulo z Kolegium Św. Jana Kantego, [1918]. PMA.

"Gwiazdkowe zakupy Pani Słodkowskiej." *See* Paryski, *Świąteczne zakupy Pani Słodkowskiej.*

Haiman, Mieczysław. "Wojtkowa dola" (Wojtek's fate). In *Kalendarz zjednoczenia na rok 1921,* 81–86. Chicago: Nakł. Zjednoczenia Polskiego Rzymsko-Katolickiego w Ameryce, [1920]. PMA.

Hodur, Franciszek. "Faryzeusze i Saduceusze: Powieść osnuta na tle stosunków polskich religijno-społecznych" (The Pharisees and the Sadducees: A novel based on Polish religious-social conditions). *Straż,* 17 April–30 October 1897.

———. *Faryzeusze i Saduceusze: Powieść osnuta na tle stosunków polskich religijno-społecznych.* Scranton: Druk. "Straży," 1899. BJ, UMN.

———. [Chrystomir Cień, pseud.]. "Ksiądz-bandyta: Powieść z obecnej doby na tle stosunków polsko-amerykańskich" (The bandit priest: A novel based on current Polish-American conditions). *Rola Boża,* 19 July 1930–14 March 1931.

———. [Chrystomir Cień, pseud.]. "Ksiądz jednooki: Opowieść współczesna na tle stosunków pol.-amerykańskich" (The one-eyed priest: A contemporary tale based on Polish-American conditions). *Rola Boża,* 18 April–20 August 1927.

———. *Nowe życie: Listy do matki i listy od matki* (New life: Letters to a mother and from a mother). Scranton: Druk. "Straży," 1905. BJ.

Iwanowski, Fr[anciszek]. "'Od nagłej, a niespodziewanej': Obrazek amerykański" ("From a sudden and unexpected": An American picture). In *Kalendarz związkowy informacyjno-encyklopedyczyny (na rok) 1915,* 80–82. Chicago: Dziennik Związkowy, 1914. BN, IBP, PMA, UMN, UPITT.

Jabłoński, Hieronim. "Dzieci wisielca: Powieść z czasów ostatniego powstania" (The hanged man's children: A novel from the times of the last uprising). In *Dzień święty,* vol. 4. Chicago: Druk. i nakł. Gazety Katolickiej, 1886. 612+.

———. "Kłopoty Pana Bencwała" (Mr. Knucklehead's troubles). In *Dzień święty*(?).

"Jak to Filip Kapusta filozofał?" (How did Philip Cabbage philosophize?). *Praca* (Wilkes-Barre), February 1920, 20. PMA.

Janusz. *See* Neuman, Kazimierz.

Jax, Antoni. "Zatruty placek Wielkanocny, albo 'Trzeba kłamać, gdy tego potrzeba wymagać . . .': Humoreska amerykańska" (The poisoned Easter cake, or "Lie when you have to . . .": A humorous American story). *Gazeta polska w Chicago,* 4 April 1912.

"Jeden dzień u polsko-amerykańskiego redaktora (humoreska)" (A day at the Polish-American editorial office: A humorous story). *Książka roczna Ameryki-Echa na 1917r,* 283–85. Toledo: Paryski, [1916]. CCSU, PMA, UPITT.

Jesień, W. S. "Historja pewnego artykułu" (The story of a certain article). In *Kalendarz "Bicza Bożego" 1912,* 21–25. Chicago: Bicz Boży, [1911]. PMA.

Józef. *Dzielny Michałek sierotka: Opowiadanie z życia polskich robotników w Ameryce* (Brave Mikey the little orphan: A story from the life of Polish workers in America). Scranton: Nakł. Towarzystwa Przyjaciół Polskiej Narodowej Szkoły, n.d. PMA, UMN.

Jużo de Kugelmacher [pseud.]. "Bigos chicagoski" (Stew Chicago-style). *Djabełek,* November 1933, 29.

K., A. "Kącik Bazylego Szturkajły" (Basil Poker's corner). *Ameryka-Echo,* 18 January–15 February 1908.

———. "Kącik Bazylego Szturkajły." *Rózga,* December 1909. PMA.

———. "Listy Bazylego Szturkajły" (Basil Poker's letters). *Ameryka-Echo,* 27 July 1907–17 January 1908.

———. *Listy Bazylego Szturkajły do żony w starym kraju i jej odpowiedzi* (Basil Poker's letters to his wife in the old country and her replies). Toledo: Paryski, [c. 1907].

———. [K., Ant.] "Pożegnalna mowa: Polsko-amerykańskiego salonisty nad grobem kolegi" (The farewell speech: A Polish-American saloonkeeper at his friend's grave). In *Rózga,* 1 January 1910. PMA.

———. "Pożegnalna mowa: Polsko-amerykańskiego salonisty nad grobem kolegi." *In Wielki wybór humoru,* 131.

———. [K., Antoni.] "Amerykański polak w Galicji" (An American Pole in Galicia). In *Kalendarz amerykańsko-polski illustrowany na rok 1913,* 91–96. [Toledo: Paryski, 1912.] PMA.

———. *Amerykański polak w Galicyi: Nadzwyczaj zabawne opowiadanie o podróży zbogaconego chłopa do starego kraju* (An American Pole in Galicia: Extraordinarily funny story about a rich peasant's journey to the old country). Toledo: Paryski, 1912. PMA, UMN.

K., T. *Przygody Lejbusia w Ameryce, czyli Przez cierpliwość do szczęścia i bogactwa* (Lejbus's adventures in America, or Patience leads to happiness and riches). Stevens Point, Wis.: Bracia Worzałłowie, 1912. OSS, PMA.

Karaś, Józef. "Serce Pomorza" (The heart of Pomorze). In Waldo, *Czyn zbrojny,* 289–95.

Karasiewicz, J[ózef]. "Dla ojczyzny" (For the fatherland). *Dziennik polski,* 15 August 1914.

Karłowski, W[iktor]. *Na dalekim zachodzie: Szkic z życia wychodźców* (In the far west: A sketch from the life of emigrants). Chicago: Dyniewicz, 1885. PMA.

Kmieciak, Michał. "Wielka niegodziwość" (A great wickedness). *Dziennik związkowy/Zgoda,* 22–25 March 1909.

———. "Z ciężkich dni: Wspomnienie z niedalekiej przeszłości" (From difficult days: Memories from the recent past). *Dziennik związkowy/Zgoda,* 25–27 June 1908.

Konom-dojde [pseud.]. "Sherlock Holmes." *Bicz Boży,* 28 March 1909. PMA.

"Kruk, który krukowi wyrządził krzywdę (Kruk, who double-crossed the crooks). In *Kalendarz humorystyczny Bicza Bożego 1914 r,* 118–25. Chicago: Bicz Boży, [1913]. BAL, PMA.

Kruszka, Wacław. "Na progu dwudziestego wieku: Różowe widoki na przyszłość Polski.—Fantazja p.t. Ostatni Yankee w Ameryce" (At the threshold of the twentieth century, rosy views on the future of Poland—A fantasy entitled The Last Yankee in America). In *Siedm siedmioleci, czyli Pół wieku życia: Pamiętnik i przyczynek do historji polskiej w Ameryce,* 1:293–300. 2 vols. Poznań/Milwaukee: Nakł. autora, Czcionkami Drukarni Św. Wojciecha w Poznaniu, 1924. BN, BUW, CCSU, HFC, MLS, MU, OX, PMA, SMOL, STU, SUNYBU, UKS, UMN, UND, UPITT, UWM, WHS.

Krwawe róże, czyli Występna miłość szaleńca, który porwał mężowi młodą żonę i chciał ją zmusić, aby go kochała (Bloody roses, or The forbidden love of a crazy man who stole a man's young wife and tried to make her love him). [Toledo: Paryski], 1911. UPITT.

"Kubuś Stołownik: Historja prawdziwa z życia emigranta polaka w Buffalo, N.Y." (Jakey Boarder: A true story from the life of an emigrant Pole in Buffalo, N.Y."). *Dziennik dla wszystkich,* 3 February–9 February 1928.

L. "Tchórz" (The coward). *Dziennik chicagoski,* 30 May 1900.

———. "Testament Wuja Jacentego" (Uncle Jacenty's will). *Dziennik chicagoski,* 7 April 1900.

Laudyn, Stefania. *Galerja obrazów z krainy dolara* (A gallery of portraits from the land of the dollar). Chicago: Polish American Publishing Co., n.d. BJ, PMA, UPITT.

———. [Stebor, A., pseud.]. "Adwokat amerykański" (The American lawyer). *Rodzina polska,* 9 March–16 March 1916. PMA.

———. [Stebor, A., pseud.]. "Biały murzyn" (The white Negro). *Rodzina polska,* 27 July–3 August 1916. PMA.

———. [Stebor, A., pseud.]. "Chłop (pisany przed trema laty)" (The peasant, written three years earlier). *Rodzina polska,* 8 June 1916. PMA.

———. [Stebor, A., pseud.]. "Chłopak (z życia polsko-amerykańskiego)" (The boy: From Polish-American life). *Rodzina polska,* 13 April–20 April 1916. PMA.

———. [Stebor, A., pseud.]. "Chwila osobliwa (z życia polsko-amerykańskiego)" (A peculiar moment: From Polish-American life). *Rodzina polska,* 23 March 1916. PMA.

———. [Stebor, A., pseud.]. "Doktorka" (The woman doctor). *Rodzina polska,* 11 May–25 May 1916. PMA.

———. [Stebor, A., pseud.]. "Swięta patrona" (The patron saint). *Rodzina polska,* 15 June–13 July 1916. PMA.

———. "'The Woman Doctor' in *Gallery of Portraits from the Land of the Dollar: A Collection of Stories Based on Polish-American Life.*" Trans. Karen Majewski. In *Something of My Very Own to Say: American Women Writers of Polish Descent,* ed. Thomas S. Gladsky and Rita Holmes Gladsky, 67–72. Boulder: East European Monographs, 1997.

———. [Stebor, A., pseud.]. "Zatracony (nowelka z życia polsko-amerykańskiego)" (Lost: A story from Polish-American life). *Rodzina polska,* 13 January–20 January 1916. PMA.

———. [Stebor, A., pseud.]. "Zbuntowana (z życia Polonii w Ameryce" (In rebellion: From the life of Polonia in America). *Rodzina polska,* 24 February 1916. PMA.

Lekarka obłąkanych zbrodniarką (The criminal-asylum keeper). [Toledo: Paryski], 1911. PMA.

Łempicki, S[tanisław]. "Franek Cichy: Nowelka polsko-amerykańska na tle obecnej wojny europejskiej" (Frankie Silent: A Polish-American story based on the current European war). In *Kalendarz związkowy na rok 1919,* 136+. Chicago: Dziennik Związkowy i Zgoda [1918]. PMA.

"List Antka Kręcigęby z piekła do Frycka Kusego w Detroit" (Antek Crookedface's letter from hell to Fritz Kusy in Detroit). *Dziennik polski,* 17 August 1907.

"List Bartka Pacygi z Chicago" (Bart Pacyga's letter from Chicago). *Ameryka-Echo,* 10 May 1910.

"List Bazylego Knychta z Hameryki do żony w Ciemnym Potoku" (Basil Knycht's letter from America to his wife in Black Spring). *Dziennik polski,* 12 August 1907.

"List Kaśki Bazylowej z Ciemnego Potoka w starym kraju do Bazylego Hnychta w Ameryce" (Kasia's letter from Black Spring in the old country to her husband, Basil Hnycht, in America). *Dziennik polski,* 5 August 1907.

"List Kejdy Jałochy do Dziana Sochy" (Katie Heifer's letter to John Plow). *Rózga,* 6 August 1910. PMA, UPITT.

"List Wojtka Kopicy austryacko polskiego wojaka" (Letter of Wojtek Haystack, an Austro-Polish soldier). *Rózga,* 5 February 1910. PMA.

"List z Ameryki" (Letter from America). *Dziennik polski,* 21 October 1907.

"List z Ameryki do starego kraju" (Letter from America to the old country). In *Wielki wybór humoru,* 133.

———. *Rózga,* 1 January 1910. PMA.

"Listy Dziana Sochy do Panny Jałochy" (John Plow's letters to Miss Heifer). In *Wielki wybór humoru,* 241.

———. *Rózga,* 24 April–25 June 1910. PMA, UPITT.

"Listy Wojtka do starego kraju" (Wojtek's letters to the old country). *Dziennik chicagoski,* 2 February–7 April 1898.

"Listy z końca świata" (Letters from the end of the world). *Gwiazda polarna,* 16 November 1929–10 May 1930.

Łukaszkiewicz, Czesław. *Anioł stróż i djabeł stróż: Powieść satyryczna* (Guardian angel and guardian devil: A satirical novel). Toledo: Paryski, 1931. CCSU, CPL, KSU, SMOL, UPITT.

———. "Anioł stróż i djabeł stróż: Powieść satyryczna." *Ameryka-Echo,* 29 March–12 June 1931.

———. "Bielmo" (The cataract). Boston: n.p., 1918. In *Kuryer bostoński*(?).

———. *Dziwna dziewczyna: Powieść z życia polsko-amerykańskiego* (The strange girl: A novel from Polish-American life). Toledo: Paryski, 1923. BN, CCSU, SMOL, SUNYBN, UPITT.

———. "Dziwna dziewczyna: Powieść z życia polsko-amerykańskiego." *Dziennik polski,* 21 April 1923+.

———. "Dziwna dziewczyna: Powieść z życia polsko-amerykańskiego." Rev. ed. *Ameryka-Echo,* 23 November 1930–22 March 1931.

———. *Księży chleb: Powieść z życia polsko-amerykańskiego* (Priestly bread: A novel from Polish-American life). Toledo: Paryski, 1919. PMA.

———. *Księży chleb: Powieść z życia polsko-amerykańskiego.* 3d ed. Chicago: Nakł. Księgarni Ludowej, 1921. CCSU, UPITT.

———. *Księży chleb: Powieść z życia polsko-amerykańskiego.* Rev. ed. Toledo: Paryski, 1930. BN, MLN, PMA, SMOL, UMN, YUL.

———. "Księży chleb: Powieść z życia polsko-amerykańskiego." *Ameryka-Echo,* 27 October 1929–30 March 1930.

———. *Listy Księdza Świeczki, w roku Pańskim 1928 i 1929: Przegląd spraw pobożnych, plebanych i parafjalnych* (Father Candle's letters, in the year of Our Lord 1928 and 1929: A review of religious, rectory, and parish affairs). Toledo: Paryski, 1930. PMA.

———. "Listy Księdza Floryana Świeczki" (Father Florian Candle's letters). *Ameryka-Echo,* 30 October 1927–27 January 1946.

———. "O wszystkiem i o niczem: Rozmowy Głupkowiaka z Mędrkowiakiem" (About everything and nothing: The conversations of Blockhead and Half-Wit). *Dziennik polski,* 6 January–22 June 1923.

———. "Przygody Głupkowiaka z Mędrkowiakiem" (The adventures of Blockhead and Half-Wit). *Ameryka-Echo,* 30 October 1927–27 January 1946.

———. *Przygody Głupkowiaka z Mędrkowiakiem, w roku Pańskim 1928 i 1929: Wesoły przegląd spraw polskich w Ameryce* (The adventures of Blockhead and Half-Wit, in the year of Our Lord 1928 and 1929: A merry review of Polish matters in America). Toledo: Paryski, 1929. BN, CCSU, UPITT.

———. *Ucieczka grzesznych: Powieść z życia polsko-amerykańskiego* (Refuge of sinners: A novel from Polish-American life). Toledo: Paryski, n.d. BAL, BN, UPITT.

———. "Ucieczka grzesznych: Powieść z życia polsko-amerykańskiego." Rev. ed. *Ameryka-Echo,* 3 August–16 November 1930.

———. *Zakonny welon: Powieść z życia polsko-amerykańskiego* (The nun's veil: A novel from Polish-American life). Chicago: 1920. CCSU.

———. *Zakonny welon: Powieść z życia polsko-amerykańskiego.* Toledo: Paryski, 1930. CPL.

———. "Zakonny welon: Powieść z życia polsko-amerykańskiego." *Ameryka-Echo,* 16 April–27 July 1930.

———. *Zakonny welon: Powieść z życia polsko-amerykańskiego.* Rev. ed. Toledo: Paryski, 1935. MCM, PMA, SMOL, UPITT.

Marcinkiewicz, Adam. *Pan redaktor w zalotach: Humoreska na tle stosunków amerykańskich* (The editor's courtship: A humorous story based on American conditions). Detroit: W Drukarni przy Seminaryum Polskiem, 1894. SMOL.

———. *Pan redaktor w zalotach: Humoreska na tle stosunków amerykańskich.* Toledo: Paryski, 1910. BAL, BN, PMA, SMOL, SUNYBU, UMN.

———. "Pan redaktor w zalotach: Humoreska na tle stosunków amerykańskich." *Rózga,* 15 January–19 February 1910. PMA.

"Marja Wanda Le Ford: Wychowanka sierocińca naszego w Ameryce, St. Zjed." (Maria Wanda Le Ford: A ward of our orphanage in the United States of America). *Gość niedzielny,* 4 January–26 April 1925. PMA.

Marnota [pseud.]. "Papuga" (The parrot). In *Kalendarz Bicza Bożego 1913,* 135–38. Chicago: Bicz Boży, 1912. PMA.

"Maszyna piekielna: Z życia anarchistów amerykańskich" (The hellish machine: From the life of American anarchists). *Dziennik chicagoski,* 31 March 1900.

"Mąż panem domu: Humoreska" (The husband rules the roost: A humorous story). In *Wielki kalendarz uniwersalny, czyli Powszechny dla wszystkich stanów polskiego narodu na rok 1920,* 2:253–55. [Stevens Point, Wis.: Bracia Worzałłowie] Nakł. i Druk. Polskiego Wyd. Kalendarzy Europejskich, [1919]. PMA.

Mężobójczyni: Nadzwyczaj zajmująca powieść (The husband killer: An unusually interesting novel). [Toledo: Paryski], 1911. UPITT.

"Misye Pani Kasprowej" (Mrs. Kasprowa's missions). In *Księga roczna Ameryki-Echa na rok 1919,* 145–58. Toledo: Paryski, 1918. PMA, UPITT.

"Mnich i żyd" (The monk and the Jew). *Dziennik związkowy/Zgoda,* 5–6 February 1908.

Moje przygody w Ameryce; Bal w Milwaukee (My adventures in America; the ball in Milwaukee). Toledo: Paryski, [c. 1912].

Morawski, Wojciech. *Na dwóch półkulach: Szkic powieściowy na tle prawdziwego zdarzenia* (On two continents: A novelistic sketch based on true events). Chicago: Nakł. Zjednoczonej Prasy Polskiej w Ameryce, 1907. BN, CCSU, PMA, SMOL, SUNYBU, UC, UMN.

Mord w wagonie: Obrazek z życia polsko-amerykańskiego (Murder on the train: A picture from Polish-American life). [Chicago: Dyniewicz], 1914. Not extant?

———. Chicago: Polish American Publishing Co., n.d. PMA.

Morska, Celina. "Błogosławiony deszcz" (Blessed rain). *Jaskółka,* November 1927, 43–46. PMA, UPITT.

Nagiel, Henryk. *Kara Boża idzie przez oceany: Powieść na tle stosunków polskich w Ameryce* (God's punishment crosses the ocean: A novel based on Polish conditions in America). Chicago: Druk. Spółki Wyd. Polskiego w Ameryce, 1896. FP, HU, MU, MNU, PLH, PMA, PWA, SIUE.

———. "Kara Boża idzie przez oceany: Powieść na tle stosunków polskich w Ameryce." *Dziennik dla wszystkich,* 14 February–9 June 1912.

Nastal, Stanisław. "Pierwsza fala" (The first wave). In Waldo, *Czyn zbrojny,* 158–63.

———. "W nieznane jutro" (In an unknown tomorrow). In Waldo, *Czyn zbrojny,* 175–79.

Nesterowicz, Melania. "Historya białego domku" (The story of the little white house). *Ameryka-Echo,* 21 December 1907.

———. "Hot-Cha-Cha: Opowiadanie z życia młodzieży polskiej w Buffalo" (Hot-Cha-Cha: A story from the life of Polish young people in Buffalo). *Dziennik dla wszystkich,* 21 May–31 July 1934.

———. "Pan Krzywda" (Mr. Harm). *Ameryka-Echo,* 31 August 1907.

———. *Pan Krzywda.* Toledo: Paryski, 1908. Not extant?

———. *Pan Krzywda.* Chicago: Dyniewicz, 1911. BN, PMA.

———. "Siódme przykazanie" (The seventh commandment). *Ameryka-Echo,* 27 July 1907.

———. "Sprzedawaczka z Broadwayu" (The salesgirl from Broadway). *Dziennik dla wszystkich,* 14 November–20 December 1932.

———. "Sprzedawaczka z Broadwayu." *Jaskółka,* August 1933–June 1934. PMA, UPITT.

———. *Sprzedawaczka z Broadwayu.* Detroit: Unity Press, 1937. EPFL, HU, NYPL, SMOL.

———. "Sprzedawaczka z Broadwayu." *Tygodnik świat polski,* 1 October 1993–26 August 1994.

———. "Stella z Buffalo" (Stella from Buffalo). *Dziennik dla wszystkich,* 8 December 1926–21 May 1927.

———. "Tajemnica nieślubnego dziecka" (The secret of the illegitimate child). *Dziennik dla wszystkich*(?).

———. "Z życia analfabety" (From the life of an illiterate). *Ameryka-Echo,* 13 July 1907.

———. "Z życia analfabety." *Rolnik,* 26 July 1907.

———. *Z życia analfabety.* Toledo: Paryski, 1908. Not extant?

———. *Z życia analfabety.* Chicago: Dyniewicz, 1911. PMA.

[Nesterowicz, Stefan]. "Listy Hyacynta Poczciwiny z ziemi obiecanej do redakcyi 'Echa polskiego'" (Hyacinthe Goodfellow's letters from the promised land to the editorial office of the *Polish Echo*). *Ameryka-Echo,* 11 May–14 December 1912.

———. *Listy Hyacynta Poczciwiny z ziemi obiecanej do redakcyi "Echa polskiego"* [Toledo: Paryski], 1913. SMOL, SUNYBU, UMN.

Neuman, Kazimierz [Dada, pseud.]. "Fatalna przygoda: Gawęda" (The fatal adventure: A tale). *Dziennik chicagoski,* 24 December 1900.

———. [Dada, pseud.]. "Gawęda tygodniowa" (Weekly tales). *Dziennik chicagoski,* 16 September–9 December 1899.

———. [Janusz, pseud.]. *Moi trzej przyjaciele: Nowela (z teki Janusza)* (My three friends: A short story from Janusz's notebook). Chicago: Druk. J[an] I[gnacy] Migdalski, 1895. IBL, PMA.

———. [Janusz, pseud.]. "Moi trzej przyjaciele: Nowela (z teki Janusza)." *Dziennik chicagoski,* 1–12 December 1902.

———. [Janusz, pseud.]. *Mój spadek w Ameryce* (My inheritance in America). Published with *Moi trzej przyjaciele,* 57–77. Chicago: Druk. J[an] I[gnacy] Migdalski, 1895. IBL, PMA.

———. "Mój spadek w Ameryce." In *Sztandar polski* (Bay City, Mich.?).

———. [Janusz, pseud.]. "Moja nowelka (z teki Janusza)" (My short story, from Janusz's notebook). *Dziennik chicagoski,* 19–20 August 1899.

———. [Dada, pseud.]. "Niezależne piekło: Opowiadanie sędziego" (An independent hell: A story of the Judgment). *Dziennik chicagoski,* 22 September 1900.

———. [Janusz, pseud.]. "Wyprawa po Zośkę (szkic węglem)" (Campaign for Sophie: A sketch in coal). *Dziennik chicagoski,* 21 December 1897.

Niedźwiedzki, H. "Niespodzianka na gwiazdkę: Obrazek życia krawca polskiego w Nowym Jorku" (The Christmas Eve surprise: A picture of the life of a Polish tailor in New York). In *Kalendarz amerykańsko-polski illustrowany na rok zwyczajny 1891,* 124–36. Toledo: Paryski, 1890. BPP, PMA.

Niemir, Jan. *Jak się zemścił borowy Zielonka nad Wojtkiem Bruchyłą: Powieść ludowa poznańsko-amerykańska* (How Greenie the gamekeeper got revenge on Wojtek Bruchyła: A Poznań-American folk novel). Chicago: Dyniewicz, 1881. Not extant?

———. *Jak się zemścił borowy Zielonka nad Wojtkiem Bruchyłą: Powieść ludowa poznańsko-amerykańska.* 2d ed. Chicago: Dyniewicz, 1890. ML, OSS, PMA.

Nowina, B. "Noga Pani Marcinowej" (Marcin's wife's leg). *Jaskółka* June 1929. 22–27. PMA, UPITT.

"Obiad na farmie" (Dinner on the farm). In *Wielki wybór humoru,* 201–2.

———. *Rózga,* 16 April 1910. PMA.

"Odpowiedź Dziana Sochy, na list Kiejdy Jałochy" (John Plow's answer to Katie Heifer's letter). In *Wielki wybór humoru,* 243–44.

———. *Rózga,* 23 April 1910. PMA.

"Odpowiedź Kiejdy Jałochy, na list Dziana Sochy" (Katie Heifer's answer to John Plow's letter). In *Wielki wybór humoru,* 242+.

———. *Rózga,* 9 April–30 April 1910. PMA.

Ofiara hypnotyzmu: Historya nieszczęśliwej dziewczyny, która padła ofiarą zbrodniczego hypnotyzmu (A victim of hypnotism: The story of an unlucky girl who fell victim to a criminal hypnotist). [Toledo: Paryski], 1911. PMA, SUNYBU, UMN.

Ograbiacze trupów: Obrazek z życia polsko-amerykańskiego (The corpse robbers: A picture from Polish-American life). [Toledo: Paryski], 1911. CCSU.

———. [Toledo: Paryski], 1916. PMA.

———. Chicago: Polish American Publishing Co., n.d. PMA.

Orłowski, Józef. [Tomasz Plon, pseud.]. *W żelaznych kleszczach: Powieść oryginalna w trzech częściach na tle prawdziwych wydarzeń współczesnej wojny europejskiej* (In iron pincers: An original novel in three parts based on true events of the current European war). Chicago: Polish American Publishing Co., 1915. CCSU, CLP, CPL, LC, OSU, PMA, SMOL, UMN, UPITT, UWI, WSU.

Osada, Stanisław. *W dniach nędzy i zbrodni: Powieść z życia Polaków w Ameryce Północnej* (In days of misery and crime: A novel from the life of Poles in North America). Chicago: Smulski, 1908. Not extant?

———. *W dniach nędzy i zbrodni: Powieść z życia Polaków w Ameryce Północnej.* Milwaukee: Nakł. Nowin Polskich, 1908. LC, SMOL.

———. *W dniach nędzy i zbrodni: Powieść z życia Polaków w Ameryce Północnej.* 2d ed. Chicago: Smulski, 1909. SMOL, SUNYBU, UPITT.

———. "Wycieczka do Kościuszkowa: Fantazja z niedalekiej przyszłości" (An excursion to Kościuszków: A fantasy from the not-too-distant future). In *Kalendarz związkówy na rok 1910,* 53–58. Chicago: Związek Narodowy Polski w Stanach Zjednoczonych Północnej Ameryki, 1909. PMA, UPITT.

———. *Z pennsylwańskiego piekła: Powieść osnuta na tle życia naszych górników* (From a Pennsylvania hell: A novel based on the life of our miners). Chicago: Smulski, 1909. MNU, OSU, SMOL.

———. "Z Pennsylwańskiego piekła: Powieść osnuta na tle życia naszych górników." *Dziennik polski,* 1 April–20 May 1909.

Ostrowski, Janusz. "Na krwawy bój!" (In bloody battle). In Waldo, *Czyn zbrojny,* 56–72.

"Pan Ipski: Jak się z zielonego stał żółtym w Ameryce; Jego przygody" (Mr. Ipski: How a greenhorn turned golden in America; his adventures). *Ameryka,* 21 December 1889.

Paryski, Antoni A. "Gwiazdka" (Christmas Eve). *Ameryka,* 21 December 1889.

———. "Gwiazdkowe zakupy Pani Słodkowskiej" (Mrs. Sweet's Christmas shopping). *Ameryka-Echo,* 4–11 January 1908.

———. "Pogoń za mordercą" (In pursuit of a murderer). *Ameryka,* 28 January 1893.

———. *Świąteczne zakupy Pani Słodkowskiej: Opowiadanie na tle stosunków polsko-amerykańskich* (Mrs. Sweet's holiday shopping: A story based on Polish-American conditions). Toledo: Paryski, 1908. BAL, BN, SUNYBU, UMN.

———. *Wilia rodziny Drzazgów: Ciekawy i wzruszający obrazek z życia rodziny polskiej* (The Splinter family's Christmas Eve: An interesting and moving picture from the life of a Polish family). [Toledo: Paryski], 1913. PMA, SUNYBU, UMN.

Pięć powiastek: Amerykanka; Sprzedana dusza; Poza grobem; Sen matki; Kapitał u biednych (Five short stories: The American girl; The sold soul; Out of the grave; A mother's dream; Capital among the poor folks). Toledo: Paryski, [c. 1912]. Not extant?

Piekielny zegar: Powieść kryminalna (The hellish clock: A crime novel). N.p., 1911. UPITT.

———. Chicago: Polish American Publishing Co., n.d. CCSU, SMOL.

Piotrowska, Helena. *See also* S[awicka], Helena.

———. *Na progu nowego życia* (On the threshold of a new life). 1903. Not extant?

———. "Pijak" (The drunkard). *Ameryka,* 11 May–1 June 1895.

P[iotrowska], Helena. "Z nędzy" (From misery). *Ameryka,* 10 October 1896.

Plon, Tomasz. *See* Orłowski, Józef.

Pobóg, Iza. "Ich syn: Nowela na tle amerykańskich stosunków" (Their son: A short story based on American conditions). *Gazeta polska w Chicago,* 24 March 1910.

———. "Odzyskane pamiątki na cmentarzu: Nowela polsko-amerykańska" (The memento recovered at the cemetery: A Polish-American story). *Gazeta polska w Chicago,* 10 November 1910.

Poczciwy ministrant (The good altar boy). Erie, Pa.: B. Weiner, 1919. PMA.

"Pod pręgierzem okropnych podejrzeń" (In the pillory). In *Wielki kalendarz uniwersalny, czyli Powszechny dla wszystkich stanów polskiego narodu na rok 1920,* 2:135–55. [Stevens Point, Wis.: Bracia Worzałłowie] Nakł. i Druk. Polskiego Wyd. Kalendarzy Europejskich, [1919]. PMA.

"Podwójna zemsta" (Double revenge). *Rózga,* 14 May 1910. PMA.

"Pojedynek dwuch księży" (Duel between two priests). In *Kalendarz humorystyczny Bicza Bożego 1916,* 67–72. Chicago: Bicz Boży, [1915]. BAL, PMA.

"Polacy w Chicago: Popierajmy swoich! Stach i Józef (Podsłuchane rozmowy)" (Poles in Chicago: Let's support our own! Stach and Józef [an overheard conversation]). *Dziennik chicagoski,* 15 February 1898.

"Policzek" (A slap in the face). In *Wielki kalendarz uniwersalny, czyli Powszechny dla wszystkich stanów polskiego narodu na rok 1921,* 1:141–43. [Stevens Point, Wis.: Bracia Worzałłowie] Nakł. i Druk. Polskiego Wyd. Kalendarzy Europejskich, [1920]. PMA.

"Polska sierota (historya z życia pierwszych osadników polskich w Ameryce" (The Polish orphan: A story from the life of the first Polish settlers in America). In *Kalendarz maryański dla Polaków w Ameryce na rok 1918,* 74–94. N.p.: Polskie Wyd. Kalendarzy Europejskich, [1917]. PMA.

"'Polskie wiece z komedjami': Obrazek polsko-amerykański. 'It's fun to be fooled, it's more fun to know!'" (Polish comedies: A Polish-American picture). In *Książka roczna i kalendarz "Ameryki-Echa" na rok 1935,* 169–70. Toledo: Ameryka-Echo, 1934. PMA, UMN, UPITT.

Popławski, Piotr. *Z Bostonu pod Równe* (From Boston to Równe). 1938. Not extant?

"Porwana w noc poślubną" (Kidnapped on her wedding night). *Dziennik dla wszystkich,* 12 September–7 November 1936.

Porwana w noc poślubną: Dzieje miłości i cierpienia niewinnych serc (Kidnapped on her wedding night: A story of the love and suffering of innocent hearts). 6 vols. Detroit: Krystyna Osiecka, 1988.

"Pożar na okręcie: Opowiadania z życia wychodźców do Ameryki" (Fire aboard ship: Stories from the life of emigrants to America). *Kalendarz związkowy na rok 1919,* 126–30. Chicago: Dziennik Związkowy, 1918. BN, PMA, UPITT.

Prawdzic [pseud.]. "Gawędy prawdzica" (A truth teller's tale). *Dziennik związkowy/Zgoda,* 13 June 1908.

"Proboszcz polsko-amerykański w niebie: Rzecz wesoła na temat naszych parafialnych stosunków" (The Polish-American rector in heaven: A humorous tale about conditions in our parishes). *Narodowiec,* 4–11 February 1914.

"Przygody polskiego detektywa: Romans kryminalny z życia polsko-amerykańskiego w Buffalo" (Adventures of a Polish detective: A crime novel from Polish-American life in Buffalo). *Dziennik dla wszystkich,* 5 November 1928–27 May 1929.

Przyprawa, Jan J. "Ostatni etap" (The last stage). In Waldo, *Czyn zbrojny,* 240–59.

Pszczoła, Janusz. "Nauka się opłaca: Obrazek z życia polsko-amerykańskiego" (Education pays off: A picture from Polish-American life). In *Księga roczna Ameryki-Echa na rok 1919,* 102–4. Toledo: Paryski, 1918. PMA, UPITT.

———. "Z rodu Kugaty Czubate: Obrazek z walk partyjnych pomiędzy Polakami w Ameryce" (From the Kugata Czubata clan: A picture from the partisan fight among Poles in America). In *Księga roczna Ameryki-Echo na rok 1919,* 275–79. Toledo: Paryski, 1918. PMA, UPITT.

Rabusie grobów: Nadzwyczaj sensacyjna powieść, osnuta na tle stosunków amerykańskich (The grave robbers: An unusually sensational novel based on American conditions). [Toledo: Paryski], 1912. PMA, SUNYBU, WPL.

Romanowska, Felicja. "'Stary pedlarz': Szkic z życia wychodźców polsko-amerykańskich" (The old peddler: A sketch from the life of Polish-American emigrants). In *Kalendarz związkowy na rok 1910*, 92–93. Chicago: Związek Narodowy Polski w Stanach Zjednoczonych Północnej Ameryki, 1909. PMA, UPITT.

Romanowska, Stanisława. "Malkontenci: Szkic ze stosunków czykagoskich" (The malcontents: A sketch from conditions in Chicago). In *Kalendarz związkowy na rok 1910*, 32–36. Chicago: Związek Narodowy Polski w Stanach Zjednoczonych Północnej Ameryki, 1909. PMA, UPITT.

———. *Nad Michiganem* (On Lake Michigan). Chicago: Nakł. Wydziału Oświaty ZNP, 1903. BJ, BN, UMN, UPITT.

———. *Nad Michiganem*. Lwów: Słowo Polskie, 1903–4. SMOL.

"Rozmowa pajęczników przez telefon" (The clowns' telephone conversation). *Dziennik polski*, 17 December 1907.

"Samochód a zdrowie" (Good health and the automobile). In *Wielki kalendarz uniwersalny, czyli Powszechny dla wszystkich stanów polskiego narodu na rok 1927*, 2:99–102. [Stevens Point, Wis.: Bracia Worzałłowie) Nakł. i Druk. Polskiego Wyd. Kalendarzy Europejskich, [1926]. PMA.

"Samouczek M. Rosenbauma: Nowela" (M. Rosenbaum's handbook: A short story). *Straż*, 26 October 1901.

S[awicka], Helena. "Miłość Kasi" (Kasia's love). *Ameryka-Echo*, 7 November 1896–2 February 1897. *See also* Piotrowska, Helena.

"Scherlock Holmes i kometa" (Sherlock Holmes and the comet). *Bicz Boży*, 5 June 1910. PMA.

"Ściany mające uszy" (The walls have ears). In *Kalendarz związkowy na rok 1928*, 92–94. Chicago: Dziennik Związkowy, [1927]. PMA.

Sclavus [pseud.]. "Sąd ostateczny" (The last judgment). *Bicz Boży*, 18 March 1912. PMA.

"Sen starego kawalera" (An old bachelor's dream). *Dziennik dla wszystkich*, 6–11 May 1914.

Sichrawa, Mieczysław. "Po lepszą dole" (For a better day). In Waldo, *Czyn zbrojny*, 11–17.

Simplex, A. E. [pseud.]. "Biznes czy idea (szkic o piśmiennictwie polsko-amerykańskim)" (A business or an idea: A sketch about Polish-American writing). In *Książka roczna Ameryki-Echa na rok 1919*, 137–44. Toledo: Paryski, 1918. PMA, UPITT.

"Skaplerz Zosi awanturnicy: Sensacyjna powieść osnuta na tle życia codziennego" (The scapular of Sophie the adventuress: A sensational novel based on everyday life). *Dziennik dla wszystkich*, 1 February–1 March 1938.

Skarga, Paweł J. "Kuszenie nocy" (Temptations of the night). In *Święta rodzina:*

Kalendarz dla rodzin chrześcijańskich 1929, 35–39. [Stevens Point, Wis.: Bracia Worzałłowie] Nakł. i Druk. Polskiego Wyd. Kalendarzy Europejskich, [1928]. PMA.

———. "Nie zabijaj (nowelka)" (Thou shalt not kill: A short story). In *Wielki kalendarz uniwersalny, czyli Powszechny dla wszystkich stanów polskiego narodu na rok 1925,* 2:187–92. [Stevens Point, Wis.: Bracia Worzałłowie] Nakł. i Druk. Polskiego Wyd. Kalendarzy Europejskich, [1924]. PMA.

———. "W niewoli u pustelnika, czyli Przygody trojga polskich dzieci w lasach północnego Wisconsinu" (In slavery at the hermit's, or The adventures of three Polish children in the Wisconsin north woods). *Kuryer polski,* 26 June–3 July 1927.

———. "Złota tarcza polaków" (The Poles' golden shield). *Dziennik polski,* 12 March 1923.

Ślisz, Stanisław. "Emigrant" (The emigrant). In *Ojczyzna.*, ca. 1885–1887?

———. "Obcy w rodzinnym kraju" (A foreigner in his native country). In *Ojczyzna,* ca. 1885–1887?

———. "Pod pokładem" (Below deck). In *Ojczyzna,* ca. 1885–1887?

———. "Z miłości" (Out of love). In *Ojczyzna,* ca. 1885–1887?

"Sługa Boży: Powieść osnuta na tle stosunków polsko-amerykańskich" (The servant of God: A novel based on Polish-American conditions). *Straż,* January–October 1902.

Słupski, Zygmunt. *Czwarty lipca: Szkic do powieści z życia amerykańskiego* (The Fourth of July: A sketch of a novel from American life). Bay City, Mich.: Druk. Prawdy, 1897. BJ, OSS.

———. *Politykier: Powieść odznaczona pierwszą nagrodą na konkursie literackim im. M. Kopernika* (The politician: A novel awarded first prize in the Copernicus literary competition). Chicago, 1894.

———. *Politykier: Powieść odznaczona pierwszą nagrodą na konkursie literackim im. M. Kopernika* [Part] 1, *W "starym kraju"* (In the old country). 2nd ed. Poznań: M. Niemierkiewicz, 1894. Not extant?

———. [S. de Pillar, pseud.]. *Z życia Polaków w Ameryce: W raju: Szkic do powieści przez S. de Pillar, odznaczony drugą nagrodą na konkursie literackim im. M. Kopernika* (From the life of Poles in America: In paradise: The sketch of a novel by S. de Pillar, awarded second prize in the Copernicus literary competition). Bay City, Mich.: Druk. Prawdy, 1897. BJ, BN, OSS.

Spisek zbrodniarzy, czyli Nieudany zamiar zamordowania detektywa i zasłużona kara złoczyńców (The criminals' plot, or The failed attempt to murder a detective and the criminals' well-deserved punishment). [Toledo: Paryski], 1911. BAL, SMOL, SUNYBU.

"Spóźniony żal" (Late regrets). In *Książka roczna Ameryki-Echa na 1917r,* [514–16]. Toledo: Paryski, [1916]. CCSU, PMA, UPITT.

Stachowicz, S. Z. "Wyprawianie rekrutów" (Outfitting the recruits). In Waldo, *Czyn zbrojny,* 151–55.

Staniewski, Alfons J. [Ajotes, pseud.]. *Ciekawe gawędy Macieja Grzędy: Z różnymi ludźmi o różnych polsko-amerykańskich sprawach* (The interesting tales of Matt Seedbed: With various people, concerning various Polish-American matters). Toledo: Paryski, 1911. CCSU, MLS, SMOL, SUNYBU, UMN, UPITT, YU.

———. "Ciekawe gawędy Macieja Grzędy: Z różnymi ludźmi o 'Ameryce-Echu'" (The interesting tales of Matt Seedbed: With various people, concerning *Ameryka-Echo*). *Ameryka-Echo,* 2 February–6 May 1911.

———. *Sen na jawie, czyli Uwagi starego emigranta nad stosunkami polsko-amerykańskimi* (The daydream, or An old emigrant's observations on Polish-American conditions). Toledo: Paryski, 1911. PMA, SMOL, SUNYBU, UMN.

———. "Sen na jawie, czyli Uwagi starego emigranta nad stosunkami polsko-amerykańskimi." *Ameryka-Echo,* 13 May–10 June 1911.

Stanisław. *See* Dangel, Stanisław.

Stary Związkowiec [The Old Alliancer, pseud.]. *Trzech pachciarzy: Obrazek z życia* (Three Jewish tenants: A picture from life). N.p., 1913.

Staś, Helena. *Anioł miłosierdzia: Obrazek z życia polsko-amerykańskiego* (The angel of mercy: A picture from Polish-American life). Chicago: Dyniewicz, 1907. BN, PMA.

———. "Anioł miłosierdzia: Obrazek z życia polsko-amerykańskiego." *Dziennik polski,* 16 February 1907.

———. "Anioł miłosierdzia: Obrazek z życia polsko-amerykańskiego." *Gazeta polska w Chicago,* 28 February–21 March 1907.

———. "Dziecię Ameryki: Powieść fantastyczna XX wieku" (A child of America: A twentieth-century fantasy novel). *Ogniwo* 2, 17 (September 1910)+. PMA.

———. *Marzenie czy rzeczywistość: Obrazek polsko-amerykański* (Dream or reality: A Polish-American picture). Chicago: Dyniewicz, 1907. CCSU, PMA.

———. "Marzenie czy rzeczywistość: Obrazek polsko-amerykański." *Dziennik polski,* 20–27 May 1907.

———. "Marzenie czy rzeczywistość: Obrazek polsko-amerykański." *Gazeta polska w Chicago,* 29 August–12 September 1907.

———. *Moje koraliki: Powiastki dla dzieci polskich w Ameryce* (My coral beads: Stories for Polish children in America). Milwaukee: Druk. Kuryera Polskiego, 1921. BN, UMN.

———. "'More about What Hurts,' *In the Human Market: A Polish-American Sketch.*" Trans. Karen Majewski. In *Something of My Very Own to Say: American Women Writers of Polish Descent,* ed. Thomas S. Gladsky and Rita Holmes Gladsky, 73–75. Boulder: East European Monographs, 1997.

———. *Na falach życia, czyli Moc zmartwychwstania* (On the waves of life, or The power of the resurrection). Chicago: Dyniewicz, 1907. BN, PMA.

———. "Na falach życia, czyli Moc zmartwychwstania." *Dziennik polski,* 28–30 March 1907.

———. "Na falach życia, czyli Moc zmartwychwstania." *Gazeta polska w Chicago,* 4 April–16 May 1907.

———. *Na ludzkim targu: Szkic polsko-amerykański* (In the human market: A Polish-American sketch). Chicago: Autorka, 1910. PMA, UMN.

———. *Na ludzkim targu: Szkic polsko-amerykański.* Warsaw: Księgarnia St. Sądowskiego, 1911. BN, BUW, PMA.

———. "Nad powierzchnią wezbranych fal (poświęcone wspomnieniu W. . . .)" (Above the swelling waves [dedicated to the memory of W.]). *Ogniwo,* November 1910, 210–11. PMA.

———. "Podczas wakacji" (During vacation). *Ogniwo,* November 1910, 226–28. PMA.

———. "Polish Trunks." Trans. Karen Majewski. *Gwiazda polarna/GP Light,* July 1998.

———. *Polski pień: Obrazek z życia polsko-amerykańskiego* (The Polish trunk: A picture from Polish-American life). Chicago: Dyniewicz, 1907. CCSU.

———. "Polski pień: Obrazek z życia polsko-amerykańskiego." *Dziennik polski,* 19–21 March 1907.

———. "Polski pień: Obrazek z życia polsko-amerykańskiego." *Gazeta polska w Chicago,* 23 May–6 June 1907.

———. [Wasza Kaśka, pseud.] "Rezon Kaśki" (Kasia's self-confidence). *Ogniwo,* September 1910+. PMA.

———. "Spełnienie" (Fulfillment). *Dziennik polski,* 6–8 August 1907.

———. "Tajemnica magicznego pokoju" (The secret of the magic room). *Dziennik polski,* 21 September 1907.

———. *Tajemnica Polskiej Róży: Powiastka z życia amerykańskiego* (The secret of Polish Rose: A story from American life). Not extant?

———. *W domu psiega prawa* (A dog's life). Chicago: Nakł. autorki, 1908. Not extant?

———. *Wędrówka dwojga zakochanych* (The wanderings of two sweethearts). Not extant?

———. "Wspomnienia z agentury Ameryki-Echa: Błogosławienie" (Reminiscences of an *Ameryka-Echo* agent: The blessed). *Ameryka-Echo,* 18 April 1908.

Stebor, A. *See* Laudyn, Stefania.

Stefański, Leonard. "Sokoli rekrut" (The Falcon recruit). In Waldo, *Czyn zbrojny,* 32–42.

Swojski, Jan [pseud]. *Ludzie znajomi których nie znamy: Typy wielkich i małych działaczy polskich w Ameryce* (Acquaintances whom we don't know: Types of great and small Polish activists in America). Toledo: Paryski, 1927. PMA, SMOL, UPITT.

———. "Ludzie znajomi których nie znamy: Typy wielkich i małych działaczy polskich w Ameryce." *Ameryka-Echo*, 1 December 1926–26 June 1927.

Szczutowski, Henryk. "Dlaczego nie zostałem cygarnikiem: Z pamiętnika 'Grinola.'" (Why I didn't become a cigar maker: From the memoir of a greenhorn). *Ameryka-Echo*, 27 June 1908.

———. "Dlaczego nie zostłem [*sic*] fireman'em: Humoreska" (Why I didn't become a fireman: A humorous story). *Bicz Boży*, 19 June 1910. PMA.

———. "Dlaczego nie zostałem posłem? Humoreska" (Why didn't I become an envoy? A humorous story). In *Kalendarz robotniczy na rok 1913*, 63–65. New York: Robotnik Polski, 1913. PMA.

———. "Dziki człowiek w Coney Island: Humoreska" (The wild man at Coney Island: A humorous story). *Bicz Boży*, 1 August 1910. PMA.

———. "Gdzie była moja żona?" (Where was my wife?) *Bicz Boży*, 12 June 1910. PMA.

———. "Ja, moja corka i jej narzeczony: Humoreska z pamiętnika 'Grinola.'" (Me, my daughter, and her fiancé: A humorous story from the memoir of a greenhorn). *Ameryka-Echo*, 20 June 1908.

———. "Kiedy się sprzedałem" (When I sold myself). *Bicz Boży*, 3–10 April 1910. PMA.

———. "'Lolly pops': Humoreska." *Bicz Boży*, 3–19 July 1910. PMA.

———. "Moi sąsiedzi" (My neighbors). *Bicz boży*, 17–24 April 1910. PMA.

———. *Mój pierwszy "Thanksgiving Day": Z pamiętnika "Grinola"* (My first Thanksgiving day: From the memoir of a greenhorn). [Toledo: Paryski], 1908. SMOL, SUNYBU, UMN.

———. "Mój pierwszy 'Thanksgiving Day': Z pamiętnika 'Grinola.'"*Ameryka-Echo*, 9 May 1908.

———. "Moje wiosenne marzenie: Humoreska" (My spring reverie). *Bicz Boży*, 1–8 May 1910. PMA.

———. "Pisanie humoreski (zamiast humoreski)" (On writing humorous stories [in place of a humorous story]). In *Kalendarz robotniczy na rok 1912*, 66–72. New York: Robotnik Polski, 1911. PMA.

———. "Sto nagrody, czyli Zeznanie człowieka spoczywającego na łożu śmiertelnym" (A hundred prizes, or The deposition of a man on his deathbed). *Bicz Boży*, 31 July 1910. PMA.

———. "W pogoni za członkami 'czarnej reki'" (In pursuit of members of the Black Hand). *Bicz Boży*, 15–22 May 1910. PMA.

———. “Z namowy mojej żony miałem zostać redaktorem: Humoreska” (My wife made me become an editor). *Bicz Boży,* 5 December 1909. PMA.

———. “Złote Husarzy Ks. Romualda Pacankiewicza: Humoreska” (The golden Hussars of Father Romuald Pacankiewicz). *Bicz Boży,* 9 May 1909. PMA.

Szczypawka. *See* Chełchowski, Telesfor.

Szpaczek, Jan. “Kłopoty z mieszkaniem” (Problems with an apartment). In *Kalendarz narodowy 1918,* 146–56. Chicago, [1917]. PMA.

Szwajkart, Stanisław. “Lila.” In *Zgoda,* ca. 1881?

Tajemniczy mnich: Nadzwyczaj zajmująca powieść (The mysterious monk: An unusually entertaining novel). [Toledo: Paryski], 1911. PMA.

Tarczyński, Rudolf. “Testament żołnierza” (A soldier’s last will and testament). In Waldo, *Czyn zbrojny,* 186–99.

Them., Stef. “Kozioł ofiarny” (Sacrificial lamb). *Jaskółka,* January 1933, 8–9, 14. PMA, UPITT.

Truszkiewicz, Franciszek. “Nasza podchorążówka” (Our military college). In Waldo, *Czyn zbrojny,* 117–31.

“Trzy nikle” (Three nickels). *Dziennik chicagoski,* 21 April 1900.

“W noc wigilijną” (On Christmas Eve night). In *Kalendarz maryański na rok Pański 1926,* 71–76. N.p.: Polskie Wydawnictwo Kalendarzy Europejskich, [1925]. CCSU, PMA, UPITT.

Wachtl, Karol H. *Podarek nowy: Dla polskiej dziatwy w Ameryce* (A new gift: For Polish children in America). Stevens Point, Wis.: Bracia Worzałłowie, 1918. BAL, CCSU, SUNYBU.

Waldo, Artur L. *Czar miasta Kościuszko: Opowieść na tle prawdziwych wydarzeń* (The charm of the town of Kosciuszko: A novel based on true events). Chicago: Dziennik Zjednoczenia, 1936. ACPL, BN, BUW, CCSU, LO, NYPL, PMA, SMOL, UC, UMN, UWMD.

———. “Idziemy pod broń” (We’re taking up arms). In Waldo, *Czyn zbrojny,* 24–31.

———. “Jeden z wielu” (One of many). In Waldo, *Czyn zbrojny,* 313–18.

———. “Maguda.” In Waldo, *Czyn zbrojny,* 144–50.

———. *Obrazki z Ameryki* (Pictures from America). Not extant?

———. *Ochotnik z Ameryki* (The volunteer from America). 1921. Not extant?

———. “Pierwszy posiew” (The first seeds). In Waldo, *Czyn zbrojny* 18–23.

———. “Ratman.” In Waldo, *Czyn zbrojny,* 200–232.

———. “Sierocy grosz” (An orphan’s penny). In Waldo, *Czyn zbrojny,* 138–43.

———. *Za kulisami: Powieść na tle życia aktorów* (Behind the scenes: A novel based on the life of actors). Not extant?

———, ed. *Czyn zbrojny Polonii Stanów Zjednoczonych w nowelkach, gawędach, i opowiadaniach wojskowych* (The armed effort of U.S. Polonia in novellas, tales, and short stories). Chicago: Nakł. Dziennika Zjednoczenia, 1938. BGU, BJ, BN, BUW, HIS, MLN, NYPL, PMA, SMOL, UPITT, UWMD.

Walus, F. J. "Jedzie ich więcej" (They go onward). In Waldo, *Czyn zbrojny*, 180–83.

———. "Mobilizacja Polonii" (The mobilization of Polonia). In Waldo, *Czyn zbrojny*, 134–37.

———. "Na krwawej rubiery" (On the bloody border). In Waldo, *Czyn zbrojny*, 270–88.

———. "Nasz obóz zima" (Our winter camp). In Waldo, *Czyn zbrojny*, 164–67.

Watra[-Przewłocki], Józef. "A iż cię nie opuszczę aż do śmierci" (Until death do us part). *Nowiny polskie*, 30 April–12 May 1927.

Watra-Przewłocki, Józef. "Trafił dobry na lepszego" (He met his match). In *Wielki kalendarz uniwersalny, czyli Powszechny dla wszystkich stanów polskiego narodu na rok 1919*, 2:179–80. [Stevens Point, Wis.: Bracia Worzałłowie] Nakł. i Druk. Polskiego Wyd. Kalendarzy Europejskich, [1918]. CCSU, PMA, UPITT.

Wedda, Józef. "Zbrodnia: Nowelka" (The crime: A short story). *Dziennik polski*, 27 January 1911.

Widmo w zbroi: Opowiadanie o złym bracie, który w starym zamku urządzał strachy, aby przerazić bogatego brata i odebrać mu majątek (The phantom in armor: The story of an evil brother who set up fake ghosts in an old castle to terrify his rich brother and take his fortune). [Toledo: Paryski], 1912.

Wielki kalendarz uniwersalny, czyli Powszechny dla wszystkich stanów polskiego narodu na rok 1920 (Great universal calender, for the entire Polish nation). 2 vols. Stevens Point, Wis.: Bracia Worzałłowie] Nakł. i Druk. Polskiego Wyd. Kalendarzy Europejskich, [1919]. PMA.

Wielki wybór humoru: Największy wybór najzdrowszego humoru, żartów, dowcipów, fraszek, anegdot, opowiadań, i wierszyków (Big book of humor: The greatest selection of the healthiest humor, jokes, witticisms, trifles, anecdotes, stories, and verses). Toledo: Paryski, n.d. CCSU, SMOL.

Włamywacze: Powiastka wykazująca, że najsprytniejszy zbrodniarz pozostawi zawsze po sobie ślady i na zasadzie poszlak zostanie ujęty i ukarany (The burglars: A story demonstrating that the cleverest criminal always leaves clues, and on the basis of this evidence is caught and punished). [Toledo: Paryski], 1911. UPITT.

Włóczęga. *See* Yolles, Piotr P.

Woicki, Józef. "Tydzień prawdy" (Truth week). *Dziennik związkowy/Zgoda*, 17 January 1908.

Wójcik, J. "Kto starszy, kura czy jaje? Wspomnienia z pola pracy oświatowej wydaw. A. A. Paryskiego" (Which came first, the chicken or the egg? Reminiscences from the educational work of publisher A. A. Paryski]. *Ameryka-Echo*, 20 May 1911.

———. "Przygody agenta: W jaki sposób i wśród jakich warunków odbywa się obecnie praca oświatowa A. A. Paryskiego" (The adventures of an agent: In what manner and under what conditions the educational work of A. A. Paryski is carried out). *Ameryka-Echo,* 23 July 1910–18 March 1911.

Wróg ludzi: Historya o okrutnym doktorze, który dla doświadczeń zabijał dzieci (Enemy of the people: The story of a cruel doctor who killed children for his experiments). [Toledo: Paryski], 1911. SUNYBU, UMN.

Wrotnowski, Bronisław [Marjan Bronisławski, pseud.]. "John Neewen: Powieść kryminalna" (John Neewen: A crime novel). *Jaskółka,* March 1929–April 1930. PMA, UPITT.

———. "Szlakiem dolara: Przygody dwóch młodych Polaków w Ameryce." (On the trail of the dollar: The adventures of two young Poles in America). *Jaskółka,* November 1927–January 1929. PMA, UPITT.

———. "Szumowiny: Powieść sensacyjna na tle stosunków amerykańskich" (The scum: A sensational novel based on American conditions). *Jaskółka,* November 1930–May 1932. PMA, UPITT.

———. *Szumowiny: Powieść sensacyjna na tle stosunków amerykańskich.* Stevens Point, Wis.: Bracia Worzałłowie, 1933. PMA.

"Wujcio z Ameryki" (My uncle from America). *Dziennik polski,* 31 May 1921.

Wydziedziczona, czyli Losy pewnej hrabianki: Powieść z życia rzeczywistego (The disinherited, or The fate of a certain countess: A story from real life). Toledo: Paryski, 1914. CCSU, NYPL, PMA, SMOL, UMN.

Yolles, Piotr P. [Włóczęga, pseud.]. "Trzy matki" (Three mothers). *Nowy świat,* 10 March–15 May 1930.

"'Z owoców ich poznacie je': Powieść z życia polsko-amerykańskiego" (By their fruits ye shall know them: A novel from Polish-American life). In *Kalendarz franciszkański na rok Pański 1914,* 55–89. Pulaski, Wis.: Miesięcznik Franciszkański, 1913. FP, PCI, PMA, UMN.

Zaborska, Tekla. "Po prace do biura" (Looking for work in an office). *Ameryka,* 29 August 1896.

Zagroda, Jerzy. *Kara Boska, czyli Księże dziecko w Ameryce* (God's punishment, or The priest's child in America). Toledo: Paryski, 1896. Not extant?

———. "Kara Boska, czyli Księże dziecko w Ameryce." *Ameryka,* 23 November 1895–4 January 1896.

Zahajkiewicz, Szczęsny. "Krzyżyk: Opowieść napisana dla Kalendarza polsko-amerykańskiego" (The crucifix: A short story written for the *Polish-American Almanach*). In *Kalendarz katolicki na rok zwyczajny 1895 dla ludu polskiego w Ameryce,* 70–82. Chicago: Nakł. Spółki Wyd. Polskiego w Ameryce, [1894]. PMA.

———. "Kura . . . jajko zniosła" (The chicken laid an egg). *Dziennik chicagoski,* 5 October 1913.

———. "Pamiętniki nieszczęśliwego" (The memoirs of an unfortunate man). *Dziennik chicagoski,* 29 September 1913.

Zasławska, Alina. "Spotkanie" (The meeting). *Dziennik związkowy/Zgoda,* 19 December–23 December 1908.

Zawadzki, Marian. "W niewoli u anglików" (In slavery to the English). In Waldo, *Czyn zbrojny,* 73–81.

Żuławski, Czesław. *Powrót (W osiemnastą rocznicę)* (The return, on the eighteenth anniversary). 1938. Not extant?

Secondary Sources

Andrews, Theodore. *The Polish National Catholic Church in America and Poland.* London: SPCK, 1953.

Anstruther, F. C. *Old Polish Legends.* New York: Hippocrene, 1991.

Barszczewski, Stefan. *Czerwony mesyasz* (The red messiah). Warsaw: Gebethner i Wolf, 1913.

———. *Obrazki amerykańskie* (American pictures). Warsaw: M. Arct, 1905.

———. *Polacy w Ameryce: Zarys obecnego stanu wychodźtwa polskiego w Stanach Zjednozonych* (Poles in America: A sketch of the current state of Polish emigration in the United States). Warsaw: M. Arct, 1902.

Barth, Frederick. Introduction to *Ethnic Groups and Boundaries: The Social Organization of Cultural Differences,* 9–39. Boston: Little, Brown, 1969.

Bartosz, Adam. Papers, 1917–1975. Milwaukee Urban Archives, University of Wisconsin-Milwaukee.

Bautro, Adam F. "Wspomnienia z lat 1891 do 1926" (Reminiscences, 1891 to 1926). *Jedność-Polonia,* 25 December 1926.

Blejwas, Stanislaus A. "Old and New Polonias: Tensions within an Ethnic Community." *Polish American Studies* 38, 2 (1981): 55–83.

———. "Stanisław Osada: Immigrant Nationalist." *Polish American Studies* 50, 1 (1993): 23–50.

———. "Voiceless Immigrants." *Polish American Studies* 45, 1 (1988): 5–11.

Bobrowski, Tadeusz. *Praca oświatowa, jej zadania, metody, organizacja: Podręcznik opracowany staraniem Uniwersytetu Ludowego im A. Mickiewicza* (Educational work, its tasks, methods, and organization: A handbook created through the endeavors of the Adam Mickiewicz People's University). Kraków: Michał Arct, 1913.

Bolek, Francis. *Who's Who in Polish America: A Biographical Dictionary of Polish-American Leaders and Distinguished Poles Resident in the Americas.* 3d ed. New York: Harbinger House, 1943.

Borun, Thaddeus, comp. *We, the Milwaukee Poles: The History of Milwaukeeans of Polish Descent and a Record of their Contributions to the Greatness of Milwaukee.* Milwaukee: Nowiny Pub., 1946.

Brooks, Jeffrey. *When Russia Learned to Read: Literacy and Popular Literature, 1861–1917.* Princeton, N.J.: Princeton University Press, 1985.

Brożek, Andrzej. *Polish Americans, 1854–1939.* Trans. Wojciech Worsztynowicz. Warsaw: Interpress, 1985.

Brzoza, Jan. *Powrót z Ameryki* (Return from America). Warsaw: Ludowa Spółdzielnia Wydawnicza, 1966.

Bujak, Franciszek. *Żmiąca: Wieś powiatu limanowskiego: Stosunki gospodarcze i społeczne* (Żmiąca: A village in the Limanowski district: Economic and social conditions). Kraków: Gebethner i Spółka, 1903.

Bukowczyk, John. *And My Children Did Not Know Me: A History of the Polish-Americans.* Bloomington: Indiana University Press, 1987.

Bukowski, Andrzej. *Działalność literacka i społeczna Hieronima Derdowskiego w Ameryce (1885–1902) z dodatkiem dwóch nieznanych jego utworów pt.: "Jasiek z Kniei i Szymek z Wiela w podróży do Ameryki" oraz "Listy z podróży" po osadach polskich w Ameryce* (Hieronim Derdowki's literary and social activity in America, with the addition of two unknown works, "Jasiek from Knieje and Szymek from Wiele on the way to America" as well as "Letters from a journey" around the Polish settlements in America). Gdańsk: Gdańskie Towarzystwo Naukowe, 1961.

Chametzky, Jules. "Styron's *Sophie's Choice,* Jews and Other Marginals, and the Mainstream." *Prospects* 9 (1984): 433–41.

Chełminski, David Gwidon. "From *Gwiazda* to the *Ameryka-Echo:* Antoni Alfred Panek/Paryski and His Publications." *Polish Heritage* 35, 1 (1984): 4–5.

Chojnacki, Władysław, and Wojciech Chojnacki. *Bibliografia kalendarzy polonijnych, 1838–1982* (A bibliography of Polonian calendars). Wrocław: Zakł. Narodowy im. Ossolińskich, 1984.

Chojnacki, Wojciech. "Antoni A. Paryski (1864–1935): Wydawca polski w Ameryce" (Antoni A. Paryski: A Polish publisher in America). Biographical file. Polish Museum of America. Typescript.

———. *Bibliografia wydawnictw zwartych Polonii amerykańskiej, 1867–1900* (Bibliography of American-Polonian publications). Prace Polonijne, no. 14. Warsaw: PWN, 1991.

———. "Czytelnictwo, piśmiennictwo i działalność wydawnicza polskiej grupy etnicznej w USA w latach 1870–1939" (The Polish ethnic group's reading, writing, and publishing activity in the U.S.A.). *Przegląd polonijny* 1, 2 (1980): 115–23.

Chrzanowska, Helena. "Sixty-Four Years of Polish Book Publishing in Chicago." In *Poles of Chicago, 1837–1937,* 189. Chicago: Polish Pageant, 1937.

Cienciala, Anna M. "Foundations of Polish-American Scholarship: Karol Wachtl." *Polish American Studies* 50, 1 (1993): 51–73.

Cuba, Stanley L. "Polish Amateur Theatricals in America: Colorado as a Case Study." *Polish American Studies* 38, 1 (Spring 1981): 23–49.

Cygan, Mary E. "A 'New Art' for Polonia: Polish American Radio Comedy during the 1930s." *Polish American Studies* 45, 2 (1988): 5–21.

———. "Political and Cultural Leadership in an Immigrant Community: Polish American Socialism, 1880–1950." Ph.D. diss., Northwestern University, 1989.

Czarnik, Oskar Stanisław. "Wybory beletrystyczne 'Dziennika chicagoskiego' w latach 1921–1926 i 1938–1939: Z problemów rozpowszechnienia literatury w środowisku polonijnym" (*Dziennik chicagoski*'s literary selections: Of the problems in disseminating literature in Polonia). In *Kultura skupisk polonijnych: Materiały z sympozjum,* ed. Oskar Stanisław Czarnik and Krzysztof Groniowski, 166–89. Warsaw: Biblioteka Narodowa, 1981.

Davies, Norman. *God's Playground: A History of Poland.* 2 vols. New York: Columbia University Press, 1982.

———. *Heart of Europe: A Short History of Poland.* Oxford: Clarendon Press, 1984.

Dearborn, Mary. *Pocahantas's Daughters: Gender and Ethnicity in American Culture.* New York: Oxford University Press, 1986.

Denning, Michael. *Mechanic Accents: Dime Novels and Working-Class Culture in America.* London: Verso, 1987.

Di Pietro, Robert J., and Edward Ifkovic, ed. *Ethnic Perspectives in American Literature: Selected Essays on the European Contribution.* New York: Modern Language Association, 1983.

Dodatkowy katalog książek, Bibljoteki Polskiej w Domu Narodowym Polskim w Chicopee, Mass. (Supplemental book catalog, Polish Library at the Polish National Home in Chicopee, Mass.). Chicopee: Komitet Bibljoteki i Polskiej Rady Oświatowej, 1934. PMA.

Dolan, Jay P. *The American Catholic Experience: A History from Colonial Times to the Present.* Notre Dame, Ind.: Notre Dame University Press, 1992.

Dunikowski, Emil Habdank. *Wśród Polonii w Ameryce: Druga serya "Listów z Ameryki"* (Within Polonia in America: A second series of "Letters from America"). Lwów: Księgarnia P. Starzyka, 1893.

Duszak, Thomas. *Towarzystwo Czytelni Polskiej, 1898–1998: The Centenary of the Polish Library Association, Wilmington, Delaware.* Camp Hill, Penn.: Plank's Suburban Press, 1998.

Dziembowska, Janina, ed. *Pamiętniki emigrantów: Stany Zjednoczone* (Emigrant memoirs: United States). 2 vols. Warsaw: Książka i Wiedza, 1977.

Eile, Stanisław. *Literature and Nationalism in Partitioned Poland, 1795–1918.* London: Macmillan, 2000.

Elliott, Robin. "The Eastern European Immigrant in American Literature: The View of the Host Culture." *Polish American Studies* 43, 2 (1985): 25–45.

Erdmans, Mary Patrice. *Opposite Poles: Immigrants and Ethnics in Polish Chicago.* University Park: Pennsylvania State University Press, 1998.

Estreicher, Karol. *Bibliografia polska dziewiętnastego stulecia: Lata 1881–1900* (Bibliography of Polish nineteenth-century publications). 2 vols. Kraków: Spółka Księgarzy Polskich, 1906; 2d ed. 16 vols. Kraków: Uniwersytet Jagielloński, 1959–91.

Federal Works Agency. Work Projects Administration (Illinois). *Chicago Foreign Language Press Survey Records,* 1936–41.

Ferraro, Thomas J. *Ethnic Passages: Literary Immigrants in Twentieth-Century America.* Chicago: University of Chicago Press, 1993.

Fine, David. *The City, the Immigrant, and American Fiction, 1880–1920.* Metuchen, N.J.: Scarecrow, 1977.

Flisiński, Wacław Stefan. *Rys dziejowy i historyczny prasy polonijnej w Ameryce, w latach 1842–1972* (Historical sketch of the Polonian press in America). New York: author, 1973.

Fox, Paul. *The Polish National Catholic Church.* Scranton: School of Christian Living, 1961.

Francič, Mirosław. *Komitet Obrony Narodowej w Ameryce, 1912–1918* (The National Defense Committee in America). Wrocław: Zakł. Narodowy im. Ossolińskich, 1983.

Gans, Herbert. "Symbolic Ethnicity: The Future of Ethnic Groups and Cultures in America." In *On the Making of Americans: Essays in Honor of David Riesman,* ed. Herbert J. Gans, 193–221. Philadelphia: University of Pennsylvania Press, 1979.

Gardaphé, Fred L. *Italian Signs, American Streets: The Evolution of Italian American Narrative.* Durham: Duke University Press, 1996.

Gąsiorowski, Wacław. *Ach, te chamy w Ameryce* (Oh, those yokels in America). Warsaw: Dom Książki Polskiej Spółka Akcyjna, 1935.

Gieysztor, Aleksander, et al. *History of Poland.* 2d ed. Trans. Krystyna Cękalska et al. Warsaw: PWN, 1979.

Gladsky, Thomas S. *Princes, Peasants, and Other Polish Selves: Ethnicity in American Literature.* Amherst: University of Massachusetts Press, 1992.

Greene, Victor. *American Immigrant Leaders, 1880–1910: Marginality and Identity.* Baltimore: Johns Hopkins University Press, 1987.

———. *For God and Country: The Rise of Polish and Lithuanian Ethnic Consciousness in America, 1860–1910.* Madison, Wis.: State Historical Society, 1975.

Grotnik, Casimir J. *An Index to Rola Boża, God's Field.* Scranton: Polish National Catholic Church, Commission on History and Archives/Bishop Hodur Biography Commission, 1989.

Grzebień, Ludwik, ed. *Burzliwe lata Polonii Amerykańskiej: Wspomnienia i listy Misjonarzy Jezuickich, 1864–1913* (The stormy years of American Polonia: Reminiscences and letters of Jesuit missionaries, 1864–1913). Kraków: Wyd. Apostolstwa Modlitwy, 1983.

Haiman, Mieczysław. *Polacy w walce o niepodległości Ameryki: Szkice historyczne* (Poles in the battle for American independence: Historical sketches). Chicago: Nakł. Polskiej Katolickiej Spółki Wydawniczej, 1931.

———. *Zjednoczenie Polskie Rzymsko-Katolickie w Ameryce, 1873–1948* (The Polish Roman Catholic Union in America). Chicago: ZPRK, 1948.

Hapak, Joseph T. "Recruiting a Polish Army in the United States, 1917–1919." Ph.D. diss., University of Kansas, 1985.

Hering, Alfons. "Dzieje 'Gwiazdy Polarnej'" (The history of *Gwiazda polarna*). In *Gwiazda polarna, 75 lat w służbie Polski i Polonii,* ed. Thomas Francis Hering, 11–29. New York: Poray, 1983.

Jacobson, Matthew Frye. "Martial Art: Literature and Romantic Militarism in Turn-of-the-Century Polonia." *Polish American Studies* 51, 1 (1994): 5–19.

———. *Special Sorrows: The Diasporic Imagination among Irish, Jewish, and Polish Immigrants in the United States.* Cambridge, Mass.: Harvard University Press, 1995.

Kantowicz, Edward R. *Polish-American Politics in Chicago.* Chicago: University of Chicago Press, 1975.

K[arasiewicz], J[ózef]. "Los pracownicy pióra" (The fate of a literary laborer). *Zgoda,* June 1947; repr. from *Dziennik polski,* Detroit. Biography file, Melania Nesterowicz. PMA.

Karłowiczowa, Jadwiga. *Historia Związku Polek w Ameryce* (History of the Polish Women's Alliance in America). Chicago: ZPA, 1938.

Kister, Hanna. *"Pegazy na kredytowej": Wspomnienia* (Pegasus on credit: A memoir). Warsaw: Biblioteka Syrenki, 1980.

Klein, Kathleen Gregory. *The Woman Detective: Gender and Genre.* Urbana: University of Illinois Press, 1988.

Klimaszewski, Bolesław. "American Polonia in Domestic Polish Literature of the Nineteenth and Twentieth Centuries." *Polish-Anglosaxon Studies* 3–4 (1992): 219–27.

———. *Pod znakiem potu, łez, i dolara: Polonia amerykańska w zwierciadle literatury polskiej* (Under the sign of sweat, tears, and the dollar: American Polonia as reflected in Polish literature). Kraków: Uniwersytet Jagielloński, 1990.

———. "Sami o sobie? Obraz wychodźcy polskiego w literaturze polonijnej" (By ourselves about ourselves? The picture of Polish emigration in Polonian literature). *Przegląd polonijny* 17, 1 (1992): 91–110.

Kłossowski, Andrzej. *Historia książki polskiej za granicą: Problemy badawcze* (A history of the Polish book in foreign lands: Research problems). Warsaw: Biblioteka Narodowa, 1980.

———. "Śmiałym los sprzyja" (Fate favors the bold). In *Na obczyźnie: Ludzie polskiej książki,* ed. Andrzej Kłossowski, 164–207. Wrocław: Zakł. Narodowy im. Ossolińskich, 1984.

Knothe, Maria Anna. "Recent Arrivals: Polish Immigrant Women's Response to the City." In *Peasant Maids—City Women: From the European Countryside to Urban America,* ed. Christiane Harzig, 301–38. Ithaca: Cornell University Press, 1997.

Koscielski, Regina. "Illiterate Peasants I Have Known." *Tygodnik świat polski* (Detroit), 26 April 1991.

Kowalczyk, Edmund L. "'Pike' Landusky, Montana Frontiersman." *Polish American Studies* 4, 1–2 (1947): 16–18.

Kowalik, Jan. *The Polish Press in America.* San Francisco: R and E Research Association, 1978.

Kruszka, Wacław X. *A History of the Poles in America to 1908.* Part 1. Trans. Krystyna Jankowski. Ed. James S. Pula. Washington, D.C.: Catholic University of America Press, 1993. Originally published as *Historya Polska w Ameryce.* 13 vols. Milwaukee: Druk. Spółki Wydawniczej Kuryera, 1905.

Krzyszkowski, Joseph. "Anthony Jax—A Forgotten Playwright." *Polish American Studies* 9, 1–2 (1952): 17–23.

Krzyżanowski, Julian. *A History of Polish Literature.* Trans. Doris Ronowicz. Warsaw: PWN-Polish Scientific Publishers, 1978.

Książka pamiątkowa czterdziestolecia pracy dziennikarskiej Czesława Łukaszkiewicza, 1905–1945 (Czesław Łukaszkiewicz, forty years of work in journalism). Chicago: n.p., 1945.

Książki polskie: Polish Books. Chicago: Chicago Public Library, 1926. PMA.

Kubiak, Hieronim. *The Polish National Catholic Church in the United States of America from 1897 to 1980: Its Social Conditioning and Social Functions.* Kraków: Uniwersytet Jagielloński, 1982.

Laudynowa, Stefania. *Kwestja polska i inne: Listy polityczne "Polki," drukowane w gazecie* Ruś *od 1(14) października 1904 r. po 10 (24) listopada 1907 r.* (The Polish question and other matters: Political letters of "A Polish Woman," printed in the newspaper *Ruś,* 1(14) October 1904–10(24) November 1907.] Warsaw: n.p., 1908.

Ledbetter, Eleanor E. *The Polish Immigrant and His Reading.* Chicago: American Library Association, 1924.

Leonard, John Williams, ed. *Woman's Who's Who of America: A Biographical Dictionary of Contemporary Women of the United States and Canada, 1914–1915.* S.v. "Piotrowska, Helena." New York: American Commonwealth, 1914.

Loryś, Maria. *Historia Związku Polek w Ameryce* (History of the Polish Women's Alliance in America). 2 vols. Chicago: ZPA, 1980–81.

Łukaszkiewicz, Czesław. *Moskalofile (ich pochód przez nasze dzieje)* (Moscow-lovers: Their march through our history). New York: Nakł. autora, 1915.

———. *Nauczyciel wychodźtwa [sic]: Antoni A. Paryski (1865–1935)* (Teacher of the emigration: Antoni A. Paryski). Toledo: Ameryka-Echo, n.d.

M. Andrea, Sister. "America in the Polish Novel." *Polish American Studies* 3, 1–2 (1946): 13–20.

Maciuszko, Jerzy. "Polish-American Literature." In *Ethnic Perspectives in American Literature: Selected Essays on the European Contribution,* ed. Robert J. Di Pietro and Edward Ifkovic, 163–82. New York: Modern Language Association, 1983.

Mackiewicz, Józef, Jerzy Wyszomirski, Stanisław Mackiewicz, and Walerian Charkiewicz [Felicja Romanowska, pseud.]. *Wileńska: Powieść kryminalna* (Wilenska: A crime novel). London: Kontra, 1995.

Magocsi, Paul R. *Rusyn-American Ethnic Literature.* Cambridge, Mass.: Harvard Ukrainian Research Institute, 1978.

Mazurkiewicz, Casimir J., and Victor Turek. *Alfons J. Staniewski, 1879–1941: A Chapter in the History of the Polish-Language Press in Canada.* Toronto: Polish Alliance Press, 1961.

Miaso, Józef. *The History of the Education of Polish Immigrants in the United States.* Trans. Ludwik Krzyżanowski. New York: Kosciuszko Foundation, 1977.

Michalski, Thomas A. "The Prussian Crucible: Some Items in the Cultural Baggage of Prussian Polish Immigrants." *Polish American Studies* 42, 2 (1985): 5–17.

Mierzyńska, Zofia. "Rozmowa z Zofią Mierzyńską" (Conversation with Zofia Mierzyńska). Interview by Edward Dusza. *Gwiazda polarna,* 15 November 1986.

———. *Wakacjuszka* (The vacationer). 4 vols. Chicago: Z. and L. Song, 1985.

———. *Zawód: Hałskiper* (Occupation: Housekeeper). Chicago: Index, 1989.

Milostan, Harry [Natsolim, pseud.]. *The Errant Nun: "Peaceful Peninsula" in Turmoil.* Mount Clemens, Mich.: Masspac Publishing, n.d.

Miłosz, Czesław. *The History of Polish Literature.* 2d ed. Berkeley: University of California Press, 1983.

———. "Separate Nations: Poetry and the People." *New York Times Book Review,* 11 October 1987, 43.

Nagiel, Henryk. *Dziennikarstwo polskie w Ameryce i jego trzydziestego-letnie dzieje: Referat przeznaczony na Wystawę Kościuszkowską 1894r. we Lwowie* (Polish journalism in America and its thirty-year history: A lecture presented at the 1894 Kosciuszko display in Lwów]. Chicago: Nakł. Komitetu Centralnego Obesłania Wystawy Lwowskiej przez Polonię Amerykańską, 1894.

———. *Tajemnice Nalewek (z cyklu "Krwawe Dramaty")* (Secrets of Nalewki, from the "Bloody Dramas" cycle). Warsaw: Gebethner i Wolff, 1911.

Natsolim. *See* Milostan, Harry.

Nesterowicz, Stefan. *Travel Notes.* Trans. Marian Moore Coleman. Cheshire, Conn.: Cherry Hill Books, 1970. Originally published as *Notatki z podróży po Ameryce Północnej.* Toledo: Paryski, 1909.

Newman, Katherine. "An Ethnic Literary Scholar Views American Literature." *MELUS* 7, 1 (1980): 3–19.

Nir, Roman. *Catalog of the Polish American Archives at Orchard Lake.* 4 vols. Orchard Lake, Mich.: Central Archives of American Polonia in Orchard Lake, 1996–1999.

Olszyk, Edmund G. *The Polish Press in America.* Milwaukee: Marquette University Press, 1940.

Opalski, Magdalena, and Israel Bartal. *Poles and Jews: A Failed Brotherhood.* Hanover, N.H.: Brandeis University Press, 1992.

Orłowski, Józef [Tomasz Plon, pseud.]. *O chłopską skórę.* Milwaukee: Druk. Nowin Polskich, 1920.

Orłowski, Leon. *Reymont w Ameryce: Listy do Wojciecha Morawskiego* (Reymont in America: Letters to Wojciech Morawski). Warsaw: Państwowy Instytut Wydawniczy, 1970.

Orton, Lawrence D. *Polish Detroit and the Kolasinski Affair.* Detroit: Wayne State University Press, 1981.

Orzechowski, Emil. *Teatr polonijny w Stanach Zjednoczonych* (Polonian theater in the United States). Wrocław: Zakł. Narodowy im. Ossolińskich, 1989.

Osada, Stanisław. *Jak się kształtowała polska dusza wychodźtwa w Ameryce* (How the Polish emigrant spirit was formed in America). Pittsburgh: Sokół Polski, 1930.

———. *Prasa i publicystyka polska w Ameryce* (The Polish press and journalism in America). Pittsburgh: n.p., 1930.

———. "Towarzystwo Literatów i Dziennikarzy Polskich w Ameryce Północnej" (The Society of Polish Writers and Journalists in North America). In *Sprawa polska w Ameryce Północnej na Pierwszym Zjeździe Towarzystwa Literatów i Dziennikarzy Polskich w Syracuse, NY w dniach 2 i 3 października 1911 r.*, 9–20. Chicago: Dyniewicz, 1912.

Osada, Stanisław, and Adam Olszewski. *Historia Związku Narodowego Polskiego* (History of the Polish National Alliance). 6 vols. Chicago: Związek Narodowy Polski, 1957–67.

Øverland, Orm. *Immigrant Minds, American Identities: Making the United States Home, 1870–1930.* Urbana: University of Illinois Press, 2000.

Panek, Leroy Lad. *Probable Cause: Crime Fiction in America.* Bowling Green, Ohio: Bowling Green State University Popular Press, 1990.

Parot, Joseph John. *Polish Catholics in Chicago, 1850–1920: A Religious History.* De Kalb: Northern Illinois University Press, 1981.

Paryski, Antoni [Parysso, Antoni, pseud.]. *Nieposłuszna* (The disobedient girl). Chicago: Dyniewicz, 1886.

Pawlowska, Harriet M., ed. *Merrily We Sing: 105 Polish Folksongs.* Detroit: Wayne State University Press, 1983.

Peterson, Brent O. *Popular Narratives and Ethnic Identity: Literature and Community in "Die Abendschule."* Ithaca: Cornell University Press, 1991.

Pienkos, Donald E. *For Your Freedom through Ours: Polish-American Efforts on Poland's Behalf, 1863–1991.* Boulder: East European Monographs, 1991.

———. *One Hundred Years Young: A History of the Polish Falcons of America, 1887–1987.* Boulder: East European Monographs, 1987.

———. *PNA: A Centennial History of the Polish National Alliance of the United States of North America.* Boulder: Eastern European Monographs, 1984.

Pigoń, Stanisław. "Główne problemy literatury ludowej" (The main problems of folk literature). In *Na drogach kultury ludowej: Rozprawy i studia* (Toward a folk culture: Debates and studies), ed. Tomasz Jodełka-Burecki, 212–35. Warsaw: Ludowa Spółdzielnia Wydawnicza, 1974.

Pobóg, Iza. *Cawboy* (Cowboy). Lwów, 1911.

———. *Cudowny kamień* (The miraculous stone). Chicago: Smulski, [1912].

Pochmann, Henry. "The Mingling of Tongues." In *Literary History of the United States,* ed. Robert E. Spiller et al., 676–93. 3d ed., rev. London: Macmillan, 1963.

"Początki literatury nowopolskiej w północnej Ameryce" (The beginnings of a new Polish literature in North America). *Przegląd emigracyjny* (Lwów), 1 May 1894.

Polish American Publishing and Importing Company. *Katalog księgarni Polish American Publishing and Importing Co.* (Bookstore catalog). Chicago: Polish American Publishing, n.d.

Polski słownik biograficzny (Polish biographical dictionary). Wrocław: Zakł. Narodowy im. Ossolińskich, 1935–.

Porter, Brian. *When Nationalism Began to Hate: Imagining Modern Politics in Nineteenth-Century Poland.* New York: Oxford University Press, 2000.

Przewłocki-Watra, Józef. *John Big Foot (w krainie złota i krwi): Z cyklu "Polacy na szlakach świata.* (John Big Foot: In the country of gold and blood: From the "Polish Trails around the World" cycle) Warsaw: Rój, n.d.

———. *Prawdziwy mężczyzna: Powieść* (The real man: A novel). Poznań: Wielkopolska Księgarnia Nakładowa Karola Repeckiego, 1928.

Pula, James S. *Polish Americans: An Ethnic Community.* New York: Twayne, 1995.

Redliński, Edward. *Dolorado.* Chicago: Contemporary Images, 1984.

———. *Szczuropolacy* (Rat-Poles). Warsaw: BGW, 1994.

Romanowska, Felicja. *See* Mackiewicz, Józef, et al.

Rosienkiewicz, Marcin. *Dialogues to Facilitate the Acquisition of the English Language by the Polish Emigrants / Rozmowy, do ulatwienia nauki jenzyka angielskiego, dla emigrantow polskich.* Philadelphia: n.p., 1834.

[Rosiński, Wiktor]. *Antoni A. Paryski: Życie, prace, i czyny, 1865–1935* (Antoni A. Paryski: Life, works, and achievements). Toledo: Ameryka-Echo, [1945].

Roy, Jacek. "Marylin Monroe z Greenpointu: Powieść detektywistyczna z serii złota trzynastka" (Marilyn Monroe of Greenpoint: A detective novel from the Golden Thirteen series). *Panorama,* 1995.

Samsel, M. Ancilla. "Polish Catholic Book Publishing in the United States and Its Distribution during the Period 1871–1900." M.S. thesis, Catholic University of America, 1957.

Sanders, Irwin, and Ewa Morawska. *Polish-American Community Life: A Survey of Research.* New York: Polish Institute of Arts and Sciences in America, 1975.

Schreiber, Helena Chrzanowska. *Dzieje jednej instytucji wydawniczej* (The history of one publishing institution). N.p, 1959.

Schultz, Rima Lunin, and Adele Hast, eds. *Women Building Chicago, 1790–1990: A Biographical Dictionary.* Bloomington: Indiana University Press, 2001.

Segel, Harold B., ed. *Stranger in Our Midst: Images of the Jew in Polish Literature.* Ithaca: Cornell University Press, 1996.

Shell, Marc, and Werner Sollors, eds. *The Multilingual Anthology of American Literature: A Reader of Original Texts with English Translations.* New York: New York University Press, 2000.

Sienkiewicz, Henryk. *Za chlebem* (After bread). New York: R. F. Fenno, 1897.

Sollors, Werner. *Beyond Ethnicity: Consent and Descent in American Culture.* New York: Oxford University Press, 1986.

———. "Immigrants and Other Americans." In *Columbia Literary History of the United States,* ed. Emory Elliott, 568–88. New York: Columbia University Press, 1988.

———. "Literature and Ethnicity." In *Harvard Encyclopedia of American Ethnic Groups,* ed. Stephan Thernstrom, 647–65. Cambridge, Mass.: Belknap Press, 1980.

Spiller, Robert E. "The Cycle and the Roots: National Identity in American Literature." In *Toward a New American Literary History: Essays in Honor of Arlin Turner,* ed. Louis J. Budd, Edwin H. Cady, and Carl L. Anderson, 3–18. Durham: Duke University Press, 1980.

Spottswood, Richard K. "The Sajewski Story: Eighty Years of Polish Music in Chicago." In *Ethnic Recordings in America: A Neglected Heritage*, 133–73. Washington, D.C.: Library of Congress, 1982.

Staś, Helena. "Dla dobra literatury poslko-amerykańskiej [*sic*]" (For the good of Polish-American literature). *Dziennik polski*, 21 August 1907.

———. *Kobieta wobec Chrystusa* (A woman before Christ). [Milwaukee, 1915].

———. "Marya i Marta" (Mary and Martha). *Głos Polek*, 29 September 1921.

Stauter-Halsted, Keely. *The Nation in the Village: The Genesis of Peasant National Identity in Austrian Poland, 1848–1914.* Ithaca: Cornell University Press, 2001.

Stone, Daniel. "Jewish Emigration from Poland before World War II." In *Polish Americans and Their History: Community, Culture, and Politics*, ed. John J. Bukowczyk, 93–120. Pittsburgh: University of Pittsburgh Press, 1996.

Stowarzyszenie Weteranów Armii Polskiej w Ameryce. *Czyn zbrojny wychodźtwa polskiego w Ameryce* (An armed act of the Polish emigration in America). New York: Wyd. Stowarzyszenie Weteranów Armii Polskiej w Ameryce, 1957.

Studnicki, W[ładysław]. "Nadzwyczajne polskie przedsiębiorstwo w Ameryce" (An exceptional Polish enterprise in America). *Ameryka-Echo*, 18 March 1911. Reprint from *Goniec* (Warsaw), 18 February 1911.

Świderska, Hanna. "Eldorado—dolorado." *Kultura*, June 1986, 115–19.

Symanski, Edward Alan. *From the Fourth Province.* Florence, Italy: Tyszkiewicz Private Press, 1952.

Symonolewicz-Symmons, Konstanty. *Ze studiów nad Polonią amerykańską* (From studies on American Polonia). Warsaw: Ludowa Spółdzielnia Wydawnicza, 1979.

Szydłowska-Cegłowa, Barbara. "Funkcje stylistyczne i artystyczne gwary polsko-amerykańskiej" (The stylistic and artistic functions of the Polish-American dialect). In *Kultura skupisk polonijnych: Materiały z II sympozjum naukowego* (Culture of Polonian communities: Materials from the Second Academic Congress), ed. Ewa Klimpel, 193–205. Warsaw: Biblioteka Narodowa, 1987.

Thomas, William I., and Florian Znaniecki. *The Polish Peasant in Europe and America.* 5 vols. Chicago: University of Chicago Press, 1918–20.

Turek, Victor. *The Polish-Language Press in Canada: Its History and a Bibliographical List.* Toronto: Canadian Polish Congress, 1962.

United States. Immigration and Naturalization Service. *Statistical Report: Illegal Alien Resident Population*, 25 November 1997.

<www.ins.usdoj.gov/text/aboutins/statistics/illegalalien/htm>.

Urbanski, Adam. "Americanism and the Polish-American Press, 1916–1925." Ph.D. diss., University of Rochester, 1974.

Wachtel, Karol. *See* Wachtl, Karol.

Wachtl, Karol. *Ciche pieśni: Poezye* (Quiet songs: Poetry). Chicago: Smulski, n.d.

———. *Pieśni orężne: Wspomnienia rymowane z lat Wielkiej Wojny* (Battle songs: Rhymed reminiscences from the years of the Great War). Częstochowa: Księgarnia A. Gmachowskiego, 1925.

———. *Polonia w Ameryce: Dzieje i dorobek* (Polonia in America: History and accomplishments). Philadelphia: Nakł. autora, 1944.

———. *ZPRK: Dzieje Zjednoczenia Polskiego Rzym.-Kat. w Ameryce* (PRCU: The history of the Polish Roman Catholic Union in America). Chicago: [PRCU], 1913.

Waldo, Artur L. "Polish-American Theatre." In *Ethnic Theatre in the United States*, ed. Maxine Seller, 387–417. Westport, Conn.: Greenwood, 1983.

———. *Rok książki polskiej w Ameryce: Referat na II-go Zjazd Polskiej Rady Międzyorganizacyjnej w Chicago 15 i 16 maja 1937 roku* (The year of the Polish book in America: A report at the Second Congress of the Polish Interorganizational Council in Chicago, May 15–16, 1937). Chicago: Nakł. Polskiej Rady Międzyorganizacyjnej, 1937.

———. *Sokolstwo: Przednia straż narodu: Dzieje idei i organizacji w Ameryce* (The Falcon movement, advance guard of the nation: The history of an idea and organization in America). 4 vols. Pittsburgh: Nakł. Sokolstwa Polskiego w Ameryce, 1956–58.

———. *Zarys historii literatury polskiej w Ameryce: Szkic bibliograficzny* (Outline history of Polish literature in America: A bibliographic sketch). Chicago: Nakł. "Dziennika Zjednoczenia," 1938.

Wepsiec, Jan. *Polish American Serial Publications, 1842–1966: An Annotated Bibliography.* Chicago, 1968.

Weredyk, Ks. *Wielka rana narodu polskiego, czyli Małżeństwa mieszane: Rzecz praktyczna nietylko dla kapłanów, ale także i dla szerszych warstw intelligentnych wszystkich trzech dzielnic* (The great national wound, or Mixed marriage: A practical matter not just for priests but for the general intelligentsia of all three partitions). Wrocław: Drukarnia "Gazety Śląskiej Ludowej," 1904.

Wilgat, Janina, ed. *Bibliografia polska, 1901–1939* (Polish bibliography). Wrocław: Zakł. Narodowy im. Ossolińskich, 1986–.

Wlodarski, Stephen. *The Origin and Growth of the Polish National Catholic Church.* Scranton: Polish National Catholic Church, 1974.

Wolanin, Alphonse S. *Polonica Americana: Annotated Catalogue of the Archives and Museum of the Polish Roman Catholic Union.* Chicago: Polish Roman Catholic Union Museum and Archives, 1950.

Wyman, Mark. *Round Trip to America: The Immigrants Return to Europe, 1880–1930.* Ithaca: Cornell University Press, 1993.

Zaborowska, Magdalena J. *How We Found America: Reading Gender through East European Immigrant Narratives.* Chapel Hill: University of North Carolina Press, 1995.

Zasławska, Alina. "Sokół: Wspomnienie lat dziecinnych" (The Falcon: A childhood memoir). *Dziennik związkowy,* 28 October 1908. Reprinted in Waldo, *Sokolstwo,* 2:492–96.

Index

Page numbers in italics refer to illustrations.